CW00644444

Dealing with Disruption

Michael Ross writes from long experience with ease and authority. His analysis of change in audiences, creative development, marketing channels and financial models in global publishing is insightful and succinct. His practical examples illustrate his argument with clarity. Michael's conclusion, that disruption challenges us by solving problems that the market – all of us – creates through the decisions we make, underpins his overarching philosophy: that no civilized society exists without the vigorous interchange of continuously minted fresh ideas.

Ian Grant, Chairman, Inpress Books Ltd;
Partner, Creative Structure Ltd

Humorous in a way only Michael Ross can be, this book thoughtfully and practically demonstrates how the digital age is disrupting the publishing industry but also brings opportunity to meet educational needs meaningfully while growing a successful business. Noteworthy case studies illustrate Ross's concepts and offer rich new ideas for providing content in innovative and exciting ways. I highly recommend this book.

Rachelle Cracchiolo, Founder, Teacher Created Materials

What do we fear? It's typically the unknown and there is nothing more fearful to an industry like a yet to be unveiled disruptive technology. Publishing executives could tell you all about that as they have ignored, feared, struggled against and ultimately embraced the digital age. Michael Ross' new book Dealing with Disruption *shines a light on the darkness that is the history of publishers dealing with these newest realities. As someone who has published several blog posts on this topic I admire what Mike has put together. Among other things it includes a matter of fact re-telling of the publishing industry's struggle with disruption. But it also includes the hope and promise of this new digital age. If nothing else it'll have a calming effect on publishing executives to counteract any lingering hysteria.*

Michael Foy, President, Publishing Search Solutions

Even though he was describing a huge, respected brand-name, Michael's open and honest account of the challenges of the digital future for Britannica have already inspired my colleague and I to consider the future for our tiny children's publisher and take advantage of the practical guidance he offers for dealing with the inevitable disruption coming our way.

Catherine Bruzzone, Managing Director, b small publishing ltd

Dealing with Disruption

Lessons from the Publishing Industry

MICHAEL N. ROSS

Senior Vice President, Education General Manager,
Encyclopaedia Britannica/Britannica Digital Learning,
Chicago, Illinois, USA

Routledge
Taylor & Francis Group

LONDON AND NEW YORK

First published 2016
by Routledge
2 Park Square, Milton Park, Abingdon, Oxon OX14 4RN

and by Routledge
711 Third Avenue, New York, NY 10017

Routledge is an imprint of the Taylor & Francis Group, an informa business

© 2016 Michael N. Ross

The right of Michael N. Ross to be identified as author of this work has been asserted by him in accordance with sections 77 and 78 of the Copyright, Designs and Patents Act 1988.

All rights reserved. No part of this book may be reprinted or reproduced or utilised in any form or by any electronic, mechanical, or other means, now known or hereafter invented, including photocopying and recording, or in any information storage or retrieval system, without permission in writing from the publishers.

Trademark notice: Product or corporate names may be trademarks or registered trademarks, and are used only for identification and explanation without intent to infringe.

British Library Cataloguing in Publication Data
A catalogue record for this book is available from the British Library

Library of Congress Cataloging in Publication Data
Names: Ross, Michael N., author.
Title: Dealing with disruption : lessons from the publishing industry / by
   Michael N. Ross.
Description: Farnham, Surrey, England ; Burlington, VT : Gower, [2016] |
   Includes bibliographical references and index.
Identifiers: LCCN 2015025555 | ISBN 9781472456878 (hardback) |
   ISBN 9781472456885 (ebook) | ISBN 9781472456892 (epub)
Subjects: LCSH: Publishers and publishing. | Electronic publishing.
Classification: LCC Z278 .R66 2016 | DDC 070.5—dc23
LC record available at http://lccn.loc.gov/2015025555

ISBN: 9781472456878 (hbk)
ISBN: 9781315575926 (ebk)

Typeset in Palatino Linotype
by Apex CoVantage, LLC

To my three children—and wonderful disruptors—
Monica, Rachael, and Daniel

Contents

List of Figures		*ix*
Acknowledgments		*xi*
About Michael N. Ross		*xiii*
Preface		*xv*
Introduction		1
1	Digital Publishing Comes of Age	9
2	Life after Print	21
3	The Print-to-Digital Continuum	35
4	Tools to Change By	49
5	Towards a Global Idiom	59
6	Brand and Reputation Matters	85
7	The Virtue in a Virtual Town Hall	97
8	Luck is Not a Strategy	109
9	Making a Deal with Best Practices	129
10	Consumption Models	149
11	The Lion and the Mouse: The Professional vs. the Amateur	163
Epilogue		175

Appendix A: International Book Fairs   *181*
Appendix B: A URL A–Z for Information on Publishing and Licensing   *185*
Appendix C: Sample Licensing Agreement   *193*

Bibliography   *207*
Index   *209*

List of Figures

4.1   Britannica Map of the World, circa 1902   55

5.1   Smokey Bear   66

6.1a   Encyclopaedia Britannica corporate logo   87
6.1b   Britannica Digital Learning logo   88
6.2   *Merriam-Webster's Scrabble Dictionary* cover   94

11.1   Infographic 1: Britannica's editorial process   166
11.2   Infographic 2: Britannica's editorial team   167

Acknowledgments

Throughout the process of writing this book, I'm thankful to the many people who were eager to see it published. In particular, I appreciate the support I received from Kristina Abbotts, my tireless and patient editor at Gower, who was an enthusiastic advocate from the beginning of the project, believed in my personal narrative, and sold it to the Gower team—who, in turn, gave me the reprieve I needed to finish, and did a fine job of bringing the book to market.

I want to thank all of my colleagues at Britannica, whose talent and dedication to quality publishing and the education field make me optimistic about the future of our industry. A special thanks goes to Steve Kapusta, who provided some of the digital image files that appear in the book; Kate McCowen, who produced the cover art and internal design elements; and above all Ruth Kos, executive assistant *par excellence*, who double-checked many of the facts. Still, any errors are entirely my fault.

Also, my heartfelt gratitude goes out to my friends and partners in the industry who were kind enough to take the time to offer their personal experiences with disruptive technology and change, and how they not only adapted but, in most cases, set the pace for others to follow: Julio Abreu, of A+ Media; Catherine Bruzzone, of b Small Publishing; Bill Evans, of Evan-Moor; Neal Goff, of Egremont Associates; John Ingram, of the Ingram Content Group; Andy Lieb, of the JRL Group; Deanne Mendoza, of Teacher Created Materials; John Morse, of Merriam-Webster; the late and great Tom Murphy; Roger Rosen, of Rosen Publishing; Barbara Russell, formerly of Options Publishing; Marlowe Teig, formerly of Berkery, Noyes; and Philip Walters, formerly of Hodder Education and Rising Stars.

Finally, I'm indebted to my wife, Kathleen, who graciously agreed to edit the manuscript with her finely developed skills as an in-house and freelance editor for several publishing companies; and our three children—Monica, Rachael, and Daniel—who kept me disciplined, focused, and, through their own hard work, determination, and optimism in their pursuits, provided the motivation that I needed to keep from procrastinating and to get on with it.

About Michael N. Ross

Michael Ross is the Senior Vice President, and Education General Manager, at Encyclopaedia Britannica, Inc., where he heads the sales and marketing activities in North America, the U.K., Europe, the Middle East, and Africa. Prior to joining Britannica in 2002, he was the Executive Vice President and Publisher of World Book, Inc., and has held executive positions at other publishing companies, including NTC Publishing Group, now part of McGraw-Hill. He began his publishing career as an editor for Time-Life Books and spent three years at the company's Tokyo bureau.

Throughout his career, Michael has worked in all areas of publishing, including editorial, technology, product development, sales, and marketing. His products and publications have had worldwide circulation and have won the highest industry awards, including the Distinguished Achievement and the Golden Lamp Awards from the Association of Educational/American Publishers, now the AAP; the GLI Award, presented at the Bologna Children's Book Fair; *Learning Magazine*'s Teacher's Choice Award; *PC Magazine*'s Editor's Choice Award; Parent's Choice Award; *Family PC*'s Top 100 Award; and the Software & Information Industry Association's Codie Award.

Michael served on the executive committee and the board of directors of the Association of Educational Publishers (AEP), including a term as President from 2002 to 2003. He also serves on the advisory boards of Teacher Created Materials and A Pass Education. In October 2002, he was inducted into *Printmedia*'s Production Executives' Hall of Fame, and in December 2009, he was inducted into AEP's Educational Publishing Hall of Fame.

Michael's other books include *Publishing without Borders* (2003) and *Publishing without Boundaries: How to Think, Work and Win in the Global Marketplace* (2007). He also occasionally blogs for Britannica's website. He is a frequent speaker at international conferences on electronic publishing, strategic alliances, marketing, product development, and licensing.

He has a B.A., *summa cum laude,* from the University of Minnesota; an M.A. from Brandeis University; and a certificate from Stanford University's Advanced Management College.

Michael would be delighted to receive comments and feedback on this book or discuss your particular interests in publishing. Please contact him at: michaelnross@comcast.net.

Preface

In 2007 I wrote a book entitled *Publishing without Boundaries*, which focused on global publishing and the emergence of digital solutions. My goal was to encourage publishers to look beyond ink on paper and to take advantage of the digital options that were available at that time. Opportunities in new markets, both foreign and domestic, and in new formats were not being fully exploited. Since then, however, digital technology has evolved exponentially. The playbook that provided publishers with a way forward less than a decade ago is no longer applicable. Today, publishers are challenged by the abundance of options to pursue, many of which are in constant motion. My aim in *Dealing with Disruption* is to rewrite that playbook to help publishers in particular—and businesses in general—take advantage of new opportunities that have resulted from innovation in production and manufacturing, the wider use of the Internet, and the role of disruptive vendors in the supply chain that have gone from being upstarts to entrenched businesses.

Technology has enabled publishers and content creators of all kinds to go to market faster than ever before and to reach larger and more disparate audiences. Consumers have become more comfortable with using digital products, so publishers have been encouraged to invest a greater percentage of their resources in information technology. The Internet is used as much for accessing, downloading, and streaming content as it is for surfing, searching, and shopping. At the same time, the appetite for physical books remains strong, even though the majority of print sales have moved from bricks-and-mortar boutiques to Internet warehouses.

If we look at a timeline of technological innovation and change in the publishing industry, for more than 500 years after Gutenberg's invention of the printing press in 1452, nothing jumps out as a truly disruptive change agent—an event or series of events that dramatically altered the normal way in which we consumed information and knowledge—until the arrival of digital technology in the mid-1990s. Innovations in production, printing, marketing, and distribution began to challenge the hegemony of long-established business models.

At that time, all areas of publishing experienced a perfect storm of dramatic change, which created an atmosphere of uncertainty as to who would be the winners and losers. The direction of digital publishing wasn't evident. Further, the weakening of technology stocks that occurred in the mid- to late 1990s added to the confusion and slowed the adoption of technology-driven business solutions. Even by the end of the decade, it wasn't clear that the rapid ascendency of businesses like eBay and Amazon were signs of a permanently upward trend.

In the education sector, tech had yet to deliver on many of its promises. Most classrooms of the 1990s looked not unlike they did in the 1890s. A teacher stood at the front of the classroom, a chalkboard in the background, 35 or so students in desks facing her or him, each with a printed textbook, pencil, and paper. Maybe the teacher had an overhead projector, but probably not an interactive whiteboard or laptop—and certainly not a mobile device. If there were computers in the school, they were likely to be in a computer lab, as if the machines themselves were an experiment with indeterminate applicability. Software incompatibility and clumsy multimedia hardware configurations (including laserdisc players) caused many adopted technology "solutions" to fail. Schools spent millions on programs that were quickly obsolesced by the next big thing.

Apple, education's tech darling, was yet to bounce back from near-obscurity after a propitious start. Its stock was trading at around $15 a share and Steve Jobs was still in exile. When Jobs returned to Apple in 1997, Michael Dell, CEO of Dell Computers, was asked what he thought Jobs should do with Apple, and said: "I'd shut it down and give the money back to the shareholders."

Today, Apple is the most valuable company in the world, and not only as a software and hardware provider, but also as a producer of various publishing platforms. Google, which started life as a search engine and then became an advertising juggernaut, is also a major source of cloud-based solutions for consumers and educators. Chromebooks and tablets are in classrooms around the world. Consumers seem reluctant to choose between print and e-books and prefer to access both, so print is unlikely to go extinct as a result of more e-books in the market.

Our use of digital media continues to rise and expand. Bandwidth has greater penetration across the globe. Wireless technology can now provide an alternative to many local network issues. Customer satisfaction with digital solutions has improved, and more people are willing to pay for Web-based products that increase productivity, teach, inform, and entertain. Mobile devices are ubiquitous, and social media connects the citizens of the world through instantaneous communication. Overall, e-publishing is rooted in fertile ground; for the most part, we are convinced that technology has accelerated our ability to make better products for more people more efficiently and at lower costs. We no longer question whether digital publishing makes a difference; instead, we wonder what else we can do with it to become better informed and more empowered to innovate.

The adoption of various technologies has caused numerous changes in the publishing industry and in our relationship with information, but we have gained more than we have lost. Although digital publishing is now commonplace and some types of publishing have turned entirely digital, we continue to have a very vibrant print business. The market has helped us determine where print is viable and remains a user preference or, on the other hand, where digital solutions are more functional. Still, pricing and monetization models and distribution channels are in flux, and concerns about monopolization in distribution linger in the background.

We are now accustomed to the presence and importance of social media, user-generated content, and crowdsourcing, but we should not overestimate their value. For some types of information—financial, health, and consumer product, for example—we depend on what we believe are trusted sources. And those of us who are knowledge workers, however we define that label, are willing to pay for peer-reviewed, authoritative information and publishing services.

In the same way that we are careful about what we eat and drink, we should be equally cautious about what we feed our brains. We should be able to embrace social media and crowdsourcing without relying on them as our only sources of information. Both user-generated information and curated content have their place and value; we should react to this world of nearly infinite information without overreacting or overcorrecting.

Technology has caused disruption in publishing by improving the tools that are available to us and by increasing the participation of a greater number of people from diverse locations. My goal in this book is to explore the opportunities that disruption in the publishing industry has made possible, and how we can make the most of them.

Michael N. Ross
Chicago/London
November, 2015

Introduction

Let your sympathies and your compassion be always with the underdog in the fight—this is magnanimity; but bet on the other one—this is business.

Mark Twain, A Biography

For readers who have been observing the publishing industry for more than 10 years from the outside, either as a consumer or as a partner in the supply chain, this book may cover familiar ground. Disruption in the publishing industry has been a frequent topic of business news in general, and many business leaders and pundits have been watching the industry closely to see who will survive and in what form. Most if not all of the disruption in publishing is a direct result of the introduction of new technology, which has had a dramatic, positive effect on the production and distribution of published material, and, as a consequence, on consumer behavior as well. But what may not be as familiar are the various ways in which the publishing industry has had to adapt to changes in the market, the different business models that publishers have had to adopt to continue to grow and meet consumer needs, and how similar changes may apply to other types of business. For readers currently on the inside of the publishing industry, this book should be useful as a primer for examining the challenges and opportunities provided by technology and how professionals can exploit recent technological changes to their best advantage.

Digital publishing is no longer in its infancy. Almost every publisher today—large or small and regardless of their specialization—utilizes reliable, intuitive digital technology to create their publications, and distributes some form of digital product as part of their overall marketing strategy. At the same time, the "digitization" of the entire publishing ecosystem has also significantly altered consumer expectations. The new normal is instant access to information at increasingly lower costs, and in many cases at no cost at all. This is the expectation of a large percentage of people who obtain most of their information from the Internet.

As a result of the changes in market expectations, publishers of all kinds of information have been forced to think differently about their business. Over the last 15 years, in order to respond to changing market demands, various publishing models have emerged, most of them dependent on some type of technology. Although technology has made the mechanics of publishing in general, and Web publishing in particular, far easier, publishers now find it much more difficult to find the right business model that can satisfy market needs on the one hand and the bottom-line requirements of the business on the other. Establishing the most efficient and profitable business models has been made both more challenging and more rewarding by the numerous advancements in technology. At the same time, the publishing industry can be viewed as a kind of "petri dish" for observing change and examining disruption caused by technology. Because of the amount of change that has occurred in publishing and the sources of that change, publishing has been closely watched as an example of an industry where leaders must make strategic and tactical adjustments quickly in order to innovate, grow, and continue to create shareholder value.

The most conspicuous change in the business of publishing is the number of formats that are available to publishers, from traditional print to DVDs, to flash drives, and to the Internet. With so many choices, most of which are dependent on technology of some kind, publishing today is far more complex than when the only format available was print. However, even as the proliferation of formats has complicated the nature of the business, more opportunities have emerged for reaching a wider audience than ever before. These opportunities are available to publishers of any size. Whether our perspective is that of a small, boutique publishing house or a large, multinational corporation, opportunities to make an impact and to be profitable, even though competition has increased and the landscape has become more crowded, are plentiful.

Business leaders in every industry experience disruption that forces them to make changes in how they go to market in order to stay relevant and profitable. Some businesses make the transition from one model to another faster than others. For a variety of reasons, some do not make it at all. Businesses that are not able to adapt to changes in their commercial environment are sometimes sold in whole or in part, or just disappear altogether.

Although I have acquired intimate knowledge of how publishing companies have adjusted to market changes, I've never found it very useful to be overly concerned with which particular businesses in other industries have failed to make the necessary changes to survive, or why. Without detailed information of the inner workings of a specific business and decisions that are made in private meetings and in day-to-day activities over a period of time, we can only speculate and generalize about what management did or did not do to adjust to disruptions in the marketplace. Instead, what I think is more useful, and broadly applicable, is to identify what problems disruption attempts to solve; what opportunities result from the disruption; how and when to take advantage of these opportunities; and how experiences with disruption in the publishing industry can be applied to other businesses.

Virtually every aspect of the publishing industry has been affected by technology—from product development to sales and marketing. Personnel have also been greatly affected; people's jobs have changed or even been eliminated. Most of the disruption in the industry has occurred when technology has created efficiencies in the supply chain and, as a result, changed customer expectations and behavior. Because of various disruptions in the business, publishing professionals have been forced to re-think when and where to deploy emerging technologies to better serve their customers, who often have increasingly higher expectations.

Over the last 15 years or so, we have also seen the rise and empowerment of the amateur publisher, or self-publisher. Inexpensive, accessible, and sophisticated technology tools have enabled non-professionals—meaning anyone who is not held accountable to a set of generally accepted standards or guidelines and who does not make a living solely through publishing—to produce polished products and to reach a wide audience. Amateurs have the ability to create a magazine, book, website, blog, or post that has all of the markings of a professional publication.

With access to the Internet and mobile technology, amateurs also have more distribution outlets than was the case in the past. The backing of a professional publisher is no longer necessary to achieve visibility in the marketplace. Many of the functions that were formerly the exclusive domain of the professional publisher can now be accomplished by anyone with a computer and a connection to the Internet. Most publishing functions—composition, design, production, marketing, distribution, and sales—can be done without the aid of a professional. And they can be done quickly and inexpensively.

Amateurism does not have to be regarded as a threat to professional publishing, nor is it necessarily of lesser quality. On the contrary, it should be welcomed because it allows for an increase in the number of viewpoints and greater access to more information. The professional and the amateur can co-exist, and each has their role and value. As a society, we can benefit from the continued growth of both professional and amateur publishing. However, the more difficult task, and also a theme of this book, is how we as consumers respond to the professional and the amateur, and how their simultaneous presence in the market affects our behavior and worldview. To many of us, it may not matter whether an amateur or a professional is behind the information we consume, and in some cases there may actually be no difference. But where a difference does exist, we should be able to recognize it and make adjustments in how we react to the various outputs.

One of the most critical challenges that results from the increased access to amateur publications is to be able to differentiate them from professional, unbiased publications. We need to be able to distinguish fact and neutrality from opinion and prejudice. Of course, professional publications are not necessarily void of bias (regardless of how hard we may try, we all have our biases) and are not always more accurate than amateur publications. But in the free Internet, amateur or crowdsourced publications are simply not as accountable to the same oversight as professional publications or as incentivized by either paying readers or sponsors to correct errors, stay current, or adhere to certain social standards.

In a democracy, we don't want to appear to be advocating for censorship, so we welcome all opinions. Still, we do need to be able to make distinctions, as educated and well-informed consumers, between truth and fiction, and to be able to recognize instantly when information comes with an agenda, whether or not we share that point of view. We should be able to know who or what we can believe, or is apt to be more trustworthy.

As an executive at Britannica, I am frequently asked to differentiate our content from Wikipedia, one of the largest and most visited websites. Trying not to show my own bias, I will quickly acknowledge that Wikipedia may have accurate information on many subjects. But as an open site that can be edited by anyone, it lacks accountability and is not susceptible to the same criticism as sites that depend on customer loyalty, either in the form of subscription fees or advertising revenue driven by viewer visits. Even though Wikipedia may have editorial guidelines or suggestions, there is no real oversight or outside pressure to be less biased or to correct errors; the site's accuracy is dependent mostly on volunteers, who may or may not have a bias on the topics that they are writing on or editing, or enough expertise to improve the site's accuracy.[1]

---

1   In an article by Shane Greenstein and Feng Zhu entitled "Do Experts or Collective Intelligence
     Write with More Bias? Evidence from Encyclopaedia Britannica and Wikipedia" for the Harvard
     Business School, October 10, 2014, the authors conclude that "overall, Wikipedia articles are more
     slanted towards Democrat than Britannica articles, as well as more biased." The authors go on
     to say: "Overall, we conclude that Wikipedia articles are generally much more biased." Andrew
     J. Flanagin and Miriam J. Metzger in "From Encyclopaedia Britannica to Wikipedia," *Information,*

This leads to the issues of quality and trust in published material, and how these two essential hallmarks of highly regarded brand-name publishing houses have been commoditized and compromised in an age of free content, open-source technology, and crowdsourcing. In some cases, particularly in mass media, curated content is under siege because of the growth of amateurism and social media. The role of the professional publisher is being challenged, and issues of quality and trust are now competing with a free Internet. As a result, publishing professionals need to experiment with business models that can succeed in this kind of economic environment, where quality and trust may not be valued as much as easy access to information. These are crucial issues not only for publishing, but for all businesses, as technology enables more competitors—amateurs and professionals—to enter the marketplace and threaten existing business models.

Being able to insist on quality and trust is a dilemma for consumers, who now have an unprecedented number of choices to make. As we explore disruption in the publishing industry specifically and in the marketplace generally, we should address two key questions: How can we make the best choices out of the many that are available to us? And what will the long-term effect of these choices be on the future of publishing and our culture?

As publishing has increasingly moved to the Internet—and we see this on a daily basis with newspapers and magazines—we have also become aware that publishing has become more multicultural. There has always been a great tradition of international publishing, with the licensing and translation of books at the heart of a global appetite for multiple viewpoints and an avid exchange of ideas, knowledge, art, and creativity. The widespread use and globalization of the Internet has broken down any barriers that may have existed in that exchange. Publishing can now be instant and geographically diverse. Translation software, even with its limitations, allows content to be viewed in multiple languages with just a click or two. Even as the Internet has enabled more communication among diverse people in distant places, this has not necessarily resulted in more clarity. Languages and cultures collide on the Internet as billions of pages in hundreds of languages share common space. The promise of the World Wide Web has been achieved, even if it largely remains a Tower of Babel.

Communication & Society, April, 2011, state: "Not only does Wikipedia completely lack reliable source cues about who provides its content to all but the most savvy and diligent users, thereby rendering information content providers largely anonymous, it is further confounded with a dubious reputation about the quality of its content. Thus, the main elements of credibility—trustworthiness and expertise—are difficult to assess in the Wikipedia environment."

However, for publishers—amateur and professional alike—this ever-growing mountain of information on the Internet presents an almost infinite amount of opportunity and a genuine need to help make sense of the confusion, to divide it into readable, meaningful, attractive packages—offline and online—and to publish works of greater interest to more people and in more languages and cultures.

The international marketplace (now laid bare by the Internet) can be an invaluable resource, a source of inspiration, and a destination for tapping into additional markets and revenue streams. The global publishing community is made up of global citizens with a strong impulse to share information. Publishers, in general, are knowledge seekers, and knowledge has no boundaries. Knowing and seeing what other publishers around the world are doing is critical to creating relevant content that will be suitable for various markets.

With the growth of the Internet and online publishing, both consumer and educational markets have greater entry points for discovering more diverse and relevant content that addresses specific local needs. Experienced publishers who have never worked in the international marketplace before should consider doing so now, especially given the relative ease of reaching new audiences.

More than in the past—when only print was available as a way to represent and reach multiple markets—publishers now have a variety of ways to establish a presence in local and global markets. But in order to adjust to or grow in a constantly changing, global business environment, a publishing enterprise needs a roadmap that takes a wide range of consumer expectations into account and provides a variety of practical steps to reach those consumers efficiently.

If a roadmap is going to be useful for publishers faced with a number of unprecedented options—including print as well as online and offline digital formats—and nascent business models, it must include the fundamental elements that publishers need to consider to make sound decisions about what to do, how much to invest, what to prioritize, and what skills they need to acquire. Publishing leaders, like the heads of any business, have to make choices, and sometimes those choices are binary, such as whether to produce a book in a digital format or not. Sometimes there isn't an either/or choice to make, but rather a question of how much or how fast among a variety of options. For example, as part of a publishing plan, a decision point around how many and when books should be manufactured using print-on-demand services versus traditional web-offset or sheet-fed printing would be addressed. To simplify the effort involved in creating a roadmap, the fundamental elements of publishing (and many other businesses) today can be placed into the following categories: *business models*, such as online subscription or free-with-advertising models; *strategies*, such as co-publishing and negotiating contracts; *marketing*, such as brand development and virtual forums; *technical or production* issues, such as mark-up language or outsourcing; and *distribution* channels, such as the consumer or educational markets.

These are not meant to be exhaustive or fixed labels, and some activities may fall into one or more categories. But they should be useful for organizing the various functions of publishing and can serve as a kind of checklist toward a successful, ongoing business plan. And assuming that disruption comes from external innovation in the market rather than internal development, they should also help in making adjustments to business plans when trends in the market change direction. Marketing guru Dan Moore of Southwestern Advantage once said (and I quote him often) that "change is inevitable, *except* perhaps from a vending machine." Disruption, too, is inevitable, but in this case, I can't think of any exceptions.

Chapter 1
Digital Publishing Comes of Age

When clouds appear, wise men put on their cloaks;
When great leaves fall, the winter is at hand;
When the sun sets, who doth not look for night?
Untimely storms make men expect a dearth.
William Shakespeare, Richard III, Act II, Scene III

While most businesses must change over time to stay relevant and continue to grow, few businesses, especially if we include most forms of text-based media (newspapers, magazines, trade books, and reference works), have undergone as much change in both production methods and paths to market as the publishing industry has in the last 15 years. Better, more cost-effective technology has been central to all of this change since the turn of the 21st century. Continually improving digital tools have made production processes much more efficient. Composition, design and page-layout software have greatly improved the pre-production steps in publishing. At first, these tools only made it easier and cheaper to produce the same type of finished product—a physical book, magazine, or newspaper, for example. The real disruption, however, came when the end result was no longer a physical entity but a digital one, consumed in bytes on electronic devices (computers, tablets, and smartphones) rather than ink on paper. Once the finished product could be delivered over the Web in a digital rather than physical form, the entire publishing ecosystem changed and we saw the emergence of new players—amateurs and professionals—reaching many more customers through new distribution channels and at much lower costs than in the past. How we respond to disruption—and its social and economic consequences—is what this book is about.

We are all aware of the dramatic changes in the music industry since the early 1980s and the introduction of the compact disc. The evolution of the formats for delivering music, starting with LPs and culminating today with digital downloads and streaming, has caused long-lasting disruption in all aspects of this industry and has forced significant changes in business models. Manufacturing and distribution changes have not been trivial and have caused many long-time players to exit the business as the industry has contracted and moved to the Web. Traditional revenue streams have dried up as record labels have lost the influence that they used to have and the once-ubiquitous retailers have almost completely disappeared from the landscape. Technology has precipitated these changes, and as market forces embraced the products and services that have emerged as a result, rapidly advancing innovation in technology continued to defeat older, inefficient models. Consumers benefited by having greater access to the products that they wanted and at lower prices.

The change in the music industry that caused the greatest disruption and also the greatest benefit to consumers—by providing easy access to an almost unlimited amount of music—was the file-sharing of digital music. Prior to file-sharing, first introduced by Napster in 1999, the only aspects of the business that changed were the formats in which music was produced and consumed. The distribution channels for these formats did not change. The wholesaler or retailer could easily adjust to the different formats; they could swap one for another and stay in business. The same distribution channel that traded in LPs stayed relevant by moving, as technology and trends evolved, to eight-track tapes, to cassette tapes, and then to compact discs. But the emergence of digital downloads and, in particular, file-sharing, which later led to streaming, eliminated the need for the traditional bricks-and-mortar retailer and changed the way music is consumed today. Everyone involved in the music industry, from the artists and producers to the distributors, has had to alter the way they generate and share revenue. The demise of most bricks-and-mortar music outlets has forced artists to take more direct control over the business aspects of their craft, especially in regard to how they market and sell to consumers. Some markets, such as Japan, for a variety of social and cultural reasons, have resisted the temptation to embrace fully digital downloads and have remained loyal to CDs. Bricks-and-mortar retailers are still thriving businesses in Japan. But music industry experts generally believe that this is a temporary state and that the highly consumptive Japanese market, too, like most of the rest of the world, will eventually abandon CDs and switch to downloads and streaming.[1]

In this new digital environment, Apple is the largest player. In 2000, it introduced iTunes, an online music store where consumers could download single-track, multiple-track, or whole albums directly onto their MP3 player, which was more often than not Apple's own device, the iPod, which runs the iTunes player. Today, approximately two-thirds of all consumer music

---

1   See "CD-Loving Japan Resists Move to Online Music," *New York Times*, September 17, 2014.

transactions take place through Apple's iTunes store, which has been a major disruption to the traditional vehicles for music sales.

What iTunes did to the music industry and for the music consumer, Amazon did to the publishing industry and for the book buyer, also at about the same time (it went public in 1997). When Amazon made books available through its online store, the traditional bricks-and-mortar stores found it very difficult to compete. Some stores introduced coffee bars and tried to become more of a destination for meeting friends, studying, working, or relaxing. The original purpose of the in-store cafés was to encourage book sales. In theory, if people came to the stores to buy a cup of coffee, they would leave with a book or two in their hands. But this didn't really happen, at least not regularly enough to keep bookstores relevant for their original purpose. Coffee, or a place to hang out, became an end in itself. Now, with Amazon accessible to anyone with an Internet connection, consumers could buy the books they wanted much more easily, often at substantial discounts, delivered to them in a day or two. Convenient and cost effective, Amazon also ensured that you could get any book you wanted at any time. You no longer had to go to a bookstore to discover that the book you wanted was not available. Books were rarely if ever out of stock on Amazon's giant online store. Physical bookstores had no tangible advantage over the online alternative. And a cup of coffee was not an offering that bookstores could leverage as a consumer benefit, not with the large number of Starbucks, Costas, and other chains dotting the metropolitan areas.

In the late 1990s, Amazon may have been the new kid on the virtual block, but it quickly became a very disruptive fact of life for anyone trying to stay in the bricks-and-mortar book business. As a result, some well-known retailers went out of business, and even the biggest one, Barnes & Noble, drastically reduced the number of its stores. Within a few years of opening its online portal, Amazon was on its way to becoming the behemoth suggested by its name as the largest river in the world. By transforming the way people bought books, it created a never-before-realized revenue stream.

The existence of a massive online store, with virtually millions of books available for immediate shipping, may have had a profound negative effect on the traditional retailer, but it was well received by consumers and it was also good for most publishers. Now publishers could more effectively sell their backlist titles—older, slower-selling books that may still be relevant, but only to a small number of readers.

Slow sellers at bookstores, even when they were part of a store's inventory, were often difficult to find on bookshelves; they were hidden from view and therefore lost in a distribution model that favored best-sellers and popular publications. After a period of collecting dust on shelves or sitting in boxes in the store's backrooms, backlist titles were eventually returned to the publisher for full credit.

Merriam-Webster, which is a Britannica company, publishes the best-selling dictionaries in North America. When there were still thousands of retail booksellers in business, Merriam-Webster would receive orders for hundreds of thousands of dictionaries, from the collegiate level down to a child's very first illustrated dictionary. Periodically I would visit Merriam-Webster headquarters, in Springfield, Massachusetts, and the President of the company, John Morse, would show me stacks of boxes on the warehouse docks that had come back from various retail outlets across the country unopened. These were books that retailers had made a point of ordering, only to return them several months later.

Managers of bricks-and-mortar stores have always had a hard time deciding what to stock and were forced by economic and physical constraints to maintain a limited inventory. Even the largest stores have shelf-space limitations. Bookshelf real estate is a precious commodity and must be used for products that turn over quickly to maximize revenue per square foot. Store managers knew they could move best-sellers; for other categories, however, they had to decide which books to order from publishers by speculating as to what their customer base might have an interest in. They had to guess what people wanted, or wait for customers to request a title, and then artfully display the books so that other people might find such titles by browsing. Many customers, of course, enjoyed roaming through the shelves of a bookstore and discovering books they never knew they wanted. But it was not a very practical way to find a good read, a good book on fly fishing, or a book that they had vaguely recalled having an interest in, but didn't know the author or title.

The traditional distribution model of a bricks-and-mortar store was an inefficient vehicle for publishers to sell their backlist titles. Neither the publisher nor the bookstore owner benefited from the wasteful process of sending books from the publisher to the bookstore only to have them sent back again to the publisher unsold. The only entities that benefited from this economic yo-yo were the supply-chain shippers. But until Amazon arrived on the scene, no reliable alternative existed. The only partial, purely economic solution was for publishers to limit the number and kind of books they published and for bookstores to limit their inventory. But this did not help consumers find the titles that they wanted or to make them aware of the scope and range of titles available.

Amazon provided publishers with a perfect solution to slow-selling backlist titles. Publishers no longer had to worry about placing inventory into a store, hoping that people would find their titles, or deal with returns when those books didn't sell through. Amazon could basically stock everything, since its customers were anyone who was online and in any location—not just someone who lived in the vicinity of a certain store. It could list all of its titles in its database, making them easy to find and buy, and eliminating returns as an economic burden for publishers. It could rely on its online systems to track demand and replenish inventory accordingly. It could order books strictly from the behavioral data of a large online customer base and actual sell-through. At least in this one area of publishing, Amazon could be a better partner for publishers than the traditional bricks-and-mortar retailer.

With Amazon, consumers could also save time, energy, and transportation costs. Unless someone had a personal preference for making a trip to a bookstore—perhaps he or she enjoyed the act of physically browsing, needed to kill time, or simply did not want to shop online for personal reasons—buying a book online was far more practical. You knew immediately that the book was on its way and did not have to wonder whether it would be in stock at a bookstore.

Amazon was disruptive to bookstores because it solved problems in the supply chain. Consumers could now find books that were difficult to find before, and publishers were able to continue to publish (or keep in print) books that had only a niche audience. For the publishing industry, this gave rise to the economic viability of the so-called "long tail." A term first introduced by Chris Anderson, editor-in-chief of *Wired Magazine*, the long tail refers to products that have a low demand or low sales volume and can only be kept from being phased out through the availability of a large enough distribution channel. Amazon could provide a single-source channel that the thousands of individual bookstores, dispersed over the planet, could not.

In publishing, the long tail is very long indeed, since most books sell in low volumes; best-sellers account for approximately 80% of all book sales, so any single bookstore that stocked a variety of books beyond the best-sellers would have a building full of niche, or long-tail, titles. However, since less popular books could now be searched for by consumers on Amazon, publishers could have access to a much wider audience for slow-selling books. They could keep a small supply of these books in print for a much longer period of time, knowing that more people will find them among Amazon's giant, worldwide community. Sending books to a single distribution source and having people locate them over the Internet is a far better scenario than sending a mix of popular and slow-selling books to thousands of addresses around the world and hoping that people within physical range of these locations walk into the stores and find what they want. A large percentage of the books would end up coming back to the publisher even before they made it onto the stores' shelves. The new model, made possible by the Internet, is (show) *one to many, not* (send) *many to* (sell) *one.*

From today's perspective—taking the Internet for granted and with the enormous year-on-year growth of online shopping of all kinds—Amazon's strategy was a formula for success. But this wasn't so clear in its early years. Many people were skeptical of the online shopping experience. In 2001 at the Frankfurt Book Fair, the publishing industry's biggest rights and licensing event, I was talking to a German colleague, Peter Gutmann, who ran the international division of Bertelsmann, the largest privately held publisher as well as Random House's owner. He announced that he was going to try to buy a book on Amazon for the first time, as an experiment, just to see how it worked. He wasn't convinced that Amazon's strategy made any sense at all; his opinion was that people would insist on the non-virtual bookstore experience so they could actually thumb through a book before buying it—this being one of the quintessential pleasures of shopping for a book. His skepticism was shared by many others in the publishing industry. Traditionally the industry has been populated (and subsidized through low salaries) by people who love books. Perhaps Peter was naively channeling this love and missed the disruption that was right in front of him. Today, more than two-thirds of all book sales are made through Amazon. And books are only one of many product categories that Amazon offers.[2]

Amazon was not alone in selling books online. The largest U.S. bookseller, Barnes & Noble, also launched its website around the same time as Amazon launched its own. Others followed as well, including Waterstones in the U.K. and dozens of new startups in most major markets. But Amazon had the mind share and first-mover advantage, and remains the dominant player

---

2   According to George Packer in "Cheap Words," *New Yorker*, February 17, 2014, Amazon's current revenue from book sales accounted for only 7% of the company's $75 billion in total annual revenue.

today. It initiated the disruption that changed the industry forever. While in theory Barnes & Noble (or any of the other book retailers or wholesalers) could have led the way in changing the model in favor of online selling over physical stores, it took an outsider, primarily a technology and logistics company, to force the change and to provide a better model for selling books directly to the end user. Further, as Amazon was creating a new business and investing heavily in its backend infrastructure, it, unlike Barnes & Noble or Waterstones, did not have a legacy business to protect.

Because of their origins as booksellers and not software providers, Barnes & Noble, Borders, Books-a-Million, Waterstones (the U.K.'s largest bookseller), and other prominent book retailers should not be faulted for not recognizing early on the threat that Amazon posed to their traditional business or foreseeing the huge industry disruption that would occur for both publishers and consumers. When Amazon came on the scene, the Internet was still new to consumers and was largely used as a medium for communicating through email. It was just emerging as a place to find information and was not yet a proven platform for selling anything, let alone books. Amazon was an Internet pioneer and, as we know, pioneers often end up with arrows in their backs. In Amazon's case, though, it was the successful settler who became the landed gentry of online selling.

The advantages of buying books over the Internet went beyond convenience, and Amazon quickly convinced consumers of other benefits: being able to find any book at any time; having access to books that constitute the long tail; saving time and money by staying home and shopping; and enjoying favorable pricing, which Amazon could offer by not having the overheads typically incurred by physical stores. These benefits provided consumers with a compelling incentive to transfer their loyalty from a bricks-and-mortar store to an online startup. Soon Amazon became the most popular place to buy books. The Internet is now a mainstream medium, and Amazon proved that its platform was an efficient means for publishers to sell all of their books, best-sellers as well as backlist titles.

Online bookselling has also been a boon to the sale of used books. Hundreds of independent online bookstores as well as individuals with websites are finding it profitable to sell used books. AbeBooks, an online marketplace that launched in 1996 as the Advanced Book Exchange, features new and used books, out-of-print books, and "cheap textbooks." It claims to have millions of books for sale through its site and to be the leader in rare and hard-to-find books. Originally started in British Columbia, Canada, with European offices in

Dusseldorf, Germany, AbeBooks also has websites in the U.S, the U.K., France, Italy, Australia/New Zealand, and Spain. Not surprisingly, it was purchased by Amazon in 2008. By acquiring what may have been the largest player in the used-book business, Amazon was quickly able to gain a stranglehold on this market, remove a competitor, and avert any disruption to its own growth and strategy.

Amazon transformed the way people would buy books. It had a better mousetrap, which comprised superior logistics, an engaging online user experience, and an efficient delivery process—and it was willing to make acquisitions to scale its business and maintain dominance. But it was not the only early adopter in the book industry to take advantage of the Internet. By 2000 or soon after, in addition to the other mainstream bricks-and-mortar retailers, publishers entered the game as well and began to establish a presence on the Web, not just to promote and market their books to distributors but also to sell them direct to customers. Today thousands of publishers, booksellers, wholesalers, and individuals participate in the Internet's vast marketplace.

Alibaba—the Chinese website that combines the features of a search engine, auction house, and e-commerce site for businesses and consumers (without actually carrying any inventory itself)—stormed onto the Internet scene in 1999. Although its revenue is still a fraction of Amazon's, it went public only one year ago—had one of the biggest stock sales ever recorded—and already has a higher valuation than Amazon based on the size and expectations of the booming Chinese e-commerce industry. Still, Alibaba probably owes its rapid ascent to Amazon having first paved the way.

Amazon not only caused disruption in the publishing industry by being a centralized distribution center for physical books; it can also be credited with creating the e-book market by producing an electronic device whose sole functionality was to display digital versions of books. With the introduction of the Kindle in 2007, Amazon made two things possible at once: it sold a device that was dedicated to and ideally suited for reading e-books; and it made it easy to download an e-book anywhere at any time for only the cost of that e-book (no delivery fee and sometimes no tax), which was often less than either the hardback or paperback edition of the book. In addition, it provided the Kindle customer with free broadband, with no monthly fee or cost of accessing the Internet to download an e-book. With these innovations—free Internet access, a device that made it easy to read e-books, and a virtual store that carried just about any book available in the Kindle format at a very attractive cost—Amazon created an e-book revolution. It proved that e-books were not only a viable alternative to physical books, but that they could constitute a new market for people who didn't normally buy books or would buy fewer books if they had to visit a physical bookstore.

The Kindle, and rival e-book readers that were either in the market or were soon to enter the market, had other advantages as well. These devices could hold hundreds of books in memory, a clear advantage for people who were reading more than one book at a time or were traveling and didn't want to limit the number of books they brought along on their trips. Also, I often heard from Kindle users that they liked the fact that they could read books in public places on their devices without other people knowing what they were reading since the cover couldn't be seen. Apparently this particular feature caused a spike in the sales of Harlequin novels, where risqué covers that helped sell the books could be an embarrassment to people (mainly women) who wanted to read them on trains or buses. The e-book format has the benefit of keeping one's reading choices private.

The e-book market continued to grow rapidly after Amazon's release of the Kindle. Amazon continued to add books to its store and brought out a variety of Kindle devices. Demand continued to grow, particularly since both the Kindle devices and the e-book downloads were relatively inexpensive. Amazon's main competitor in the book market, Barnes & Noble, came out with its own device in 2009, the Nook; it was counting on both the strength of its brand as established purveyors of books and loyal customers to its physical stores to take sales away from Amazon. Then Apple released its first iPad in 2010, along with iBooks, its online bookstore, and the competitive landscape changed again. Although Waterstones doesn't have its own device, it too was selling books online and was relying on its strong brand as a premium bookseller to help sustain loyal readers in the face of global giants like Amazon and Apple.

Plenty of other companies compete in the e-book market, as online bookselling in general continues to show meaningful year-on-year growth. These include sites that sell both print and e-book versions of the same title, only print titles, or only e-books. Some of these sites, like bookstore.co.uk, are independent and global, while some are local. All of them are a result of the significant disruption in this market that, in the end, has allowed more people easy access to millions of books, many of which are finding an audience that they could never have reached without this disruption.

The e-book format has greatly expanded the overall sales of books. The Internet has made it possible to extend the reach of books in multiple formats to people who could not or would not go to a bricks-and-mortar store. This is an excellent example of disruption that has very tangible results for consumers. However, not all businesses are able to respond well when this kind of sudden change in the market occurs. Barnes & Noble may have found a way to adapt its business strategy to remain relevant and viable, but it had to make many changes in order to survive. It could not have remained a viable business if it had stuck only to its bricks-and-mortar stores. It had to adapt; it had to make the transition from one type of business to another, from a primarily bricks-and-mortar business to an online distribution business of print and e-books.

Regardless of the industry and products, with the emerging market opportunities provided by the Internet, some businesses have not been able to adapt to a new way of marketing their products and move from an offline to an online business fast enough to continue to grow at the same pace as they had in the past. They could not adopt a new model even though their primary business model and sources of revenue were contracting. The video rental store Blockbuster is one example of a big brand company that, for whatever reason, stuck to one model for too long and missed the bigger opportunity online that would soon take over. Netflix, on the other hand, which never had physical stores, was able to respond to the rapid changes in the market, first with DVDs delivered in the mail and then through streaming over the Internet, which has become, along with cable and satellite, the preferred way to consume video content.

In the case of publishing, even as e-books have grown and expanded the book business, the sales of print books have not gone away and, in some categories, are also growing. Many publishers still publish only in print formats. Many others publish both print and electronic formats. Print may continue to thrive for many years to come, especially for certain kinds of publications—popular nonfiction, fiction, illustrated children's books, and some educational books. Still, market trends indicate that all publishers should be in some state of transition and should be asking themselves what the right balance is between an offline (primarily print) and an online business—if not for the present, then for the near future.

In fact, publishers have been forced to confront many questions with the emergence of e-books, especially since more and more readers prefer them: will the demand for the printed book decline dramatically and, if so, how fast, and how can this be managed? Will e-books cannibalize the sale of print and what will happen to publishing margins as a result? Are there certain genres that are better suited to e-books than to print? Are there consumer groups with special needs, such as the site-impaired, which would benefit greatly from digital books that are audio-enabled and whose fonts can be adjusted for easier reading? Finally, can feature-rich e-books help to open new markets?

For now, and perhaps for the short term, both formats are in demand; at least there is enough of a demand for publishers to be able to produce both print and e-book products profitably. In a conversation I had with an executive at Follett, a major distributor of books to libraries representing more than 6,500 publishers, I learned that some publishers had their historically best print sales in 2014. The reality today for publishers and distributors is, as John Ingram, of the Ingram Content Group (the largest distributor of physical and digital content), described it to me at the most recent Frankfurt Book Fair: "It's not either/or, but either/*and*."

Chapter 2
Life after Print

"How did you go bankrupt?" Bill asked.
"Two ways," Mike said. "Gradually and then suddenly."
Ernest Hemingway, The Sun Also Rises

My experience over the past 35 years, with five publishing houses, has been primarily in nonfiction, educational, and illustrated reference publishing. For the last 13 years, I have been a senior vice president at Encyclopaedia Britannica and have been on the leadership team tasked with making the transition from traditional print publishing to online delivery. Any company can make this change, of course, but doing it profitably is the challenge. At no time during our transition did we sacrifice our bottom line or allow for an "investment period" in our annual P&L. Today, Britannica is entirely a digital publisher and service provider, with a variety of online products that address both the educational and consumer markets.

Due to declining sales of Britannica's main print products, the need to become a digital publisher, in part or whole, had been clear to the company several years before I arrived, though how fast the company would become primarily a digital publisher and when it would produce its last set of printed books was not a fixed point on the calendar. There had been many plans on how and when to become fully digital, some of which are still in place today, as well as several false starts. But it became evident to all of us in management more than a dozen years ago that Britannica's future was not going to depend on being a print-based publisher of general and specialized encyclopedias, even though that is precisely the type of publications the company has been known for, and what the brand predominately still stands for, in the minds of many.

Nevertheless, Britannica's evolution from print to digital publishing has been greatly misunderstood and misrepresented by almost every outsider who has attempted to describe its position relative to other publishers or explain what Britannica's management has actually done to maintain financial stability during what would end up being a 20-year journey. Some pundits, even those who should have a better understanding of the publishing landscape, are unaware of the diversity of Britannica's publications, including its legacy as one of the most prominent producers of educational videos, and did not know that Britannica has been online since 1981—when the company published the first digital encyclopedia in history, a text-only version of the *Britannica* for LexisNexis subscribers—at a time when the "Internet" was still known mostly to researchers and academics. (The term "Internet" would not be adopted until 1995.)[1]

Among both analysts and the general public, a lack of awareness exists of what many companies—not just Britannica—have been doing to adapt to the digital age. This may be the case for a variety of reasons. For one, change can be slow, especially in big companies with huge investments in legacy processes and products. Another reason may be the continual financial success of traditional products, which can result in delays in making necessary adjustments to the inevitable. An additional contributing factor is the enormous amount of information and distraction that we are bombarded with and how hard it is today to penetrate and filter out the substantial "noise" in the market. In Britannica's case, it's likely that because the brand has been so closely tied with a single product line for so long, the company's other innovations and publications, both online and off, have gone largely unnoticed by most people other than Britannica's most loyal followers. Britannica's progress in becoming a digital solution publisher demonstrates how disruptive market forces and technology can provide both an impetus and a means for making changes that increase a company's revenue, provide more opportunities for future growth, and, in the process, alter a company's identity, both internally and externally. By illuminating the path that Britannica has taken and clarifying how it is succeeding in the digital age, I hope to correct some misconceptions about the decision making that brought Britannica to its current position in the market and to provide an example that other companies might follow when faced with similar challenges.

When people think about Britannica, even today, they visualize a large set of thick volumes on a bookshelf. (The set consisted of 32 volumes to be exact, including a two-volume subject index and a single-volume topic index called the *Propeadia—Outline of Knowledge*.) This venerable set of books, known as the *Encyclopaedia Britannica*, was the gold standard in general knowledge retrieval for more than 240 years, beginning with the first printing of a three-volume

---

1   For a concise history of the Internet and its beginnings as ARPANET, see the following website: http://internetsociety.org. September 18, 2015.

set in 1768. My generation of learners, who were in school in the 1950s–1970s, relied on the "new" *Britannica* (or one of its few rivals) to get information on almost any topic and complete our homework assignments. We used these tomes in the school library during study hours and many of us—the lucky ones—had a comparable set of books at home that was purchased at an onerous cost, often over time with interest charges. But despite the heavy price relative to other home purchases and especially other books, having or using a set of these trusted sources of knowledge was essential, because there was no other way to gain fast and easy access to reliable information on a vast number of subjects. To keep up to date on world events and changing times, an annual supplement, called the *Book of the Year*, was another must-have tool for students and other knowledge seekers.

In its 20th-century heyday (from the 1950s up to 1990), Britannica was selling hundreds of thousands of sets of encyclopedias worldwide each year and millions of annual supplements.[2] The sets were sold and distributed through the now-defunct network of door-to-door salesmen and the annual supplements were delivered via the mail on a "negative-option" basis, meaning that they came to your door automatically if you had purchased a set of encyclopedias; your choice was either to pay for the book after it arrived or return it. Most people (roughly 90% from year to year) kept the book and sent in their checks. The company had very little bad debt from these sales, because customers either eagerly anticipated receiving the books every year or didn't want the hassle of returning them. Either way, these yearbooks represented a major publishing program and supported a substantial editorial, production, manufacturing, and distribution effort. Customers were sold on the idea that the annual supplements were a way to keep their sets up to date, which, at the time, was true and an actual benefit. Still, from a business preservation point of view and in order to increase the lifetime value of the customer, the negative option marketing of this product was ingenious. A positive option approach—sending customers an announcement first and asking if they wanted to receive the book—would have resulted in many more cancellations. At least that was the theory. Thus, sales of the annual supplements represented a highly profitable revenue stream that had a built-in base of millions of owners of the *Britannica* worldwide.

---

2   Sales of the *Britannica* continued to increase through the 1980s and peaked in 1990, when the company printed approximately 165,000 sets. Since each set contained 35 individual books, including the two-volume index and the *Propaedia*, Britannica was selling more than 5.7 million books, not including the annual supplements and other print products. Four years later, sales of the printed books declined by 50%.

Stores did not carry multivolume encyclopedias. The door-to-door sales channel was the only way by which you could acquire these essential products for learners of all ages.[3] This distribution system, though labor-intensive and often mocked, was, at the time, the most efficient way of selling this type of product. Having the encyclopedias stockpiled at bookstores would not have been practical for several reasons: the logistics of transporting them from the store (each set required three heavy boxes); the absolute cost of the product, which would prevent spontaneous purchases; and the price disparity between its cost and every other item in a bookstore. Even if purchasing a set of encyclopedias was anxiety-producing for some customers, having them at home on the bookshelf was the equivalent of participating in a cultural phenomenon and a shared experience among *Britannica* owners—mostly an aspirational class of parents—who wanted to give their children an advantage so that they could excel in school, attend college, and have a better chance at success in life. For millions of people who owned the *Britannica*—generally regarded as *the* gateway to knowledge—this mindset was not a myth but a fact, as unlikely as that may seem now in an era of instant access to many times the amount of information than could ever be organized and printed in a fixed set of books.

The first technology that disrupted this model and started the process of a different, less cumbersome, and more efficient way to deliver encyclopedic content was the CD-ROM. In the early 1980s, Britannica's management—with genuine excitement—realized that software, and the ability to provide access to a large amount of content in a digital format, could change the way in which content-heavy products like encyclopedias were produced, distributed, and consumed. In addition to fitting the entire contents of an encyclopedia onto one or more discs, the benefits that software could provide were manifold. Using the new technology, content-rich products could now include video, sound, and animation. Search and browse functions could replace an index, which most people either ignored or didn't know how to use correctly or easily. The content could also be updated more often and at a reduced cost. As a result, software and information technology were viewed and appreciated early on as enormously beneficial to the editing process and to consumers. Even during the early days of CD-ROM development, management viewed the new technology as a potentially high-growth area of publishing, with the ability to reach many

---

3 Some encyclopedias, like Funk & Wagnalls' *New Standard Encyclopedia*, were available in supermarkets on a "continuity" model. The volumes were released gradually over time. The first few volumes were heavily discounted to encourage purchases. Subsequent volumes were at full price. Depending on the release dates of the volumes, it would take months to acquire an entire set.

more people at lower costs. The business models that would make growth sustainable, however, were still not yet developed.

While management was working on software business models, it was also preoccupied with how the resulting digital products would affect the legacy print business. In the 1980s, the print business was not only highly profitable; it was still growing every year. Of course, there were concerns and debates about cannibalization, especially among the salesforce, which made a living on print sales and feared the potential disruption to their livelihood. Still, management enthusiastically pursued the new technology, not because they knew exactly how to market the products or how fast the technology would improve, but because they believed that the new format would be transformational for consumers by providing a more up-to-date, accessible, and engaging product. They felt strongly that Britannica had to embrace the new technology because they realized it would be better to cause disruption from within the company (if that's what introducing new technology into the product line would mean) than to be disrupted by a competitor. Unfortunately, as I will discuss, additional market forces were in play—particularly with the development and marketing of CD-ROMs bundled with computer operating systems and the appearance of a non-traditional player in the encyclopedia business—that would make this strategy harder than the Britannica team could imagine and more urgent to implement.

Britannica's initial effort to provide encyclopedic content with images, movement, and sound was not based on the *Britannica* itself, but on the *Compton's* database, another Britannica property, which had less text and fewer volumes in print (26 versus 32). By using *Compton's*, management was wagering that an engaging digital product could be produced that would take advantage of the available technology, but would not necessarily threaten the print revenue from the *Britannica*, its flagship product. Also, during the early stages in CD-ROM technology (before the arrival of DVDs), it would have taken several CD-ROMs to contain all of the *Britannica*, especially with the addition of other media.

The result, in 1989, was the world's first multimedia encyclopedia on a single CD-ROM. *Compton's Multimedia Encyclopedia* hit the market through the computer software outlet Tandy/Radio Shack and sold for $850, which was roughly the same price as the *Compton's* print set. Although the product represented a successful publishing effort, in that it worked as planned on computers and users liked it, the business model was not sustainable: the price was too high (many consumers were reluctant to assign the same value to a single disc as they did to 26 volumes on a shelf, in spite of the extra bells and whistles that could be built into the software), which lowered overall demand; the distribution channel was limited; producing multimedia for the CD-ROM was expensive and time-consuming; the extra editorial effort required to produce both the CD-ROM and the print set strained the available resources; and the technology was still evolving. Most publishers in the early days of developing computer-driven digital products were well aware of the general acceptance of Moore's law—which states that the processing power of computers would double every year—and recognized that CD-ROMs would improve quickly and would eventually become obsolete. And for Britannica, the question of what to do with its main, iconic property, the *Britannica*, was perennial. The company could not keep its most sought-after asset as a print-only product forever and prevent it from having a digital life. The *Compton's* product was excellent and a reasonably good first step in multimedia publishing, but it would never match the reputation or represent the value proposition (and demand the high price point) of the *Britannica*. Management had a new imperative: in order to ensure a continuing strong market for an encyclopedic product, the *Britannica*, universally regarded as best of class, would have to be made available on the medium of choice. Before this could be made a reality, the company would have to decide which digital medium would be used, how fast the product could be converted to a digital format, how many media assets it should contain, the optimal price, and the most efficient distribution channel. Surely the door-to-door channel, which depended on personally selling to individuals, would not make sense for a product that was designed to be viewed via a disc on computers rather than on 32,000 pages bound into 32 volumes on a bookshelf and at a fraction of the cost.

Although discussions about converting the *Britannica* to a digital format—with the risk of negatively impacting the value of the print product—were troubling for the salesforce and caused plenty of internal squabbling, management continued to invest in the new technology, which had many advantages over print—some that were easily achievable at the time and others that were rapidly evolving—that needed to be explored. Experimentation with the technology and marketing models continued in spite of the protests of some naysayers, whose main motivation was only self-preservation. The company had an obligation to protect the brand, not the door-to-door salesforce. Yes, the consumer salesforce had always been a huge asset to the company, but the digital era, because of the type of products it heralded, was going to be far less dependent on it. Although the speed with which the market would adopt the new technology was yet to be determined, the salesforce was in denial about the inevitability of digital products replacing the print set. In many situations where change is not universally embraced, denial, as the axiom goes, is not just a river in Egypt. The new technology would be a major disruption not only to the traditional product format and the channel that brought it to millions of customers around the world, but also to a way of life for thousands of people.

In 1993, four years after the launch of the *Compton's Multimedia*, the entire *Britannica* text (without images or sound) was put on two CD-ROMs, and sold only to other publishing companies and businesses as an annual license for $2,100 per year—with the promise that the following year's product would be fully updated and therefore merited the annual fee.

In 1994, compression technology made it possible to launch the same *Britannica* product on a single CD-ROM, which was then distributed to the consumer market for $895, and would drop even further to $495 a year later—though even this price was too high to compete in the cut-throat consumer market. Meanwhile, the price of *Compton's* was lowered to $100 in order to maintain a differentiation in value with the *Britannica*, to make the product more accessible to consumers, and to compete with other CD-ROM products that had started to appear on the market.

Also in 1994, *Britannica Online* debuted on the Internet at www.eb.com, which was initially available only to educational institutions. With the introduction of the online product, the company was now juggling several different formats (print and digital, offline and online) and several pricing models (including annual subscriptions for its online product), with two different databases, in an effort to discover the extent of the demand and where consumer preferences might be headed. All three formats—print, CD-ROM, and online—were profitable, and each format had meaningful market acceptance and a different user base. The print products were still selling well, particularly in schools and libraries, where digital consumption was slow to catch on, and in overseas markets, especially Asia, where computer penetration and broadband availability still lagged behind the U.S. and European markets. Since print revenue was still strong, the company felt it could experiment with digital technology and various price points without seriously risking the cannibalization of its primary revenue streams.

Still, Britannica's management realized that all three formats—especially as the price points of each format continued to diverge—could not live side by side forever. Keeping all formats in the marketplace over time would strain resources and would put pressure on profit margins. But it was too early in the lifecycle of the new technologies to be able to read clear signals from the market as to which products would continue to be in demand and at what price.

However, Britannica, and other reference publishers that were also experimenting with multiple formats, could not delay making a major commitment to digital publishing. The bold and unexpected entrance into the CD-ROM field of an outsider caused a major disruption in the industry and forced them to move faster. This unanticipated publishing disruption occurred when Microsoft launched a series of reference products on CD-ROM.[4] Microsoft viewed CD-ROM technology as a way to showcase the consumer utility of the PC and as an opportunity to consolidate its position as the provider of Windows, the leading computer operating system. CD-ROM—and, later, DVD—technology, with the ability to deliver media-rich text on PCs, helped to make the case for why consumers should own PCs at home. When Microsoft was considering the kind of CD-ROM products it should produce to build a consumer base for PCs, an encyclopedia was a logical choice, since it was the one product that a large number of consumers—proven over decades—either had or wanted in their home, especially if it could be purchased at an attractive price point from a local retail store or bundled with a new computer. If Microsoft could develop its own multimedia encyclopedia, using its advanced software capabilities, it would be able to create a greater demand for the home use of PCs, which would be a boon for Microsoft, since its Windows operating system was on every PC shipped except for Apple computers. At the same time, by producing CD-ROMs with the kind of content associated with encyclopedias, Microsoft—without having this objective as part of its corporate strategy—would, as a consequence, become a major reference publisher in addition to a technology company.

In 1993, after almost six years of delays, Microsoft came out with *Encarta*, its own multimedia encyclopedia based on content that it licensed from Funk & Wagnalls. It was well aware that the contents of Funk & Wagnalls' *New Standard Encyclopedia*, remembered as a supermarket product and not a serious reference work, could not compete in terms of size and prestige with the *Britannica*, or even with *Compton's*, which was widely known as a Britannica brand, revised and edited by the same team of Britannica professionals. But Microsoft also knew that it didn't need to match Britannica's editorial quality. It set out to make an engaging mass-market product that showcased the utility of the

---

4   Called the Microsoft Bookshelf, the CD-ROM consisted of a dictionary, thesaurus, the *Chicago Manual of Style, Bartlett's Quotations*, and the *World Almanac*.

computer as well as software innovation, and that could be made available at computer-software stores for under $100. In addition, now consumers had an even more compelling reason to buy a new PC: they could get CD-ROMs bundled with the new machines that virtually replaced print products that cost more than $1,000.

When *Encarta* appeared on the market, the CD-ROM wars began in earnest, because Microsoft was no ordinary publisher or competitor. It had deep pockets. It could recruit the best editors and designers in the business. It could make a legitimate effort to improve the Funk & Wagnalls' database by throwing more money at it than any ordinary publisher could conceive of doing. In fact, it aggressively recruited talent from Britannica and other reference publishers, several of whom were my colleagues at the time, and brought them together with top-notch Microsoft engineers. To attract skilled talent from the publishing industry and move them to Redmond, Washington, Microsoft's headquarters, it showered editors with stock options, bonuses, benefits, and salaries rarely available at traditional publishing houses. For ordinary editors, joining Microsoft was like winning the lottery, especially for industry veterans who had not imagined the kind of opportunities that Microsoft could offer. Because of the size of its core business, Microsoft didn't even have to make money on the CD-ROMs or DVDs and could continue to build a senior staff and invest in product development, while, at the same time, lowering prices at retail or bundling the CD-ROMs with new PCs to increase its market share. This product category was viewed as a loss leader to Microsoft for the purpose of selling more computers with Windows, which, as a marketing strategy, was a major problem for encyclopedia and traditional reference publishers, like Britannica, whose main business was constructed around the profitable publishing of quality editorial products—even as the format for delivering these products evolved.

With pressure from Microsoft, as it aggressively marketed *Encarta*—in computer stores, bundled with computers, and all over the world in several different languages—Britannica finally abandoned the strategy of protecting the *Britannica* by using only the *Compton*'s database as a competitive, consumer-driven product. Management knew that if it was going to continue a two-centuries-old history of owning the encyclopedia space and retain its position as the world's leading encyclopedia publisher, it needed to go to market with its best product in all formats. In 1997, the company launched the *Britannica Multimedia Encyclopedia* at $100 to go head-to-head with *Encarta*, which at that time was selling for $70 when sold as a stand-alone product.

The CD-ROM/DVD wars continued for another 10 years (Microsoft finally withdrew *Encarta* from the market in 2009). But Microsoft and Britannica, along with the other encyclopedia publishers like Grolier and World Book, had very different stakes in this business. For Microsoft, *Encarta* achieved its objective—not of being the best encyclopedia on the market, which was never the goal—but of creating demand for and loyalty to Windows across the globe.[5] It didn't set out to beat Britannica at the encyclopedia business. However, as a consequence of its size and power, it forced a leading publisher, albeit in a specialized field, to reinvent its business. For the consumer market, the number-one disruption that came out of the CD-ROM/encyclopedia wars was getting *Encarta* free with the Windows operating system. When this offer was made available, it represented a threat—not only to encyclopedia publishers in particular but to all publishers—that was simply unprecedented. For reference publishers, this was a Darwinian moment. How could any business survive in an environment where a competitor, for whatever reason, was willing to invest a great deal of money and resources in a product and give it away for free? And not just any product, but one that was an acceptable or "good enough" alternative to a product that for decades (more than two centuries) had a high perceived value in the market. Yet this free-with-the-computer offer was the model that some publishers had to face in the early days of digital publishing.

Senior management of other publishers and businesses that were not personally affected by this specific disruption at the time should have taken note, for this model, which married content with technology, foreshadowed other new models that would cause disruptions in publishing. Encyclopedia publishers, because of the nature of their product line—consisting of expensive, multivolume print sets that, in digital form, offered a variety of benefits to consumers—were the first to be challenged from an outsider and forced to make rapid changes in their products and in their distribution channels. But the rest of the industry would find their business models equally shaken as digital publishing matured. It just took longer.

For encyclopedia publishers, the CD-ROM/DVD format would soon be replaced almost entirely by the Internet.[6] In 1999 Britannica launched britannica.com, a site specially created for consumers. Its educational products, sold mostly to colleges and universities, continued to evolve. At this point, Britannica was

---

5   See *The Microsoft Way* by Randall Stross for a discussion on how and why Microsoft developed *Encarta*.

6   Where broadband is not reliable, it is still a useful medium today and, for many types of media-rich content, is preferable to print.

responding to the needs of both consumers and educational institutions with two different websites. Both sites became popular. Consumers had a choice of viewing a version of *Britannica* free with advertising or subscribing to the entire *Britannica* (with additional premium features) and no advertising. Now, three viable formats and various business models competed for market attention: print, mostly a library purchase; DVDs, sold in stores or bundled with computers; and online products for consumers and institutions. Britannica's management knew that juggling all three of these formats was not sustainable: too many separate editorial and production efforts competed for valuable resources; and the results did not provide the optimal solutions for the market.

Market conditions were beginning to emerge that would determine the viability of these formats. As a result of the widespread availability of inexpensive or free encyclopedias on DVDs and computers, including the company's own products, Britannica's print business started to decline in the early 1990s, and then more precipitously between 1993 and 1999 when Microsoft's *Encarta* was dominant. Management understood that this print business, once lost, would not return. Both DVDs and the Internet provided a better experience for consumers at much lower prices. And because of the promise of the Internet, even as early as 2000, with the advantages it offered of providing up-to-date content to users from any computer at any time, Britannica's management was well aware that DVDs too would eventually become obsolete.

Between 2001 and 2006—I joined the company in 2002—we accelerated the development of new and specialized reference and learning websites for different audiences and markets. K-12 schools, universities, public libraries, and consumers each had a Britannica website tailored to their specific needs and uses, with prices that were aligned with the requirements of these markets. In 2006, Britannica reached a tipping point, where more than half of the company's revenue came from digital products (DVDs and websites). Website revenue was particularly promising and was growing at a rate of about 18% each year. Print was in a perpetual downward slide. We accepted the fact that eventually we would have to eliminate the print products altogether. Up until 1997, the decline in print revenue was still gradual. The sales of individual sets declined more rapidly than the gross revenue as we raised prices to mitigate revenue and profit erosion. But based on the trends, we could see that both print sales and revenue would drop to unacceptable levels sometime in the near future. As the Internet became a place for more robust development and as more people flocked to it in the early 2000s, DVD sales declined dramatically; the DVD-ROM, a relatively new technology, was about to take its place next to the laserdisc and become digital technology's latest equivalent of the dodo.

No one at the management level of the company, especially by 2002, thought that the demand for the print product would experience a rebirth or that digital delivery over the Internet was just a fad. On the contrary, we projected that by no later than early in the second decade of the new century, print would come to an end, as the decline was perceptible year on year and then month on month. Simultaneously, we were experiencing steady growth in our website revenue, even though it wasn't at the same pace as the decline of print revenue. We anticipated that at some point the lines would cross on a graph and Web revenue would outpace and replace print revenue.

We were preparing our business and the new financial models for the inevitable—we just didn't know exactly when we would terminate print production and place all of our confidence in a digital future. However, we did know that we had to make that decision before the bottom fell out of the market, meaning that we wanted to avoid being stuck with a warehouse full of print sets—a huge investment in inventory—which we could not sell or would be forced to sell at fire-sale prices. If we were going to stop printing, we wanted the timing to be as close to the actual end of the consumer demand for print as possible, but also in line with the increased demand of our Web services. We wanted to avoid the plight of Mike Campbell in Hemingway's novel *The Sun Also Rises*, who described the two ways he went bankrupt: "Gradually and then suddenly."

Our main print product had been in a gradual decline for a decade, but we knew that if we did not act at the optimal time, the "suddenly" would happen; we did not want to be caught off-guard. Our goal was to time the end of our print business, as best we could, so that the impact on our P&L would be minimal. That moment came in 2012. We had gone to press with the *Britannica* for what would be the final printing in 2010 and had fewer than 10,000 sets left in all of our global locations. By this time, revenue from our websites was strong enough to sustain and grow the business. In February 2012, we announced to the public that when the last *Britannica* set was sold, there would be no additional print-runs. The sets sold out in less than 30 days, most likely because consumers wanted to own a piece of history—the last printing of the venerable *Britannica* print set.

The end of an era precipitated the beginning of a new business, which would be entirely digital and distributed over the Internet. By producing relevant products and exercising flexibility in the way in which those products could be delivered, Britannica was able to weather the storm of two powerful disruptions to its business. The company had been in the print business for more than 247 years and the DVD business for 10 years. Both formats were made obsolete by the Internet—one gradually and one rapidly. Will the Internet be obsolesced, eventually, by something else? As good stewards of the Britannica brand and as good business people, we should expect that it will and should plan for further disruption. We don't know at this point if or how the Internet will be displaced. Mobile technology is a growing trend now, but it too relies on the Internet. And we are fully immersed in responsive design, which allows users to access our products on any device, anywhere, and at any time. Learning platforms are also being used increasingly by schools and libraries to allow students and patrons to search multiple databases from a single query. Usage is a key metric for demonstrating product value; our goal, in order to continue to be relevant, is to be the first stop in any search on any subject. Publishers can demonstrate their value by showing that consumers use their products frequently, get the information they seek, and view those products as reliable, affordable, engaging destinations that deliver on their promise.

Chapter 3
The Print-to-Digital Continuum

There is a tide in the affairs of men
Which taken at the flood leads on to fortune;
Omitted, all the voyage of their life
Is bound in shallows and in miseries.

William Shakespeare, Julius Caesar, *Act IV, Scene III*

Digital publishing strategies vary greatly depending on the publisher's specialization. Trade publishers approach the marketing of digital content differently from educational publishers or publishers of professional titles in the fields of health or law, for example. The output can be as simple as e-book versions of print publications, released either at the same time or after the print editions have hit the market. Some publishers believe that delaying the availability of the e-book version positively impacts the sales of the hardcover versions. Others, particularly textbook publishers, are bypassing printed revisions of their books and releasing new editions only as e-books. Educational publishers who have a strong demand for their print publications, particularly those written for younger learners, might provide PDF versions of the same books—sometimes enhanced with video or animations—on discs. The content of these CD-ROMs or DVDs are often downloaded onto school networks where teachers and students can access them on computers or interactive whiteboards. This often satisfies a "technology requirement" established by school districts or learning authorities. Others are creating collections of e-books on specific topics and selling them on a subscription basis as a classroom solution. A growing number of e-book apps are primarily targeting parents of pre-school and primary-age children. Publishers are testing the market's appetite for digital versions of books as well as responding to the demand for content on various devices, especially mobile devices, including tablets and smartphones.

Very few general trade publishers today are releasing their titles only in print formats.[1] Some companies may favor either print or digital outputs, but for the most part, mainstream publishers are on a continuum that includes

---

1   "E-books Outsell Print Books at Amazon." *New York Times*, May 19, 2011.

both. This book, for example, will be available in print or as an e-book, and will be compatible with the Kindle, Nook, and Kobo, and with other Android and Apple (iOS) devices as well. For some types of publishing, especially multivolume and specialized reference titles, digital formats have replaced print altogether. At the far, *digital* end of the print-to-digital continuum are database publishers, like Britannica, described in the previous chapter, whose publications are continuously updated and revised, and expand regularly—and are available as a daily Web service to millions of readers simultaneously, 24/7. An equivalent print version of this kind of publication—which is delivered over the Internet—is not feasible. (Newspaper content is also published daily as an Internet service, but it is different, since the content is almost entirely replaced every day—with the older articles sent to a retrievable archive—and a print version is also available.) Further, a clear distinction exists between database and e-book publishing, each of which creates different consumer expectations. E-books, though digital, are still "books," meaning they are finished, static products released at a specific time and are not subject to change. They have their own ISBNs (International Standard Book Numbers), but are otherwise identical to, and look just like, the print versions. Physical books do not come with future updates or changes, and consumers do not expect any when they buy one. The same should be true of the e-book version. The only way in which an e-book "changes" is when a new edition is released. In other words, when consumers buy e-books, they should not expect that they would receive a new edition of the book or future updates with the initial purchase. The situation is very different, however, with online information services, or databases, where the expectation is not only that the content changes over time, but also that the information is always up to date. And since most online databases are purchased on a subscription basis, the expectation is that all updates, revisions, and enhancements come with the subscription price.

These examples of print and digital publishing revolve around economic models that are still in flux. Database publishing's own cost structure is very different from that of either a printed book or an e-book. Publishers that only produce databases may have eliminated the cost of printing and physical inventory storage and distribution, but the additional costs of code development, Web application maintenance, platform support (either third-party licenses or proprietary software), and broadband, as well as constant updating, consume much of those savings and put their own strain on profit margins.

Similarly, marketing both print and e-books has its own share of challenges, especially in trying to align consumer expectations with the prices of the print and e-book versions of the same title. Most consumers assume that e-books, simply because they do not use ink on paper—and generally contain exactly the same content as the print versions—cost less than their physical counterparts to manufacture and distribute, and therefore should be priced much lower than their hardcover equivalent. <u>Users also still have the perception that a digital product does not have the same tangible value as a physical book</u>, even though other costs, especially with highly illustrated books—including conversions to the various e-reader formats, technology storage costs, software licensing fees, and metadata development—basically replace (though perhaps not entirely) the costs of producing print products. However, consumers are not likely to consider these factors when making their purchasing decisions. Consumers do not see the outputs of these investments in the finished product in the same way they do with the physical materials in a printed book.

Another challenge for the publisher is the current sales volume of e-books. The revenue generated from many categories of e-book titles is not yet substantial enough to deliver the necessary return on investment (ROI) to cover all costs; therefore, publishers depend on print sales to subsidize a portion of the development of the digital content. For many educational publishers, whose markets are slow to change and where print remains the preferred medium, current demand for digital books does not cover the high costs of producing and integrating the rich content, which often contains interactive images and highly designed layouts. As a result, e-book development almost always follows the publishing of the print product and for now is not likely to be a stand-alone activity.

Still, e-book sales are rising year on year. The most economically promising aspect of e-book publishing is the reduction in variable costs associated with the delivery of finished e-books to the end user. The number of e-books purchased and downloaded has little impact on the publisher's cost structure; the total cost to the publisher is the same whether multiple copies or only one copy is downloaded. On the other hand, several variable costs with print books are impossible to avoid, which make them much more expensive than e-books to produce and, consequently, put the long-term viability of some categories of printed books at risk. For example, for every print book produced, approximately one-third of the costs can be attributed to the paper stock alone. The publisher incurs this cost on every single copy produced. In the case of an e-book, the cost to the publisher is the same whether it sells hundreds of copies of an e-book or only one copy. And even though e-books accrue costs that are outside those of the print product, most of these, with the exception of technology storage fees based on server space, are one-time costs. Taking into consideration only the investment in paper, print books are significantly more expensive for the publisher to produce than e-books—at least 33% more.

Where a publisher resides on the continuum from print to digital output is likely to change over time. In the future, for most publishers, an increasing share of their revenue, as well as profits, will come from digital publishing. Some publishers might be able to remain dependent on print for a longer period of time than others. But the trends are clear: as is the case with newspapers, magazines, encyclopedias, and other multivolume reference works, market preference for digital versions of all types of publications is increasing, and this fact, along with the lower variable costs associated with e-books, will influence publishers to ride the digital market wave more aggressively.[2]

The year-on-year growth in digital publishing does not mean that print revenue is being cannibalized completely or that print will go out of favor quickly—or, from a consumer's point of view, that print isn't necessarily a preferred format for some uses and publications. Print revenue is not shrinking at the same rate that digital publishing is growing. In some segments of the industry, especially the education market, both print and digital revenue are growing. And even as digital revenue grows in this market segment, print still accounts for the majority of sales.

In looking for persistent trends and watching for market tipping points as well as growth opportunities, publishers should be aware of the difference in how fast various publishing companies—particularly in the education market sector—are growing in terms of revenue and profit based on how deeply invested they are in digital products. According to *Education Market Research* (EMR), companies can be placed into two groups, "high" digital and "low" digital, depending on how much of their publishing program consists of print versus digital formats. In a study that EMR conducted in 2013, "high" digital players outperformed "low" digital players in terms of orders, volume of leads, and growth outlook.[3] The same study noted that digital product sales grew 1.8% in 2012, whereas non-digital sales actually declined by 4.9%. In short, digital products are growing faster than non-digital. On the other hand, the study also concluded that while digital is on the rise, print is "holding its own." So at least for now, the two formats can co-exist as they address different market preferences, expectations, priorities, and economic climates. Still, "holding its own" is not a formula for growth, and this is where print and e-book trends differ in value.

 2   EdNet News Alert, *Software & Information Industry Association*, Tuesday, February 24, 2015.
3   *Robert M. Resnick, Education Market Research*, October, 2013.

The physical book remains the format that most publishers tend to think about first during the creative process. It is still their paradigm of intellectual property development. But that paradigm has been morphing into other forms, as market forces and user preferences are increasingly turning to a variety of digital products for information, self-help, and entertainment, mostly *TRENDS* delivered over the Internet. So although the physical book (and other print-based products) is still a profitable, marketable, and useful (and perhaps the most intuitive) format, it may not be the most widely used in an increasing number of markets. In fact, if we accept the EMR study results as a constant trend, their conclusion is that "digital products have not only gained traction, they are starting to dominate."

Keeping in mind a positive growth outlook for digital products, publishers have to determine which factors are affecting this trend and decide if more opportunities are available with digital products than with print products for addressing new market requirements, and then make adjustments that do not negatively impact their ongoing business. An upward growth trend in e-book purchases does not necessarily mean that it is time to abandon a print strategy. Pursuing both formats can be accomplished without compromising a strong and still viable legacy business. But if data clearly shows that the publisher's print business is declining over time or if going to press—even by adjusting pricing models—is just too expensive, implementing a digital strategy may be in order.

Here's an example of a publisher which was able to satisfy the needs of its traditional print customers while also responding to the growing number of digital customers—without compromising its P&L—and discovering an additional revenue stream. A+ Media, a publisher and an end-to-end developer of educational content, had been producing a member magazine for a PBS (Public Broadcasting Service) affiliate. The circulation of the magazine was growing every year, but after eight years, the client realized that higher printing costs and postage fees were exceeding its tight budget. In this case, it was a victim of its own success. The magazine, which helped to attract members—and therefore donations—was a free premium and a marketing expense that was rising every year. Julio Abreu, the President of A+ Media, suggested that the client turn the magazine into a digital product—an e-zine—to save on the costs associated with the print product, but still provide members with the content that they enjoyed and that helped to encourage continuing membership. Although the client initially wanted to drop the printed magazine completely in favor of a digital one, Julio made the case that a gradual transition from print to digital would be more strategic because the largest segment of its target audience (and most PBS viewers) was 55 years of age or older and much less willing to give up the printed magazine. As a result, it decided not to abandon the print edition, but instead reduced the number of pages from 20 to 12 and created a digital version with 24 pages as an incentive to switch to the new format.

Meanwhile, although A+ Media's revenue actually dropped due to lower printing fees, its profit margin increased with the additional fees it was able to charge for producing the digital version of the magazine. In addition, besides enjoying a reduction in its publication costs from the smaller print product, the client was also able to generate more advertising revenues from its 24-page Web-based magazine, which it linked to its corporate website. This was a clear case where the change from print to digital publishing was implemented using a transitional strategy that satisfied the lucrative donor base with an affordable print product while making a more profitable move to a digital product. The client was lucky that A+ Media had the foresight to provide a solution to a problem that would have only gotten worse over time and that could possibly have spelled the demise of a successful program. Instead, A+ Media was able to implement a strategy that could sustain the program for the foreseeable future.

For print publishers, or those mostly on the print-end of the continuum, one of the biggest constraints in their P&Ls—even if demand for their print products has not yet declined—is the fixed costs associated with traditional printing, which has always been based on an economies-of-scale model: the more you print, the cheaper each individual unit is to produce. Whether the printing takes place on large web-offset printers, which are more economical for very long print-runs (volume projects), or sheet-fed printers for shorter runs, there is always a "make-ready," or set-up, cost that is fixed regardless of the number of units produced. The make-ready cost of a print-run puts the publisher in the position of having to guess how much to print and risks having too many books (if they don't sell quickly) or too few in the event that demand is higher than anticipated. The publisher is economically incentivized to print as many books, or sets of books, as possible in order to amortize the fixed make-ready costs over the largest practical quantity of books, reducing the per-unit cost of the print-run. If the publisher overestimates the number of copies that it can sell in a reasonable amount of time, it will have more resources than necessary invested in the print-run and excess inventory that it might have to sell at a reduced price or even destroy. If it underestimates the number of units that it can sell (to keep its total investment as low as possible), it might end up with a higher per-unit cost than necessary and may be forced to try to sell the stock at above-market value or at a lower profit margin. In addition, if it sells through the print-run due to demand for the books being greater than estimated, it might have to go back to press and incur a second make-ready charge.

Web-offset printing can be more economical because it can accommodate cheaper paper stock (large rolls) than sheet-fed printing, and, as noted earlier, since paper represents one-third of the manufacturing costs, web-offset is a preferable alternative for certain types of publications. It can also support thinner paper, which is an advantage in publications with a high page count, such as phone directories. But the economics work only in cases where the publisher needs to use a lot of paper, either in very thick books, long print-runs (best sellers), or both. If books do not sell in a timely fashion, or demand unexpectedly drops, the longer print-runs end up being counterproductive.

The waste associated with having excess inventory, on the one hand, or the burden of having to pay more per unit for shorter print-runs on the other, makes this whole process vulnerable to obsolescence and susceptible to disruption. Let's take a closer, somewhat simplified, look at the fixed and variable costs of a print-run and see how this affects the publisher's decision-making process, and why even though this is a model that has been ripe for disruption, disruptive technology has not entirely solved the problem (and may not), and how digital publishing—either e-books or databases—provides an alternative solution.

Various tasks that are itemized in a print-run include text reprint plates, cover preparation and plates, and proofing. These costs are fixed regardless of the length of the print-run. There are also fixed-variable costs associated with the quantity of printing, folding, binding, and packing that are required for a specific task. In other words, fixed-variable items have both a fixed cost (a set-up fee, if you will) and a variable cost—a fixed rate multiplied by the length of the print-run. Together, these items constitute the "make-ready" cost. As an example, let's say a publisher wants to print a 10-volume set of four-color books of 200 pages each, and that the make-ready costs amount to $100,000. If the publisher prints 1,000 units, then the make-ready contributes $100 to the cost of each set, or $10 per book. If the publisher prints 10,000 units, then the make-ready only adds $10 to the cost of each set, or $1 per book. Longer print-runs generate large cost savings. However, planning for a long print-run is not always pragmatic. If the publisher decides to print 10,000 units and is able to sell only 1,000 units at the forecasted price, then it would have been much better off printing fewer units at a higher cost than carrying leftover inventory at the lower per-set cost. The publisher might be able to mitigate the higher make-ready costs associated with a shorter print-run by charging customers more for each set. But by doing this, it risks pricing the product above market value, with the unintended consequence of lowering demand even more and then being stuck with excess inventory anyway. Alternatively, the publisher risks compromising its profit margins if it keeps prices at market value or even lower.

You can see the kind of gamble that the publisher is faced with in trying to determine the optimal print-run quantity when it has a fixed cost that needs to be considered. Since the publisher is on the hook for whatever decision it makes, the result is a supply-chain parity problem, where the printer always wins and the publisher takes all of the risk. Whenever the supply chain contains an obvious imbalance—where one party takes all of the risk—an outside entity has an opportunity to provide a disruptive solution. (Recall how Amazon disrupted the bricks-and-mortar distribution channel with an online solution that was more efficient and also eliminated antiquated, wasteful steps in the supply chain.)

One attempt at a solution to the fixed-cost problem in traditional printing was introduced by print-on-demand (POD) technology. POD enables publishers to print only a handful of books instead of committing to a print-run that is longer than necessary, even if it is a relatively short one. A publisher could order a small number of POD books without having to amortize make-ready costs. With POD printing, the cost of each book is substantially higher than books produced by either web-offset or sheet-fed printing. But POD printers explain the benefits of their solution on the basis of an economic model that they define as the "total cost of ownership" (TCO). Since the publisher can order books based on actual demand instead of having to estimate what demand might be, POD technology eliminates the publisher's risk of carrying any excess inventory over a period of time. In other words, TCO means that even though the publisher is paying more for each item, in the long run, with no upfront inventory commitment, it may end up investing less to keep a title in print while satisfying demand. When deciding if POD is a solution for a specific publishing project, the publisher should consider the TCO of a print-run, including the actual printing charges; the costs of carrying inventory over time; and, possibly, having to remainder a portion of that inventory at fire-sale prices. Since POD is synonymous with "on-demand" sales, customers know and agree to the publisher's prices up-front, which means that the publisher can build in the necessary profit margins even with the lowest of print quantities. In this way, the higher unit price and lower demand are aligned in the market. For books with a limited demand—particularly specialized books such as scholarly titles or training manuals—TCO and POD are disruptive strategic alternatives to traditional print-run gambling.

For certain kinds of publishing, especially softcover, black-and-white books, or customized publications, such as photo albums, POD technology is an ideal solution. One of the pioneers in the application of this technology was John Ingram, who started Lightning Source, an entirely POD printer, as an offshoot of Ingram's book distribution business. John set out to fix the problem in the supply chain and provide publishers with an economic solution to the guessing game that went somewhat further than what was available at the time.

Lightning Source was conceived in the late 1990s and printed its first book in January 1998. According to John, this is what was so revolutionary:

> First, we truly pioneered 'one-at-a-time' printing—not short-run printing masquerading as POD. Why did we do this? Because at the time, POD was an answer to extending the in-stock availability of Ingram's wholesale business. Ingram wholesale may have shipped 40 books to a retailer or library, but it probably represented 20 to 30 different titles. Having a POD business where you had to make five or 10 books to yield one never made any sense. We needed to be able to make one at a time. From a standing start in 1998, we made about 30 million units in 2013 with an average run length of less than two units per run.

Lightning Source (and other POD printers) provided a solution to what was a significant problem for publishers. POD technology made short runs more economical (keeping TCO in mind) and, in some cases, eliminated the risk in ordering a longer print-run just to bring down the per-unit cost. But this still did not solve the problem in the supply chain where not even shorter runs were an adequate option for certain types of publications, such as multivolume sets or books with hundreds of pages, because the cost to produce the books using POD was simply too high for market conditions.

A lower-risk solution to the fixed costs and inventory problems associated with imprecise print-runs is to replace the print product with a digital one—assuming that a market for the same product in a digital format exists and that one of the barriers to higher demand is cost. Prior to digital solutions, publishing projects that required long print-runs with substantial up-front investments were simply revised and printed less frequently, and spent a longer time in the warehouse. Publishers held off as long as possible before going back to press, and, as a result, watched their copyrights age and the books turn into the publisher's equivalent of brown bananas. Even with a strong market for the contents of these books, demand would ultimately decrease as the books aged and lost perceived value. Once real digital solutions were available, however, publishers were able to establish a much better value proposition for consumers and convert even the most hesitant print customers to the digital alternatives.

Many scholarly and venerable publications that were in continual demand in niche markets no longer exist in print form, but provide users of their digital versions with a much better experience and a better value proposition. And if not for a digital solution, many of these products might simply have disappeared from the market. The *Britannica* is just one of many examples. The OED (*Oxford English Dictionary*), *Merriam-Webster's Unabridged Dictionary*, and *Westlaw* are others. *WestlawNext*—a database of case law from Westlaw going back more than 125 years—is a prime example of a successful transition of a print product into a digital service. The current publisher of *WestlawNext*, Thomson Reuters, makes a strong case for how the digital version of its former print products (journals and books) is a win-win for it and the consumer. On its website, it describes the advantages of its digital solution over its decades-long print archive and the ease-of-use and broad scope of the database as a way for researchers to go from "information to insight." Keyword searching replaces an index or table of contents. Users can research information quickly

and comprehensively with confidence that they are not missing pertinent information. While conducting a search on a specific topic, a user also receives related information to look up. When this content was available only in journal form or books on a shelf, an attorney, a typical user, might discover that the issue or volume he or she needed was being used by someone else, whereas with the online version, an unlimited number of users can have access to the entire collection simultaneously. Thomson Reuters summarizes the transformation of its text publications to technology solutions as a journey from "chaos to classified."

Curious consumer options have come to light as publishers make their way across the print-to-digital continuum. Bowker's *Books in Print* (a ProQuest publication) is, ironically, available only online. The most recent and still-available print version of *The Grove Dictionary of Art* (34 volumes for £1,425.00) appears to have been published way back in 2003 even though, according to the website, the online version is kept current with updates three times a year "to reflect the latest scholarship, with new articles and images, revised articles, additions to bibliographies, and corrections." *Blackwell Reference Online*, published by Wiley, offers subscribers an astounding 656 titles, covering more than 15 disciplines and a variety of different subscription options. Many of these titles are no longer available in print; if they were, however, even an institution would find it much more advantageous to purchase subscriptions on an as-needed basis and for a lower initial investment than the cost of the original printed volumes.

Online products distributed over the Internet are disruptive to static print products because they break several barriers at once: currency (update frequency), price, and access barriers. Now information that was available only from a select number of physical locations—like a school or library—can be accessed by the institution's subscriber base from any Internet-connected device, wherever they are. Usage of these online products increases dramatically and cost per use goes down proportionately. Younger learners—digital natives whose research skills have developed almost entirely through the use of online resources—might not relate to the humor behind baseball legend Yogi Berra's quip: "I'm not going to buy my kids an encyclopedia. Let them walk to school like I did."

Marketing models for digital products continue to evolve, but publishers now generate revenue from digital content in a variety of ways, encouraging movement toward the digital end of the print-to-digital continuum. For many types of products, the publisher may appear to be providing a lot more content for less revenue than it did with a print product. But publishers need to become more comfortable with exchanging print dollars for digital pennies; the pennies will continue to compound as usage of their digital products rises. Publishers with substantial databases are successfully selling their online products and services, either in part or whole, on a subscription basis, most often by the year, but sometimes monthly or for even shorter time periods. For some niche information services, such as product-rating services of consumer goods like cars and appliances, even "day passes" are common. For consumers, this is a useful way to experience the value of an online service at the time they need it without having to make a long-term commitment. For the publisher, this kind of short-term, small-revenue trial, or micro-charge, helps to establish customer loyalty and create goodwill, and is an excellent lead generation strategy for building a subscriber base. Both the consumer and the publisher are likely to make more substantial commitments to digital formats as digital products become more accepted and demonstrate greater value over print. A single purchase of an expensive print product can be replaced by a subscription to a digital product at a fraction of the cost. For the publisher, there is a net gain as well. With a large, growing subscriber base, subscription revenue can eventually eclipse the declining revenue from more expensive print products. Instead of having a customer who purchases a product once in every, say, five to eight years, publishers can now build an ongoing subscriber base and substantially increase the long-term value of each customer.

For many kinds of publications, the switch from print to a digital format has numerous benefits and advantages to the publisher, the buyer, and the user (when the end user is not the buyer, as is the case in libraries), but this does not mean that some positive features of print are not lost. Print reference works, for example, have several excellent qualities as well as real advantages over their digital equivalents. They do not require hardware and software to access, which can be a major disadvantage in locations where bandwidth is limited or funding for technology is inadequate; they remain accessible at all times and in perpetuity, even as they age, whereas software upgrades can sometimes limit access to some digital products over time—a major concern to archivists; they can provide a more satisfying, serendipitous browsing experience; they are often easier to read without backlighting; several volumes can be opened at once for comparing and contrasting topics; and they have an aesthetic appeal to several human senses and an intrinsic value as objects created with fine materials by skilled craftspeople. These benefits are not trivial or easily dismissed, but it appears from consumer behavior that not enough people are willing to pay the price for these attributes.

While print reference works are physically appealing when lavishly illustrated and composed in a well-designed layout, they have obsolescing limitations: they don't contain multimedia elements (video, sound, animation); they can't be easily searched or updated frequently; and they involve costly, inefficient supply-chain constraints. The disruptive technology aimed at solving the supply-chain problem is not unlike the global effort to replace petroleum-dependent cars with hybrids and ultimately all-electric models. Based on the trends, the likely end-game seems clear in both cases.

Publishers of large data sets developed over the years—and which are continually being extended and improved—can, with a digital strategy, democratize their content. They can now reach millions of users instead of thousands, who can enjoy the products—updated, enhanced, and always available—with a far lower investment than with a print product, assuming that the print version is even available. As a result of the number of advantages that the digital transformation has demonstrated in the print-to-digital continuum, the market for general and specialized digital encyclopedias and references has grown dramatically over the last 10 years, while the market for these same products in print form has declined or disappeared; many more published works will follow the same trajectory.

No doubt, some people will miss the aesthetics of a beautiful ink-on-paper product as well as the opportunity to take pride in building a library. (Is it any different, though, than physical collections of music?) But both consumers and publishers are already adjusting to this reality, and are recognizing that the benefits of digital publishing outweigh the disadvantages. As the novelist Peter De Vries remarked: "Nostalgia isn't what it used to be." I can say from first-hand experience that when we finally decided to terminate the print version of the *Britannica* in February 2012, we celebrated the event, with a multivolume-shaped cake and a champagne toast. Everyone in the company was happy to bid the print product—which was the foundation of the company for 247 years—a fond farewell.

The print *Britannica*, for us and most of our loyal customers, is firmly rooted in the past, while our present and future is digital. The content editors were thrilled because now they could see the fruits of their labor published daily, instead of every 12–18 months, by which time some of what they had written was already out of date. The production editors were happy because they no longer had to deal with "space patrol," where, in the print product, for every article or revision that took up additional space, something had to be removed. Marketing was happy because they had fresh content to promote and could also reach millions of customers around the globe, with either a robust subscription offering or an abridged product that was free with advertising. Management was happy because we no longer had to tie up revenue for months by investing in inventory. We eliminated the risky cost of a large print product and, equally as important, were able to invest instead in an engaging, up-to-date, and relevant product that was more reflective of the brand and what it stands for—a trusted source of current information of the knowledge most worth having. Customers were pleased because they could have access to the *Britannica*—enhanced with multimedia and refreshed daily—for pennies a day instead of investing thousands in a static product that may look good on a shelf, but that aged like milk, not wine. " *good quote.*

The Internet as an effective distribution channel absolutely disrupted the value of an iconic product, but it also eliminated the need to kill trees for dead wood and helped give birth to a living product that could evolve with the times and always be relevant.

Chapter 4
Tools to Change By

There are more things in heaven and earth, Horatio
Than are dreamt of in your philosophy.

William Shakespeare, Hamlet, *Act I, Scene V*

When I talk to production and managing editors or chief product officers at publishing houses about the benefits and challenges in the era of digital publishing, they cannot imagine accomplishing their goals today without the dramatic improvements in the production processes that technology has made possible. And they embrace the increased opportunities to reach new markets and audiences—especially those that prefer to consume information on electronic devices. But they regularly struggle with how best to label, organize, and store their digital assets so that they can keep track of them, locate them, and quickly know how and when they were created. More often than not, especially with publishers who have a long history of print-only publications and have only recently begun to implement a digital strategy, many of their assets may not be in any type of digital format, but rather stuck in a physical library somewhere. Often both physical documents (slides, manuscripts, mechanicals, original art and photography) and digital files are dispersed in many different locations, and production editors may find it no easier to locate digital files than older, non-digital materials.

If publishers face this problem, converting their archived print documents into a digital format isn't enough; they also have to adopt an asset management system to organize and help them find their digital files so that they can be used again. The best first step toward building a workable digital library is to begin with the most recently completed digital publications and then work backwards to address legacy products. The most recent digital productions are likely to be the easiest to convert to current standard formats and should provide a usable model for older outputs.

A good asset management system provides publishers with the flexibility they need to respond to evolving market needs. As all market segments become increasingly accustomed to consuming information in digital formats, the demand for high-quality digitized intellectual property will increase dramatically. To take full advantage of their digital content, publishers have to maintain the integrity of the complete, final publication so that it can be relaunched or repurposed, but they also need to be able to reuse the individual digital elements that comprise the original files. Publishers need to be able to respond to requests for different versions of a publication (or even parts of a publication) on demand. Just as POD provided a solution to books that might otherwise have gone out of print and therefore would be inaccessible to the market, publishers need a solution for repurposing finished files of a book for new publications that may vary from the original product.

Since digital files are easy to manipulate in almost any format, when editors identify new publishing opportunities, they can first look to reuse content that has been converted and is accessible instead of beginning from scratch. In theory, from the beginning of any project, all of the elements of a publication should be designed so that they can be reused in future products. Whether the finished product ends up in print or digital form, the elements themselves should all be digital and located in a searchable database. In order to accomplish this, the asset management system should be a common tool used by the editorial, production, and design teams. If this system is in place and continually managed, the publisher can repurpose content and respond to internal and external product requests in almost any format.

Here is how A+ Media (introduced in the previous chapter), as a result of having made the transition from print to digital platforms, was able to solve a client's problem with a successful program that was not sustainable in its current form.

Almost 30 years ago, before digital publishing solutions of any kind were available, A+ Media developed a national science writing competition sponsored by a Fortune 500 company that today receives 10,000 student entries per year. Up until five years ago, almost all of the components pertinent to the competition were print-based; official guidelines and brochures were mailed to 30,000 schools, and thousands of essays would arrive at their offices by regular ground or overnight shipping services. But as each year's print, fulfillment, and shipping costs grew, the sponsor began having second thoughts about the program's viability—despite its popularity with the schools and the goodwill it generated for the company.

At the same time that the company was seriously considering canceling the program, A+ Media reached a tipping point of its own, where digital technology was finally grounded enough in the schools, and where its own in-house capabilities to create digital media were sufficiently developed, allowing it to replace all of the print-based components of the program with digital ones. Communication about the program could be done using e-letters and e-blasts, and the guidelines and instructions, as well as the entries, could all be organized on a robust website. Their digital transformation reduced the program costs—which changed the client's thoughts about terminating the program—and also improved A+ Media's bottom line. Equally important, it was able to enhance the program's efficiency by only accepting essay entries electronically through an online entry form. This streamlined the judging process, which was critical since the number of essay entries increased dramatically.

A+ Media's experience is a good example of why publishers should focus on the quality and scope of the content they produce rather than the format of the finished product—whether it's a book, magazine, disc, flash drive, or any other output. They should regard their content as reusable intellectual property that can change form and format depending on the audience, and move freely to become part of any workflow. From the initial planning stages of a project to the production of final files, publishers should consider multiple ways in which their content might be used so that they can take full advantage of any market opportunities while also keeping track of any ownership issues or restrictions related to the content.

Publishing today should be treated as a continual process, not a one-time event. When print was the only medium available, a book was regarded as a single entity, with inseparable parts. In a digital environment, the finished product may, over time, be less valuable than its individual parts.

A positive consequence of a publishing strategy derived from this perspective is the extended lifespan of a publication, both in its original form and in its various elements. Thanks to digital publishing and, as we have seen, POD, books no longer have to go "out of print"; they can be archived, accessed at any time in the future, and distributed more easily than ever before—and repurposed as the need or opportunity arises. We can now manage books and intellectual property with an eye toward keeping them in active circulation—either as a revised work, as part of a larger work, as a new book with a completely different design, or in a different format, such as a DVD, website, mobile device, or part of a larger database. Roger Rosen of Rosen Publishing, an independent educational publishing house, is convinced that in order to address shifting user needs, the same content needs to be available in any format—print, e-book, or online. He believes that readers and knowledge seekers are still "experimenting with different formats" and publishers need to adapt their business models as customer preferences continue to evolve. From a business standpoint, he says that he can spread the cost of the original creative work over print and digital outputs, and reach more readers. In addition, he believes that digital products in particular can help solve the social problem of "equity of access." His main market is school and public libraries, and digital content that is available through the library can be accessed remotely or from the building itself if users do not have their own devices. A library that has purchased unlimited access to a certain e-book, or that has subscribed to the same content in an online database, can now serve as many patrons as may be interested in the information without a time limitation or additional cost. The same content available only in printed book form might be "checked out" by one patron and therefore unavailable to the rest of the community.

The democratization of any content or data set depends on the accessibility of its smallest practical components. An entire 300-page book may have multiple uses, but its components—chapters, graphs, charts, etc.—may have more uses in more places. Publishers should think of intellectual property as "units" of information, or content that can be linked together and then unlinked in multiple ways. These units can be treated individually, in much the same way that an entire book can be, and then reused or licensed separately from its original context. Many content types can be repurposed and reconfigured from digital files. These files should use metadata to identify the various usable components. Text, maps, music, sound, images, video, animations, illustrations, and computer code are all types of content that can be successfully used and reused in whole or in part. By themselves, they have the potential to become revenue producing "intellectual property units" (IPUs), as digital content can be adapted to fit into the growing number and variety of devices that are used to transmit and obtain information—which we can expect to only increase in the future. Viewed in this way, the individual parts of a final product may comprise a publisher's secondary currency.

cutting your content to get more from it.

As a standard component of many publications, photography provides a good example. Even before digital technology was being widely used by the publishing industry, photographs were commonly regarded as a renewable resource. Often the photographer or photo aggregator does not know where a certain image may end up, and a single photo, perhaps originally taken with a specific intent in mind, can be used in a variety of different contexts over the course of many years. Photo agencies, such as SuperStock, 123RF (meaning "royalty-free"), Universal Images Group, or Newscom, to name but a few of the many vendors that belong to a large class of image providers, know very well the value of licensing and re-licensing a single photo, and its ability to earn revenue over a long period of time without ever permanently leaving the owner's possession. All intellectual property should be viewed in this way—as IPUs with, if not evergreen, at least long-term earning potential; they can be used without being used up. In short, with the ease of transmitting digital data, all types of content (text, music, art, etc.) can follow the same model as the photograph.

The standardization of electronic files has enabled publishers to maximize the utility and value of their digital content. The adoption of certain digital standards has made digital files readable and exploitable regardless of their DNA or the original software program in which they were created. For example, with XML (Extensible Markup Language) coding, text can be tagged and its structure and parts clearly identified so that it can be used in Web documents and other electronic formats. Similarly, video files can be compressed using the MPEG (Motion Picture Expert Group) standard to make them accessible for as many uses as possible in future products at a variety of resolutions depending on the specifications of the retrieval device. Windows, iOS, or UNIX files can be made printer-ready by converting them to PDF (Portable Document Format) files, which can also be used to create e-books. By using HTML (Hypertext Markup Language) to structure or tag content, Web-based products can be presented in a responsive design that will allow viewing on any device and will be readable on large and small screens.

Since digital files are easy to convert, transmit, and distribute, completed consumer products, particularly e-books, should be protected from abuse. PDFs can easily be "stolen" if they are not locked in some way. To keep files from getting into the wrong hands or even to control the length of a license, files should be wrapped with DRM (Digital Rights Management) technology. This involves encrypting the digital code with an expiration date so that the right to use the content can terminate and the product itself, in essence, becomes unavailable. This is often used by software, music, game, and video publishers to license their content to those who may be interested in an extended trial of a product before they decide to make a purchase, or if they don't feel that they will need the program or file as a permanent part of their collection. For example, DRM is commonly used by university professors who may require certain videos as part of a course offering, but don't see a long-term value in owning them. DRM-enabled content is often priced at a substantial discount over the full ownership price, but can be licensed with an option to buy. Although DRM technology does not provide perfect protection against piracy, in most cases it can serve as a safety key that can provide full or partial entry to a product depending on the terms of use. At the very least, it can be a more economical way for consumers to try certain products rather than, for example, buying a physical DVD that may be used only once, or not at all. If Internet bandwidth is sufficient and reliable, streaming digital content is also a solution for viewing without owning or for those not interested in acquiring DRM-encrypted products. DRM encryption has generated plenty of controversy and certainly it is not foolproof. Anyone with the skill and will can crack the code and grab the digital files. Some consumer groups simply resent the idea of using products with built-in restrictions. But for most publishers that have invested a great deal of resources into creating digital content, DRM can be an important tool for safeguarding their intellectual property while maximizing market opportunities. It can provide publishers with the necessary flexibility to experiment with digital options.

In Chapter 2, I described how Britannica adapted to changes in the market by adopting technology that allowed it to transfer its content from one format to another. This would not have been possible if its content was not fully digitized, structured, and flexible. The company's willingness to sacrifice old formats for new ones—to embrace a platform-neutral strategy—which was risky at the time, provided the foundation for growth as new market preferences emerged. By following persistent market trends, Britannica was able to abandon obsolete formats for more relevant ones. An equally important benefit of being able to adapt to a changing landscape is the resulting ability to take advantage of serendipitous opportunities. These are likely to be one-off events only, in that they are not part of normal business planning, but are highly desirable when they come around. It may not be cost-effective to assign dedicated resources to search for these opportunities, but the business should be in a position to take advantage of them when they occur.

Here are two examples of how Britannica's flexible data structure, and a warehouse of reusable IPUs, enabled it to pursue new outlets for legacy content.

A large part of Britannica's asset base consists of original art, illustrations, and historical maps and photos. Although these assets were created to accompany and enhance articles for the company's main products, many of the individual pieces are so informative and aesthetic by themselves that they can stand alone as works of art. The Britannica collection of historical and contemporary images caught the attention of the developers of the Great Big Canvas (GBC) website, which offers thousands of images from a variety of well-known sources, such as National Geographic and Britain on View, as well as modern art that can be purchased in a variety of formats—wall peels, posters, prints, and canvas frames at different sizes. GBC thought that by including Britannica's collection of proprietary images on its e-commerce site, it could offer consumers a unique way to acquire decorative art that also symbolizes "trust, intelligence, and expansive knowledge on almost every subject imaginable." Through the GBC website, consumers can now own a piece of Britannica for their walls instead of their shelves. If these assets were not in a digital form—scalable and converted to a high enough resolution—Britannica would not have been able to share (or monetize) its images in this way. This particular use of these images (or my ability to use one in this book below) would not have been possible if care had not been taken to preserve the assets separately from their original purpose and make them discoverable for future use.[1]

Figure 4.1   Britannica Map of the World, circa 1902

---

1   Reprinted with permission of Encyclopaedia Britannica. © Encyclopaedia Britannica, Inc.

As a general reference publisher, Britannica has developed, written, and revised tens of thousands of articles over the decades for learners at all age levels. Primary schoolchildren require content at a different sophistication level from adults, for example, and Britannica has published separate databases to address these disparate audiences. However, this type of content segmentation—dividing the market by age or reading level—is only one way to address market needs. Publishing straddles many market categories, and rarely is a publisher able to establish expertise and brand awareness in more than a few of them. Therefore, publishers tend to specialize in a specific interest area, such as health, business, law, travel, science, or religion to name just a few examples. One large religion publisher, Faithlife Corporation, formerly Logos Bible Software, has a worldwide consumer base for its Bible and Bible-related publications. Over the years, Faithlife has licensed various products from many publishers. All of these products are then tagged to the Logos software, so users can research many different resources from one place. Its marketing strategy is to offer a variety of product packages as software downloads from its website. Consumers can choose from hundreds of resources, including bibles, maps, literature, dictionaries, encyclopedias, journals, commentaries, grammars, atlases, and translation tools among many other options, which are all integrated with its proprietary software. As new products become available, Faithlife offers them to its consumer base as add-ons, and each new product is fully integrated with the customer's base software, creating a seamless experience across a variety of content sets. Each individual digitized book or resource would not have the same utility or the same value as when they are tied together on a robust software platform.

Faithlife approached Britannica with the idea of offering a special edition of Britannica text and visual content that would provide background information to its biblical topics. It licensed thousands of articles and media assets from Britannica's database and "white labeled" it as a special *Encyclopaedia Britannica/Logos Edition*. Once the Britannica content was integrated with the Logos software, customers were able to access Britannica articles directly from the Logos platform. When a Logos user looks up "Moses" in the Logos Bible, for example, they could now retrieve a Britannica article to get more in-depth background on Moses and related subjects. In this way, for Logos users, the Britannica content is more convenient and useful when it's integrated with the Logos software than it would be as a stand-alone product. At the same time, Britannica now gains access to a consumer base that it may not have been able to reach without the Faithlife version of Britannica content.

Logos customers can choose from a variety of different resource packages depending on their interests and how much they want to spend. The most comprehensive option integrates 629 resources and, according to its website, offers the entire package to customers for approximately $3,500. If purchased separately, these same resources would cost $35,000. Obviously, this kind of synergy between completely disparate products would not have been possible in a non-digital world. In theory, all of these 629 products could exist side by side on a shelf if they all were still in print. But they are far more useful to the reader when they can be used together, fully integrated on a software platform, and accessed with a click of a mouse. They are also much more affordable in this format.

As more content providers participate in the digital environment, more opportunities like this will arise. Some of these customized opportunities will be random, one-off events. Some publishers, however, believe that opportunities to customize publications for certain markets do not have to only come "over the transom," but can actually be a strategic component of a publishing plan.

Barbara Russell, founder of Options Publishing—which was eventually acquired by Curriculum Associates—a supplemental publisher of educational materials for urban, at-risk markets, made custom publishing a strategic goal for her company as early as the mid-1990s. She believes that with the advances in technology since she ran the company, the opportunities for customized or personalized publishing are better than ever today. As a proactive part of her sales strategy, she would have her sales representatives research the specific needs of large school districts, and propose and deliver products that combined several different data sets to meet a district's unique specifications. One spring, a sales rep was asked by the head of the Houston Independent School District if Options Publishing would be willing to create a cross-curricular summer school program. The program did not exist in the form that the customer was requesting, but this was precisely the kind of project that Barbara had encouraged her sales staff to seek out. According to Barbara, her company was able to engender customer loyalty by providing a solution that other publishers either could not or would not provide: "A combination of outstanding customer service and an ability to be nimble, listen to the customer, and customize the product placed us in a position far from any of our competitors." She was able to disrupt the "one-size-fits-all" offering that is more typical of educational publishing by using technology to generate a customer-centric product that provided a unique solution to a specific problem. In her opinion: "Today's technology allows for this sort of creative marketing and selling."

Personalized publishing solutions are ways in which digital publishing distinguishes itself from print-based publishing. Even before digital publishing was widely available, educational publishers customized products for certain markets, but this was a costly process and had many limitations. It also resulted in errors that sometimes rendered the final publications useless. With digital publishing, customization and personalization has become infinitely scalable, relatively easy to accomplish, and quickly and inexpensively corrected and revised.

A common form of customization is an adaptation or translation into a foreign language, either for domestic markets or export. Many publishers in the U.S., for example, will produce the same publication in both English and Spanish. This is especially true for educational products, such as textbooks. Canadian publishers are required to publish English and French publications simultaneously. The difference between an adaptation and a translation can be significant. A strict, perhaps literal translation is required in converting literary, health, or nonfiction trade books from one language to another, whereas adaptations are preferred in, say, curriculum materials to account for the differences in teaching methods, contexts, and other content variables that would not "translate" well without significant alterations. In the case of the literal translation of a single, formerly printed work from one language to another, technology does not offer more value over traditional publishing except perhaps speed to market. However, when adapting a product into another language for use in a different cultural environment, leveraging technology is usually responsible for making the improbable possible. In the next chapter, we'll explore how to make publications originally created for one language and culture workable in another.

Chapter 5
Towards a Global Idiom

I have a prejudice against people who print things in a foreign language and add no translation. When I am the reader, and the author considers me able to do the translating myself, he pays me quite a nice compliment—but if he would do the translating for me, I would try to get along without the compliment.

Mark Twain, A Tramp Abroad

Every literate society and culture has its own publishing industry serving its internal needs. Because publishing tends to be a language- and culture-specific industry that requires intimate connection with its market, a publisher from one culture cannot easily establish a meaningful presence in another. Even when large multinationals acquire local publishing companies, domestic publishing remains fiercely independent. Publishing both springs from and influences a culture at the same time, and an outsider cannot naturally participate in this subtle and nuanced interdependency. Successful publishing, which serves the needs of its indigenous population, is largely the domain of insiders. Tastes and viewpoints are different from one language and culture to another. What is important or useful information in China or other Asian countries may not be of interest in a European language or culture and vice versa. Broad similarities and categories of common ground can be found, but the perspectives and sensibilities are likely to be different.

The majority of a culture's publishing output is produced almost entirely for domestic consumption and therefore—perhaps like the best French or Italian wines—tends to stay within a country. (The same might be said of all of the arts; examples of influences in all directions are plentiful, but that does not guarantee that unique creative outputs developed in one culture will take root in another, even when language barriers don't exist.) Unlike commodities produced and distributed by multinational brands, such as petroleum (BP), sportswear (Nike), cars (BMW), and furniture (Ikea), published work developed for one country or culture usually requires extensive adaptation before it can enter a foreign market.

Cultural idiosyncrasies and solipsism make international publishing a fascinating and challenging business, but it is also ripe with opportunity, especially in a digital environment.

For publishers to gain access to markets outside of their own, they will likely need to partner with a local entity. This could be another publisher, a distributor, a government agency, or, especially in the case of digital products, a telecom, content aggregator, or learning management system (LMS) provider. In Chapter 8 we will take a look at the mechanics of partnering. In this chapter I will discuss why partnering can be beneficial, what needs to happen in the development process to facilitate partnering, and what successful products that result from a partnership might look like.

Some partnerships can be extensive co-publishing projects that resemble joint ventures (without being an actual legal entity) and often involve a variety of departments from both parties. To make these partnerships work, both parties need to have clearly established goals and be convinced that they will achieve their goals, which will vary depending on the partner. For two publishers working together, the main goal is a positive business relationship that has the potential to prove valuable and profitable over several years. For a government agency or a school system partnering with a publisher, the primary goal might be to provide their market or constituents with a product, series of products, or content and technology solution that they could not easily create themselves, and that represents best practices based on global standards.

At Britannica, we have had several publishing partnerships where we identified and pursued goals like these. Several years ago, we began a project with a branch of the Ministry of Education of Brazil to produce an online learning environment for students in Portuguese. Although it was based on one of our existing Web-based school products and, as a result, much of it could be translated from the original database, it still had to include approximately 25% new content specifically tailored for the students of Brazil. This meant acquiring new multimedia, developing a bilingual dictionary, and writing new articles so that the product, which, through the government, would be available in every school in Brazil, was aligned to the Brazilian curricula.

Developing this project required collaboration with government officials, local Brazilian authors and educators, and a local Web design company, as well as Britannica editors, designers, developers, producers, and marketers. Key to the project's success was the willingness of the Brazilian government to provide adequate funding to ensure that the final product would meet the high standards required by both parties and the flexibility of the Britannica team to acquire additional expertise and make the necessary internal adjustments to build a customized product designed specifically for the needs of Brazilian teachers and students.

Partnership projects of this scale are not common and require mutual trust and confidence, and a willingness to work though the inevitable differences of opinion. In this case, the results turned out to be positive for both sides. The Brazilian Ministry of Education received a Web-based product that was built on the established credibility of a widely used Britannica database, and therefore greatly reduced the amount of time and money that the Ministry would have invested if it had started such a project from scratch, and Britannica gained access to a significant market with a product that was backed and validated by the Brazilian education authorities. Without the partnership, this product would most likely not have been produced since neither party would have been willing to assume the risks alone.

Some partnering projects between different language markets or cultures are less ambitious, yet also require collaboration and a realistic commitment to making specific adaptations to meet local market needs. This means that both sides need to be willing to compromise in order to bring a product to market with a reasonable investment and in a sensible timeframe.

One example of this is an image database that we have developed at Britannica that contains more than three million images and accompanying metadata that make the images easy to find using a variety of built-in search strategies, including cross-references, related keywords, and captions. The product, called *ImageQuest* and offered as a subscription service to schools, libraries, and publishers, allows users to access the images for research and to download them for any educational, noncommercial project. The product is popular with schools and libraries because it offers several benefits for this market. All of images are safe for educational use (no depictions of violence, nudity, and so on); were acquired from trusted sources like National Geographic, Britannica, Getty Images, the National Portrait Gallery (London), Bridgeman Images, the Royal Geographical Society, Newscom, and other well-known image providers; include full credit and citation information; are rendered at the same quality resolution (a standard 150 dpi and 800 pixels on the longest side); and are rights-cleared for educational use.

In addition, the images depict people, places, and things from all over the world and on a variety of subjects, and therefore, in theory, can be used by any educational institution in any country that wants to provide its teachers and students with curated images that come with proper licensing rights, are all of the same high quality, and contain no viruses, as opposed to random images found on the Internet where these attributes may not be guaranteed. Because of this, soon after we launched *ImageQuest*, we had early interest from partners in Brazil, France, Latin America, and Japan to create versions of the product in their languages. However, with millions of images, continual updating, and the enormous amount of accompanying metadata, translating the entire database into other languages would not have been practical—the effort to do so would never pay off. As a result, we designed the product in such a way—using a flexible code structure—that allowed the interface to be easily translated and converted into any language. As opposed to translating the entire database, customizing only the interface required a relatively minor translation and adaptation effort. The metadata associated with the images was then rendered into the target languages using an automated Google translation tool. This did not result in a perfect translation, but it offered a practical way for speakers of other languages to find and use the images, which was the main intent of the product.

This strategy came in handy when a partner in Wales proposed including *ImageQuest* as part of a multiproduct offering in a government tender for primary and secondary schools across the country. Our partner was a local Web developer and content aggregator who had customized a learning management system (LMS) for the Welsh school system. We both assumed that *ImageQuest* would be perfectly acceptable to the government without any adaptation, since Wales is an English-speaking country. But the Welsh government is very nationalistic about its other official language and insisted that the product be accessible in Welsh. It was happy to accept the English-language version, but only if we agreed to make a Welsh-language version available as well. By translating only the interface into Welsh, we satisfied its official language requirement and, at the same time, gave users a choice between English and Welsh with a minimum investment of time and resources. Including the Welsh version, *ImageQuest* has been "translated" into seven languages.

Projects like this should be more common than major co-publishing ventures and, with the right planning, can be facilitated relatively simply in a digital environment. If digital products are designed correctly from the start, the opportunities to meet local market needs by making minor adaptations to products originally intended for another market should increase. This type of language and culture customization would not be possible with print-based products.

These are just two examples of why, in spite of the internally focused nature of publishing, publishers should extend themselves beyond their borders and work with international partners—why large publishers should establish a beachhead in small markets, and why publishers who reside in smaller markets need to partner with publishers in larger markets to grow and acquire current, relevant products.

Here are the top three reasons why I think publishers in markets with *small* populations should aggressively partner with publishers in larger markets:

- Assuming that the content of their products is appropriate for other markets, publishers can increase their sales volume tremendously by gaining access to larger markets. In fact, depending on the scope, some publishing projects from their inception—without a subsidy from the government or some other source—may not be feasible without a *co-publishing partner*.

- A publisher may have identified an opportunity in its market worth pursuing, but also may have determined that creating the product from scratch would be too much of an investment. In this case, *adapting* an existing product from a publisher in a larger market may be the best option.

- Extremely technical, research-heavy subject areas are more likely to be covered in greater depth by larger markets where more resources are available to generate content at the right sophistication level to meet world-class expectations. This content may be better *translated* from a major market rather than initiated from the ground floor in a small market.

Here are the top three reasons why publishers in *large* markets should look for partners in smaller markets:

- The size of a market varies depending on the language, and plenty of small- to medium-sized markets can generate *incremental revenue* for a multinational publisher, even if its indigenous market is substantial enough for it to be highly profitable. No one should underestimate the potential that may be locked away in foreign markets, especially in advanced countries. Successful multinational technology companies routinely customize their software for markets of all sizes; similarly, many publishing houses have gained substantial global traction and have improved their margins by working with a handful of publishers in countries with relatively small populations.

- Many small markets, when viewed as a *collective entity*, can constitute a meaningful source of revenue.

- By having a presence in a smaller market, publishers may be able to *acquire new content* for use in their primary market.

Here are the top three reasons why *any publisher*, regardless of size, can benefit from an exchange of intellectual property (IP) and why it should partner:

- Outside markets can be a source of new ideas, innovation, and talent. *Great ideas* and skilled individuals can come from anywhere.

- Publishers in international markets can be surprisingly nimble, flexible, and cost-effective in providing services, such as software development, hosting, editorial services, composition, and printing.

- International publishing *fosters communication, cooperation,* and *understanding,* and creates a community of like-minded people who believe that sharing information and exchanging ideas may make the world a better place; at the very least, it could prove to be a *hedge against disruption.*

These are the main drivers behind a dynamic international publishing community that has only grown more robust as a result of technology and the ease with which content can be exchanged and repurposed. To those of us who have been active in the international marketplace for some time, the last bullet point above will not sound overly ambitious. In fact, most of us with extensive partner relationships—even among partners whose governments and politics may be at odds—see only similarities and a common purpose when we explore the opportunities of sharing some of the cumulative knowledge and creative interests of our individual cultures.

In order to be a player and to participate fully in the international community, publishers first need to master the nuances of their own market—and publish content according to the standards expected of high-quality publications that appeal to their primary audiences—before they can seriously consider reaching out to foreign markets. Assuming that this is the case, publishers should design their products from the outset to be, at a minimum, acceptable (preferably desirable) to an international audience. This can be done by following a few fundamental editorial and design principles or guidelines, which are outlined below. One caveat: these guidelines are not meant to be all-inclusive or definitive, but rather examples of dos and don'ts in contexts where they might apply. At the same time, even though these factors may not be the only ones to consider, I have tried to focus on what I know to be time-tested strategies. Depending on the subject matter and the intended age and interest of the audience of the final product, these guidelines should provide a reliable framework for the kind of planning necessary to make products as attractive and as adaptable as possible to a publisher in a foreign market.

References, Illustrations, and Examples

In any written work, whenever we are introducing a new topic or subject, trying to make a point as clear as possible, or drawing a comparison between disparate entities, we rely on the persuasive power of familiar examples, anecdotes, or references. Colorful comparisons, as well as references to famous people or events, naturally come from our own experiences and culture, but they sometimes run the risk of being too limited to our own culture and frame of reference to have the impact that we intend when adapted or translated into another culture or context. Mistakes of this nature can be made in a variety of situations and at any level.

Here is one well-known and high-profile example of the limitations of frame of reference. Appearing on a talk show, President Jimmy Carter described an experience he had at a speaking engagement in Tokyo. He opened his speech with a joke, waited for the translation, and was surprised at how big of a laugh he got; the joke was funny, but not that funny. After the speech, Carter asked the translator what he said exactly to make the joke translate so well into Japanese. The translator said no one in the room would have understood the joke, so he said to the audience: "President Carter just told a very funny joke; please laugh."

We rely on what we think are very common or familiar references to illustrate a concept or to make a point, but if we intend to reach a global audience and make ourselves understood without additional explanation, we should make our examples as universal as possible. Even when including examples for our own audiences and within our own culture, references can diminish in value over time, perhaps more quickly than we might think. We may assume that our frames of reference are timeless, but this is not always the case, even in what may seem to be the most indelible examples. Around 25 years ago, I was talking to a colleague, who was only slightly younger than I was, about famous songwriters, and I mentioned Paul McCartney. She stopped me and asked: "Do you mean from the band 'Wings'?" My frame of reference may have been the "Beatles"; hers was not. (Hopefully none of my readers needed to look up "Jimmy Carter.")

Seventy years ago, the Ad Council in the U.S. created an anthropomorphic bear that became an iconic character, arguably on par with, say, Mickey Mouse, Superman, and Spiderman. "Smokey Bear" was synonymous with the slogan "Only you can prevent wildfires." I grew up with Smokey Bear (as the years went by, he was often incorrectly referred to as Smokey *the* Bear) and he was ubiquitous: on billboards, TV, and radio; in post offices and comic books; and even on milk cartons. For decades, all across the country, he may in fact have served as a friendly and memorable symbol for the prevention of forest fires, but few people outside of North America are familiar with Smokey. If an American publisher is issuing a book on forest preservation and the risks of fire due to climate change, a topic with intense global appeal, Smokey Bear, as appealing and familiar as he is to many, should probably not appear in it—at least not without context—even though he would immediately come to mind to an American audience.[1]

Figure 5.1   Smokey Bear

---

1   The name and character of Smokey Bear are the property of the United States, as provided
    by 16 U.S.C. 580p-1 and 18 U.S.C. 711, and are used with the permission of the Forest Service,
    U.S. Department of Agriculture.

By being vigilant about filtering out these kinds of culture traps, publishers can make adapting and licensing their products in other languages easier. Here are a few areas where this editorial strategy applies.

When developing an illustrated product, especially one on a general interest topic such as nature, science, or geography, researchers and editors should source images from a variety of locales, not just one region. For example, when referencing lakes, mountains, or canyons, they should include well-known landmarks from Europe and Asia, instead of, say, Minnesota (called the "land of 10,000 lakes," though it actually has closer to 12,000) or Arizona (the home of Grand Canyon National Park). Street scenes, bridges, or dams should include foreign locations as well as places close to home. Natural phenomena or disasters are global events; floods occur almost everywhere in the world—frequently, unfortunately, in India, Thailand, and the Philippines—not just along the banks of the Mississippi or the Thames. Using examples from many regions of the world reflects positively on the relevance of the content for a broader global audience.

Regardless of where we live in the world, we share more things in common than there are differences among us. Even so, we don't do everything the same way. People celebrate holidays or play sports, study, and collaborate everywhere on the planet somewhat differently. Therefore, in our publications, we need to look beyond our own backyards or gardens when showing common, everyday human activities and experiences. Making this kind of effort will pay off not just in terms of relevance and appeal to foreign markets, but in intrinsic value as well. A publication that takes more of the world into consideration is, at its core, more relevant and interesting with greater lifetime value.

Some specific events or holidays to avoid—and are common to see in texts—include highly culture-bound examples, such as Thanksgiving (more than one country celebrates a version of this, for different reasons), Presidents' Day, Boxing Day, Guy Fawkes Day, Bastille Day, or the Fourth of July. With so many regional and national celebrations that take place around the world, this entire category probably should be avoided unless it is the actual focus of a publication. When it comes to using sports, soccer (called football almost everywhere else outside of North America) or basketball, instead of American (or Australian) football, are good choices. Baseball is more widespread than most people think, being very popular in the Netherlands, Asia, and the Caribbean.

For the most part, the debate around the metric versus imperial systems of measurement has been over for decades, yet for some reason the U.S. is almost alone in hanging on to the "British" imperial system, even though the British themselves have all but abandoned it. American publishers need to be aware that at least in any scientific or engineering publication, the metric system is required, and if both imperial and metric units need to be indicated, the metric designation should be listed first. Since Americans have not converted to the metric system, the same dilemma comes up when referring to the weather. The U.S. has stubbornly stuck to Fahrenheit while the rest of the world measures temperature in degrees Celsius (even though I have to admit that I do not know what it feels like outside if I'm given the temperature in Celsius, unless it's 0°C). If for some reason the Fahrenheit temperature needs to appear in the text, the temperature in Celsius should also be shown. And when illustrating electrical systems, we should be conscious of the fact that outlets are different depending on the part of the world that is being referenced, so whenever they appear in publications, visuals of electrical outlets should be created in a format that allows them to be easily replaced if necessary.

Depicting cars can be tricky since the side of the car where the steering wheel is located depends on which side of the road people drive on. In most countries, people drive on the right side of the road, so in this case Americans are with the majority—the vast majority, in fact, since it includes all of North America, most of Asia and South America, and Europe. The "outliers" include the U.K., India, Australia, and parts of Africa. However, enough people from various parts of the world drive on both sides of the street that showing cars in photos or illustrations can be a problematic editorial and production issue. In choosing photographs or providing art specifications, editors should be conscious of this cultural difference. License plates differ from country to country as well, and this too can be an immediate indicator of place, which is fine if that is both intentional and essential for the context.

Showing road signs and billboards can limit the mobility of content since place names, language, and advertising that appear on them can get in the way of communicating clearly.

When selecting photos of people or creating illustrations, an effort should be made to be as diverse as possible and represent a variety of ethnic backgrounds, age ranges, and cultures. This is a relatively easy thing to do when designing a product and harder to do at the end; it costs no more and it makes any product travel better—and demonstrates a sensitivity that is critical in international publishing. Here's a general rule of thumb that may even be a cliché: recognize and embrace the community and the community will recognize and favor one of its own.

We recently faced this situation with a licensee in Korea that created a series of 50 educational books drawn from the style of the graphic novel using our Korean content. The books have a high production value and are very attractive. The question emerged as to whether we would be interested in licensing the books and translating them into English, taking advantage of our own content and the huge investment that they made in the artwork. It sounded like a great idea, but when we examined the books, we discovered that the people depicted in the illustrations, even though they were cartoon-like characters, lacked any diversity. They were of a single type, with the same facial features and skin color. The only small attempt at diversity was green, blue, or red hair on some of the characters.

The art director made other mistakes as well, like embedding Korean writing into illustrations of buses or buildings, which meant that those pieces would have to be completely redone in any adaptation. This was a lost opportunity. If the art director and editor had planned ahead, they would have been able to leverage the substantial investment made in the art by licensing the product to other publishers in other languages. However, given the end results, the books may have been a perfect fit for the Korean market, but they would not be accepted almost anywhere in the English-language market—and probably not in most other markets.

Certain animals can also present problems. Cows are sacred in India, for example, so most depictions of them can prompt rejection of a product or cause major edits. Pigs also require special treatment in some parts of the world. (Anthropomorphic pigs, especially when they are half-dressed as they sometimes are in Western children's stories or cartoons, could cause an international scandal. In this case, "international" could refer to parts of the U.S.) Some birds and animals are found only in certain climates and regions, so how they are used and depicted should take the local geography into consideration. I once got into a debate with a publishing partner in the U.K. over the use of a rooster in an illustration. His claim was that so few British children are exposed to roosters that they shouldn't be shown in a farm scene. To me, that seemed like an excellent argument in favor of including the rooster: how about expanding our frames of reference rather than limiting them? Besides, what would the hens say about this? Don't they get any consideration? Still, this points to the issue of how closely sense and meaning are tied to familiar objects and experiences, even in situations where we might not imagine a problem.

Seasons are not as straightforward as they might seem. Not everyone experiences all four of them in the same way, and winter doesn't always mean snow and cold temperatures, while in some places that's all that it does mean. (In Chicago, we say that there are only two seasons: winter and construction.) Also, half the planet has summer while the other half has winter. What may seem like simple things to depict—a "typical" fall or winter scene, for example—depends entirely on what side of the Equator you live on.

Geo-publishing

Maps demand their own unique set of considerations. Naming conventions are not always standard due to local variations; a handful of high-profile, hotly contested boundary and territory disputes can make it difficult for cartographers to "get it right" as long as politics stand in the way. India, China, and Pakistan all have had claims on Kashmir since the partition of India in 1947, and showing the area as disputed is not an acceptable solution for any of these countries. For example, Greece and the United Nations refer to the Republic of Macedonia (the name the people who live there use) as the "Former Republic of Macedonia" (FYROM); Korea and Japan both claim rights over two tiny islands (rocks, really) about halfway between them, called Dokdo by the Koreans and Takeshima by the Japanese. The body of water between Korea and Japan is referred to as the "Sea of Japan" by the Japanese and the "East Sea" by the Koreans.

At Britannica, in 2006, we took this "difference of opinion" between the Japanese and the Koreans into serious consideration when putting together a new print atlas. We decided to include both names, in the same font size, which we thought was a fair compromise, though we did have a debate as to which label would be listed first. We ended up putting "Sea of Japan" on top, which, ironically, didn't please the Japanese. I received a very polite but unambiguous letter from the Japanese consulate asking us to change the map and include only the "correct name"; they said that showing both names was neither accurate nor an acceptable compromise. To them, the debate had been settled long ago by Japanese cartographers, and to accommodate the strong opinions on both sides, we needed a major diplomatic intervention, which was clearly not within the scope of the atlas project. (In spite of the well-documented arguments from the Japanese in their letter "proving" that the correct name was "Sea of Japan," we stuck with our naming decision. We never heard from the Koreans and, every year, from that time to the present, I receive a beautiful wall calendar courtesy of the Ministry of Foreign Affairs of Japan.) Unfortunately, this kind of labeling problem is not resolvable in a digital environment either, because although we could have created different digital versions, we would still have ended up with an editorial integrity problem.

To help maintain neutrality in the map labeling process, a cartographer who writes a blog for Lovell Johns—a respected mapping company in the U.K.—recommends deferring to the United Nations Group Experts on Geographical Names (UNGEGN), which was established in 1959 and is typically the best source for avoiding political bias as much as possible, as well as for choosing between official names and those names that are more familiar, like referring to the largest city in Vietnam as Saigon instead of Ho Chi Minh City. By using the UNGEGN's official designations for geographical locations and boundaries, editors may feel like they are relying on a neutral authority, but doing this is unlikely to satisfy everyone in all situations. In fact, products that include maps of China will be difficult to sell in mainland China unless the boundaries and designations of places like Tibet (Autonomous Region) and Taiwan comply with the strict labeling standards established by the Chinese government, regardless of what a "neutral" authority may say. For books that are printed in China—even those made for Western consumption—local vendors are sometimes instructed to make the "necessary" changes on their own, often to the dismay of publishers. The same restrictions apply to digital content in China. Although separate digital versions of the same product can be made with less cost than multiple print versions, most publishers resist the idea of making content changes that go beyond style and are counter to their editorial policies.

Using the same "bias-free" map content in local markets where these political disputes endure is not generally an option, either in print or in a digital format. And some publishers won't have enough corporate flexibility to make the editorial concessions necessary to allow the target market's requirements to prevail. This is a case where either marketing considerations will win over editorial policies or the other way round.

With a substantial business incentive to find a solution, we handled one such situation in the following manner. We had an Asian publishing partner which was adapting one of our multivolume series that had maps scattered throughout the volumes. We ran into a problem when we could not agree on how to label some of the controversial territories. Certain names that the local publisher wanted to use on the maps would have conflicted with our in-house editorial policy, and we didn't want our brand on a product that contained what we considered to be inaccurate or biased map labels. The solution was to take out all of the maps from the individual volumes, include them in a separate atlas volume, label the maps according to the local publisher's standards, and remove our branding from the atlas volume. In this way the maps didn't disrupt the editorial integrity of the entire project and the separate atlas gave the partner the marketing flexibility it needed to address the expectations of its audience. In this case, both sides were happy with the solution.

Sometimes, however, neither side can find a satisfactory compromise. Earlier in this chapter I described how we adapted *ImageQuest*, our large database of images, to comply with the Welsh government's official language requirements. One of our Chinese partners wanted to adapt the same product for the Chinese market. It was happy with our solution of converting the interface into Chinese as a way of resolving the translation problem. However, the database contains many images of Tibet, some of which depicted Tibetan protests. The Chinese insisted that we remove all of the images of Tibet before they would license, adapt, and distribute the product in mainland China. This, of course, would have meant whitewashing our editorial content and using the product as a political tool, so we declined. In this case, we couldn't find a solution that was acceptable to both parties, so we passed on having a Chinese version of the product, at least for the time being. If the situation changes (which is unlikely), we will be happy to revisit the opportunity.

Solutions to similar problems like this will depend entirely on how much content is involved, on identifying issues as early in the development process as possible, and on being open to compromising—internally and externally—to a certain degree. In the case of the multivolume product that had controversial maps, we had to convince our editorial department that the compromise that we made to be successful in this market did not represent a diminution of our editorial standards. In the case of *ImageQuest*, the compromise that the partner was proposing was unacceptable across the board, not just to the editors.

Organizing Principles for Achieving Content Flexibility

A licensing partner for multivolume products or an ordered series of books is much easier to find if the product is organized thematically rather than alphabetically. Since the spelling of terms differs from language to language, even from British English to American English, alphabetically organized products have to be completely rearranged based on the target-language spelling. This could provide a barrier to licensing simply because the licensee now has to consider the costs of changing the layouts and re-indexing in addition to translating, adapting, and localizing the content by adding new material relevant to the target market.

Thematically arranged products, on the other hand, can stay in the same sequence when translated into another language and can usually take advantage of the existing design and layout. If the design is appealing and suitable for other markets, the licensee can retain the existing layout, make full use of the color elements, and translate and adapt only the text pages, or black plate. Even with a fully digital production process, where film has been completely eliminated, retaining as much of the original design as possible is time- and cost-efficient. Although random photos or illustrations may need to be added or changed, and additional content may have to be written, the product would not require complete restructuring.

In addition, if the entire design and layout, with all of the color elements in place, can be identical for more than one language, with the only difference being the black plates, the printing of multiple languages might feasibly be ganged, or handled at the same time—or in the case of digital products, separate but virtually identical versions produced, saving money and providing better margins for each publishing partner. A thematically organized product that requires only black-plate changes allows a publisher to take advantage of the creative elements of the original publication as well as to achieve economies of scale at press time. Of course, after the first printing, assuming that individual sales efforts in different markets did not deplete the stock of all languages at the same rate, ganging multiple languages at press time may not be practical. But at least the option is available if the partner does not want to take on the printing alone and can wait for a reprint.

If a business plan calls for a product to be translated into other languages, 100% of the text elements should be put into the black plate or layer, and even captions or subtitles should not be in color or reversed out of white. Even though the finished product is transferred in the form of electronic files rather than film, the adaptation process will be easier if the text and image layers are separated. More of a design issue than a technical one, the goal of producing an attractive and innovative design within these parameters need not be sacrificed. Dorling Kindersley (DK), now part of Penguin Random House, is arguably the multinational publisher that has made the most out of this kind of co-edition publishing. Founded in 1974, it has created thousands of beautifully designed co-edition titles in 87 countries and 62 languages, mostly by mastering the process of retaining as much of the original design and illustrations as possible and only swapping out the language layer and inserting another one. Except for the text language it is in, a DK book in Polish, for example, will look exactly the same as the French, German, or English version.

I worked on a co-edition project with DK in the mid-1990s that included videos, audiocassettes, books, and transcripts for teaching English to young speakers of other languages. With a variety of components in different media, *Say It in English* was a type of pre-digital "multimedia" product that did not rely on a computer. Because the most costly, production-heavy elements of the project were the videos, the other components were designed around them. We created a slightly different version for each target country. Each language version used exactly the same visuals and we replaced only the captions and the black-plate layers of the books to accommodate a second language. By having common color layers and swapping out the different black-plate versions, we were able to produce multiple languages at the same time and amortize the printing costs over a very large print run. This allowed a small country like Norway, for example, which might only require a few thousand units, to take advantage of a much longer print-run based on the larger quantities required for France, Germany, or Spain.

Although a design that allows for the swapping-out of the black-plate layer is useful for creating most language versions, the benefit isn't as great for some languages—such as Chinese, Japanese, Hebrew, or Arabic—where the layouts have to be reversed, for starters, since the reading conventions for these languages go from right to left, not left to right. Still, the benefit of not having to shuffle every page and being able to work instead with fully composed spreads is considerable. And in the *Say It in English* example above, the same videos could be used, assuming that cultural sensitivities were taken into consideration during the shooting by utilizing neutral backgrounds and ensuring ethnic diversity.

If the primary intention from the start is to develop a product for co-publishing and licensing purposes, consideration should be given to the fact that Asian and most European languages will normally require additional space in the text areas. For example, German normally takes up to 15% more space than English does, so the design should have enough white space around the text to accommodate more lines per page. Some Asian languages will require even more space than that. Malaysian, for example, may require up to 40% more space, so a design that works equally well in Malaysian and, say, French may not be realistic. (My limited understanding is that words are doubled in Malaysian to create plurals, kind of like "cat cat" instead of "cats.") The goal is to make sure that the design is not so cluttered with media and the text so dense that the product will have to be completely redone for foreign markets. Planning for this in advance will prevent finding out later that the design might cause the partner to make unnecessary editorial compromises, expend additional resources for the adaptation, or abandon the project entirely.

Clearing Image Rights

If a publisher expects that a product is going to be adapted for another market, it should obtain worldwide rights, in all formats, digital and print, and in all languages, for third-party photos. Finding a licensing partner will be easier if the licensee does not have to renegotiate these rights or spend time and resources replacing photos and images that have too many restrictions. Securing such broad rights in advance of bringing on licensing partners will be more efficient in the long run than trying to go back to vendors later and acquire the rights as they are needed. Only the vendors benefit when publishers go back to the well every time they bring on a new partner or create a different version of the product that contains the same photos.

Buying photo rights used to be a very expensive, laborious, and frustrating task. Pricing policies among stock photo agencies and independent photographers, and the rights that they were willing to grant, varied greatly. In spite of the fact that the supply of photos has historically exceeded the demand and it still does, agencies were able to charge exorbitant prices and grant only limited rights. This was because prior to the Internet, physical photos needed to be sent back and forth from the photo agency to the publisher, making access to the photos costly and time-consuming.

Licenses to use photos almost always had restricted territories and languages, time limits, and sometimes limitations on the print-run. When e-books became popular, publishers at first assumed that the rights they purchased to use a photo in a print book included e-book rights as well. Sometimes vendors agreed with this conclusion; sometimes they didn't. On occasion, the disagreement brought the parties to court. A case could be made, at least from the publisher's point of view, that unless specified otherwise, an e-book that was identical to the original print product was just another book, and that the rights secured for print covered the digital format of the book. Agreements with photo agencies were often silent on this issue when most of publishing was print-based and little thought was given to the e-book market. Once e-books reached a critical mass in the market, agreements for the use of photos often specified three categories of rights—print, e-books, and digital (meaning use in a database)—in an effort to eliminate any ambiguity. Now that it is routine for electronic or digital publications to be produced in conjunction with a print product, the prudent policy is to make sure that all rights that are likely to be used are specified in any agreement.

The vendor landscape of photo agencies has changed dramatically over the last 10 years as a result of the digitization of content. All photo agencies now have websites for selecting photos. The photo licensing business has consolidated and is dominated by several large stock photo agencies, including Associated Press, Getty, and SuperStock. But these have plenty of competitors, such as 123RF and Fotolia, which offer millions of photos, and numerous specialized photo agencies that cover subjects like the fine arts and science in depth. A huge supply of photos is available on the market and an increasing number of agencies are willing to make it easier for publishers to find and select the photos they need, and to adjust their pricing to fit the publishers' cost structures. In addition, thanks to the Web, access to what once was difficult-to-find or unique photography has been made much easier. The ability to first view then download image files via the Web has also reduced the physical costs of photo licensing to basically zero, and has made overseas suppliers as accessible as a local vendor. Also, photos can be acquired at varying resolutions depending on their use—a higher resolution for print publications and a lower resolution for publishing on the Web.

What used to be a seller's market (because of control, not short supply) is now a buyer's market, and photo agencies cannot always demand a premium for their images; nor can they assume that they can charge incremental fees for extended rights, such as additional languages, territories, or formats.

Many photo agencies also have subscription services available where, for a monthly or annual fee, the publisher receives unlimited use of all the photos from selected collections. The rights for photos chosen from these services are normally the same as if they were bought individually—typically the life of a print or CD/DVD product, and seven to 10 years (or sometimes for perpetuity) for online use.

Although some negotiation is still required, most individual photos from the larger stock agencies can be acquired for editorial uses under extended term limits, multiple formats, and languages for around $30.00 or less per photo, depending on the quantity of photos purchased within a specified period of time. However, rare or hard-to-find photos and fine arts images, where artists' rights are involved in addition to the photo agency fees, often require special negotiation.

As an alternative model, large agencies will provide some of their photo collections on a royalty-free basis, which sometimes means paying slightly more up-front for a photo, but for use in perpetuity, in any publication, without any restrictions or further payment. Royalty-free photos can become part of a publisher's asset collection.

In addition, quality government sites, such as the Library of Congress, and non-profit associations make a wide variety of photos on a broad spectrum of subjects available for free. Some of these institutions like NASA, tourist agencies, city (or country) chambers of commerce, and publicity departments of large corporations will provide the photos for free, or for a nominal transfer fee. Or they may charge more if a higher resolution is requested.

Overall, the cost of buying photo rights is a fraction of what it was a decade ago. The current business environment necessitates acquiring photo rights as broadly, and for as long of a term, as possible so that potential partners are able to license products without the additional burden of having to clear those rights. The partner still may have to replace or add a certain percentage of photos to account for new local content, but it shouldn't have to renegotiate the rights for the photos that are already in the product. The publisher's goal should always be to remove as many barriers as possible that might prevent a licensing project from progressing.

Standardizing Formats

One of the content owner's obligations in the licensing process includes providing production files so that the licensee can make any necessary changes prior to arranging for printing, or hosting in a viewable electronic format. To ensure that this part of the process goes smoothly, files should be available in standard digital formats, such as Quark or Adobe InDesign for page layout and design, and XML to accommodate any digital platform or environment. Files can be transferred either on discs or via an FTP (File Transfer Protocol) site, a hosted, password-protected site from which partners can download text and image files. Cloud-based services will also accommodate files of any size.

Text, images, photographs, and videos should not only be in standard digital formats, but should also be tagged and indexed so that they can be easily identified and dropped into the right place during the adaptation process. Multimedia elements should be kept separate for easy translation, editing, or replacement. The publisher's information technology (IT) department needs to be an integral part of this process.

In the previous chapter, I discussed how a good asset management system is invaluable for identifying, repurposing, and keeping track of what gets licensed to partners. Numerous options, including Web-based, managed products, as well as open-source software, are available. Adopting a system that can be scaled based on how much co-edition publishing is being planned and what percentage of the publishing strategy it will occupy is most practical, especially since this area sees continuous innovation. If a publisher has valuable IP that can be used in a variety of different contexts, languages, and formats—and if licensing is part of the publisher's overall marketing strategy—then a full-featured asset management system will likely pay off.

Slicing and Dicing Content

The great advantage of digital content—organized in a way to allow use and reuse—is its adaptability: publishers can create products that were not possible before. These products can be for internal use or for licensing. We can call it slicing and dicing; others have called it "chunking," but whatever the term, the idea of creating new materials from existing assets is made possible by having accessible digital content regardless of its origin.

Publishers have been working in a print paradigm for centuries, so, in theory, a vast buried treasure of content could be mined for the Web. Tremendous investments have been made in physical assets, and publishers are now looking at ways to adapt these assets for the Web, with the understanding that the content needs to provide a different, more interactive experience as it has migrated from a print format to a digital platform.

Today, at Britannica, we create almost all of our content specifically for the Web, but we also take advantage of our 247-year history of having developed content in other formats, as I described in Chapter 2. Content development first and foremost for the Web is a relatively new phenomenon, which, in the early days of the Internet, we experienced initially with blogs and podcasts.

What about taking content that started life on the Web and creating a print product from it? Web content is structured differently, with layouts designed for screens of various sizes, images with lower resolution, and other unique qualities that do not appear in print. But at the heart of content on the Web are some of the same assets found in books. We embarked on such a project at Britannica around seven years ago. One of our most popular online databases is the youngest-level of our *Britannica School* website. When first published online, it contained approximately 4,000 media-rich articles; it has been growing ever since, with more than 6,000 today. Created uniquely for the Web at the time of its launch, the product did not have a print equivalent. But we soon received interest from customers, domestically and abroad, for a CD-ROM and a print product based on the content. The CD-ROM, which we called the *Britannica Student Encyclopedia* (BSE), became a best-seller. Encouraged by its success, we created a 16-volume print set of the same name. It too became a best-selling product and is still in print, with the latest edition having a 2015 copyright.

If we look at the online and print versions of the product together, what they have in common is not instantly evident. They look different and each has its own advantages. But they share the same heritage and the reader or user of each format benefits not only from an originally well-conceived and graphically interesting product, but also from the various adaptations that were made in order to maximize the utility of each format. For example, the print version has a very extensive index that is invaluable for finding specific content within the A–Z organization, while the online version has a variety of search options to help readers instantly find what they are looking for—and various browse features (such as a biography or subject browse) when they just want to explore.

Another benefit of having the three formats—Web, CD-ROM/DVD, and print—available was the licensing opportunities that evolved. Together the three formats became proofs of concept and alternatives for other markets that had a need for a children's encyclopedia, but did not have a large enough market to start a project on this scale from scratch. Our French partner created both a print and an online version of BSE, though it published the print version first, with about 30% new content in 20 volumes. Our partner in South Africa, also using BSE as a starting point but adding 25% additional content, created the first-ever children's print encyclopedia in the Afrikaans language, and with an accompanying CD-ROM. Various other products, including the Portuguese learning portal that I mentioned earlier in this chapter, were derived from the same BSE content. We also used the database ourselves as the basis of a new online Spanish portal. I'm sure that we will have other opportunities to repurpose the BSE content in other formats and in other languages as usage of the Internet for learning products continues to expand and as others see the value of starting with a known entity.

The number of digital outlets for quality content is growing worldwide. Websites, especially in multiple languages for international markets, represent one channel for licensing content or content modules. In addition, the opportunities are growing in both cable and wireless delivery systems for customized content, which is often presented differently from its original format and intent. Content providers now have access to a variety of channels for licensing content to both traditional and non-traditional publishers and distributors who can successfully market portions of the same content in an entirely distinct context for a specific market segment.

For licensors, the key to licensing of this type is to avoid cannibalization. As long as they are careful about what content is being licensed and to whom—and that by licensing their content, they are reaching a market that they wouldn't normally be able to reach—licensing part of their assets becomes an excellent strategy for monetizing sunken development costs.

This strategy is particularly relevant in foreign markets and, especially, in other languages. The chances of cannibalization decrease substantially as content is rendered into other languages. In fact, unless the publisher plans on undertaking the translation, delivery, and distribution of the content in foreign markets, the risks of cannibalization approach zero. For this reason, this type of licensing can be a strategic priority, especially if content can be separated into distinct elements that end up being very different from the original work, such as media on a specific subject, statistical information, or even games and quizzes.

Wireless technology has become both more accessible and less expensive, and manufacturers and telecoms are increasingly using quality content as a way to differentiate their products and services. This technology will be demanding more content for a wide range of demographics, and for a variety of purposes, including homework help and test assessment, as well as the more common hotel and restaurant selection, traffic information, and directions. With the increasing amount of innovation going on in this field, digital strategy considerations should include how content can be made applicable and even more relevant to wireless users.

In the international environment, different markets are at various stages of adopting or embracing a variety of technologies. In some markets, wireless applications have already become far-reaching and entrenched, whereas in other markets, technologies that are basically obsolete in most other places are still maintained. All of this is good news for the content provider. It represents opportunities to license content in different formats.

In some countries, such as Japan, Korea, Singapore, and the Philippines, wireless technologies have merged faster in consumer applications than they have in North America, though North America has been catching up quickly. At Britannica, for example, we've been able to license content to large consumer electronic publishers in Japan and Korea that offer handheld devices that are simply not available in North America or Europe. Some of these are wireless devices with online access to databases and others are basically stand-alone electronic "libraries."

Licensee and Licensor Vantage Points

Keeping in mind that digital content can take on a variety of sizes and formats, let's look at how both a licensee and licensor can benefit from licensing content, as well as what some of the caveats might be.

For a licensee, acquiring content from someone else provides quick access to material that might otherwise be difficult, time-consuming, and/or costly to develop. The licensee must determine that licensing content will save both time and money, and perhaps take advantage of the licensor's reputation, assuming that the content provider has a brand that is readily recognized in the marketplace. Also, forging a new relationship and gaining access to an ongoing source of quality content may have future benefits.

At the same time, licensing content can have its downsides. Normally, a content provider will not license its content on an exclusive basis, which means that the licensee is unlikely to gain a complete market advantage with that particular content. Also, a term limit on how long the license will last without additional payments or commitments is typical. And licensed material usually cannot be sub-licensed by the licensee for other purposes or to other markets. So although licensing content is often faster and cheaper than starting from scratch, it has its limitations. The licensee is leasing content, not buying it.

Therefore, the licensee must identify a strategic advantage to licensing content as opposed to making it. If, on the other hand, it recognizes a greater long-term value in owning the content, then it should consider taking the time and investing the resources necessary to create the content itself.

Here are some benefits to leasing or licensing content over owning it:

- The content is needed for a specific or narrow purpose and has little long-term or sub-licensing value.

- The content is outside of the publisher's core area of competence.

- The savings from licensing and adapting the content will be substantial over the cost of original development.

- Licensing the content will accelerate the time to market, so the licensee can take advantage of a specific market opportunity.

For a licensor, several benefits to licensing out content may accrue, particularly for small slices of content that are part of a large database and are easily disassociated from their primary or original context. Licensing generates incremental revenue and, if the content can be branded, the licensor can benefit from the additional exposure to new markets and customers.

Here are some guidelines for maximizing the upside and minimizing the downside of licensing valuable IPUs:

- The revenue from the licensed content should be significant enough to justify the resources necessary to negotiate and generate an agreement and to deliver the files.

- The adapted product should be of a high enough quality to represent the publisher's brand positively.

- The licensed content should cause little, or insignificant, channel conflict with the publisher's main business activities.

If acquired with the appropriate rights, licensed content should be considered no differently from a publisher's own content and should become part of both the product for which it was licensed as well as the licensor's general portfolio of products. If the licensed content is acquired with this use in mind, it is possible to be both the licensee and the licensor of exactly the same assets, and benefit from being on both sides of the licensing equation. Below is an illustration of this.

A Case in Point:
Treating Licensed Content as Part of an Asset Base

Several years ago at a licensing trade fair, we met a publisher of high-end graphical content for Spanish tabloid newspapers and magazines. Under contract with a client in Spain, it created an innovative series of science books using its skills as an illustrator and retained the rights to the books for all other uses. However, marketing an educational science series was outside of its core competency. It had no presence in or direct access to the education market where these books would fit best. During the course of our discussions, it wondered whether it made sense if it published the books, in Spanish, under the Britannica name—which would enable it to find a marketing partner in its markets—and, in addition, if we, in turn, would be interested in publishing the same series in English for our markets. In this exchange, we would license our brand to it, and we, in turn, would license the content from it. We agreed to this arrangement, and ended up being both a licensor (of our brand) and a licensee (of the graphical content).

The series turned out to be a big hit, not only as a print set but also as e-books. Its reputation in the educational market garnered the interest of some of our publishing partners, which resulted in several sub-licenses, including Chinese and Korean versions. So we became the licensor of a product that we had originally licensed from someone else. In addition, another one of our partners who specializes in the retail market was interested in using the illustrations and text from the books in a new interactive children's series that utilized a special "pen" or reader that, when pressed on specific points on the pages of the books, played audio recordings, including quizzes and comprehension questions, making these highly visual books also come alive with sound. In this case, our partner licensed our brand and text and sub-licensed the illustrations (from our Spanish partner) to create a product for a market that we do not normally reach or publish for directly.

These kinds of IP exchanges are possible when content is produced in a format that enables multiple uses, when companies play to their individual marketing and distribution strengths, and the parties involved are flexible in how to best approach a market—leading with the best brand for the circumstances. (Developing quality relationships and processes in licensing partnerships is discussed in more detail in Chapter 8.) Regardless of a particular company's or brand's value in its own market, a local partner may have a better brand for maximizing sales of a certain product. Whose brand takes the lead should be determined on a case-by-case basis.

Brand equity, which is often market-specific, should not be underestimated, and it can make a difference in a publisher's ability to license products or content and how much others are willing to pay for it. Brand equity is developed over time—from competitive differentiation, continual impact in a market, and customer loyalty—and it can be one of the most persuasive and valuable attributes of a publisher's IP.

In general, publishers tend to have more brand equity among their peers, business partners, or industry marketing professionals than with the general public. To increase their brand equity, publishers need to maintain a reputation for high quality, innovation, and marketing savvy within the industry itself. For the most part, publishers rarely become highly visible consumer brands. Not one publisher, for example, is on the list of the U.K.'s consumer "Superbrands" of 2015, unless we count the BBC, which is categorized as media/TV. Except in certain areas of publishing, like education and health, publishers rarely compete against one another for consumer attention and therefore don't have many opportunities to establish either their marketing or content superiority in the minds of their readers. In general trade publishing, a Coca-Cola/Pepsi battle is not likely because publishers are trying to win consumer or reader mindshare with individual titles, not compete for shelf space with other publishers like beverage or razor-blade companies. Publishers cannot build brand equity in the same way that manufacturers of consumer products do, where the Holy Grail for big brands is consumer *insistence* over simple preference—or to have a level of brand loyalty that causes people to go the extra mile to a specific store to purchase the brand they want rather than settle for what is available.

As we will see in the next chapter, publishers are better at *creating* brands than being brands. Their authors or properties, when they are successful, usually become more influential than their own imprints. And when it comes to licensing, publishers will sometimes look to other industries to create brand recognition for their products.

Chapter 6
Brand and Reputation Matters

Reputation is an idle and most false imposition; oft got without merit and
lost without deserving.
You have lost no reputation at all, unless you repute yourself a loser.
            William Shakespeare, Othello, *Act II, Scene III*

The increasing use of technology for retrieving information has been an impetus for some publishers to align their corporate name or brand more closely with digital formats and platforms, particularly as the amount of their own digital content grows as a percentage of their product portfolio. For example, Rosen Publishing, a major publisher of nonfiction library and educational books, uses "Rosen Digital" as a marketing imprint for its e-books and databases. Pearson, the largest global publisher, established "Pearson Digital Learning" to represent its offerings of instructional technologies.

Although our official corporate name is still "Encyclopaedia Britannica," seven years ago, we introduced "Britannica Digital Learning" as an umbrella imprint for all of our educational publishing activities, and have dropped the word "encyclopedia" from the branding of our digital products. We felt that the word "encyclopedia" is too closely associated with an alphabetically organized set of printed books and no longer accurately describes our continually updated, digital learning websites, which include encyclopedic content (articles, maps, photos, graphs, and charts), as well as rich multimedia, dictionaries, primary source documents, Web links, research tools, curriculum lesson plans, and multiple search features. Since we have become a completely digital company, we wanted to change the perception of our brand, at least in our marketing materials to the education market; the goal was to keep "Britannica" and join it with a more appropriate label for the kinds of products that we have been offering and plan on building in the future.

Changing consumer perception of a brand, particularly in regard to a company that has been around for 247 years and has been known for a single product for most of that time, cannot happen overnight. It requires exposing the market to new products and messaging, and motivating customers to initiate conversations about the brand among themselves and on social media. Although we never assumed that a slight change in a label and logo would instantly unseat entrenched notions of what people thought of when they heard our name, we did think that it would help nudge our brand identity away from a product that we no longer published and increase the awareness of our shift to an entirely digital product line. We also had the reasonable expectation that the experience that users had with our new products and their willingness to recommend them to others would help build awareness and alter perception.

Without mounting a major, persistent, and costly public relations campaign, the effort involved in changing brand perceptions can be like using a hairdryer to melt a glacier. But when a market undergoes a paradigm shift, aligning the company's brand with market trends and expectations is an important step in responding to disruption and in positioning the brand for future growth.

Historically, many well-known multinational companies have made name and logo changes as a way of embracing a shift in their product strategy and refocusing their brand. In the 1920s, Computing Tabulating Recording Corp became International Business Machines, and later simply IBM; Lucky Chemical Industrial Corp became Lucky Goldstar, then LG in 1995; the Nintendo Playing Card Company became Nintendo; and Apple Computer changed its name to Apple when the iPhone became its best-selling and most profitable product. As diverse as these companies are, they all made the name change in an effort to better align themselves to market trends and consumer preferences for their more technology-driven and strategic products. In hindsight, and in light of the Internet's explosive growth, "Jerry's Guide to the World Wide Web" was too quaint of a name for an ambitious search engine, regardless of how one responds today to the "Yahoo!" brand.

I think both "Encyclopaedia Britannica" (EB) and "Britannica Digital Learning" (BDL) can continue to live side by side to communicate the right corporate message depending on the market. We continue to use EB for our consumer-facing websites and BDL for our library and school markets—even overseas, where the "Encylopaedia Britannica" name is regarded as the gold standard of knowledge publications. Our licensing partners—who know our products well and license our content primarily for a young demographic—still prefer "Encyclopaedia Britannica" to "Britannica Digital Learning." They feel that the BDL name and logo may not be immediately identified with the iconic

Encyclopaedia Britannica, so they usually choose not to risk introducing any doubt in the minds of consumers and stick with the original name and full thistle logo.[1] This point of view has some validity. I have been at educational trade shows where we display banners with the BDL label and logo, and some teachers and librarians who stop by our booth ask whether Britannica Digital Learning is the "real" Britannica. You would think it would be obvious, but it isn't always, particularly with people of a certain generation who grew up with the *Britannica* in their homes.

When the choice between the two brand names and logos comes up in actual product branding discussions on licensed products, I usually let the licensee choose, and defer to its sense of what its market's preference will be—and which branding option will help them sell more products. I don't want the licensee to blame weak sales on having to be forced to use one label and logo over another. But I'm confident, when I put on my marketing hat, that a time will come when the BDL name and brand will signify in the digital space exactly what the EB name and logo has signified for more than two centuries. In the meantime, we may have to live with being slightly ahead of market perception with the use of our branding and accept the fact that it will take some time before people know us as an entirely digital company.

Figure 6.1a   Encyclopaedia Britannica corporate logo

---

1   Encyclopaedia Britannica®, Britannica, and the Thistle logo are registered trademarks of Encyclopaedia Britannica, Inc. All rights reserved. Used by permission. The thistle is a common plant in Scotland. Encyclopaedia Britannica was founded in Edinburgh, Scotland in 1768.

Figure 6.1b   Britannica Digital Learning logo

Outside of the big newspaper and magazine publishers (which reside more in the media sector), few publishers (even large ones) have the kind of consumer brand awareness that can make a significant difference in their ability to market, sell, or license products based on their name alone. In the publishing industry, authors like Stephen King or J.K. Rowling, or book series like *The Hunger Games* or *A Song of Ice and Fire* (*Game of Thrones*), have more brand awareness than the publishers that brought these properties to market.

For this reason, publishers often look to consumer brands when making licensing deals and also take into consideration how much market preference a brand might have in a specific publishing segment. For example, Disney is one of the most recognized global brands, whose products appeal to similar demographics in many cultures, and it's been an excellent brand for building successful licensees, not just in videos, games, and toys, but in the publishing industry as well. The Disney brand is often a trusted and preferred brand among parents, especially when used for products aimed at young children. We can find the Disney brand on a wide range of books and interactive e-books, handheld devices for kids, and websites in dozens of languages. Many publishers license the Disney brand to help sell their own locally produced content—from coloring books to high-end picture books. As with all successful global branding strategies, the Disney brand is promoted differently depending on the language and culture while satisfying strict corporate licensing guidelines.

Book licensing for companies like Disney, Lucas Films, Warner Bros., or Sesame Street, to name a few of the global brands with youthful demographic appeal, is not only a very big business—it's basically an industry in itself. At the same time, these successful megabrands may not be as valuable in some publishing areas as in others. With the exception of products for very young children in a few Asian markets, educational licensing, for example, is not Disney's most active publishing category. Nor does the Disney brand resonate as well in reference publishing as, say, National Geographic, Britannica, Merriam-Webster, the BBC, or Oxford University Press. With this in mind, a publisher in Korea might be better off with the Merriam-Webster brand or Oxford than Disney or Nintendo if it wanted to produce a line of dictionaries, even for young people.

Brand Alignment

Both licensors and the licensees should align a brand with a category of publishing with which the brand can be most easily associated. To differentiate a line of recreational activity books for three- and four-year-olds, for example, the Crayola or LEGO brands or the Warner Bros. cartoon characters might be good choices. Conversely, Crayola would probably not be the best choice for a series of activity books for learning writing skills. It appeals to the wrong target age group, for starters, and it doesn't have the appropriate resonance for the subject area. Sesame Street might be a better choice for educational content aimed at that age level.

As an example of good brand alignment, Dorling Kindersley (DK) used the global LEGO brand very successfully in a line of graded readers with different themes, such as exploring space or constructing a castle. These educational books combine DK's recognizable design with photographs of characters and structures made from LEGO blocks. The two brands align well because DK is a highly regarded educational publisher and the LEGO Company stands for creativity and innovation. But when producing an illustrated children's dictionary, an entirely different kind of publication, DK licensed Merriam-Webster's brand name and content.

Brands like LEGO, Crayola, and Smithsonian are examples of global brands with unusually strong equity. They are recognized as leaders in their fields and have earned substantial customer trust, which has been tested over time and often across cultures. Any one of them, even though not necessarily associated directly with educational publishing, could be used on educational products. But they need to be correctly aligned with the appropriate subjects and demographics. Because of their name recognition, they have the ability to create opportunities in a variety of market segments that may not be available with other entities.

However, in various niche-publishing categories, lesser-known yet high-value brands can have a meaningful impact in their specialty markets and can help build customer allegiance. These are companies that are well respected in their area of specialization—in some cases even across languages—but are not familiar consumer brands like Disney or Warner Bros. In fact, only a handful of brands ever attain that same lofty level of name recognition across multiple demographics. But educational publishers, such as Larousse and Universalis in France, Langenscheidt in Germany, Scholastic in the U.S., and Bloomsbury in the U.K., are all brands that, in their publishing segments, have the potential to perform better than many major consumer brands.

Some publishers in smaller markets may be big brands for consumers. If they are licensing products and have a brand that is well known in their market segment, it's important to recognize its value to customers and use it to its best advantage. At the same time, when shopping for properties to license, one goal is to uncover brands that have equity and are trusted in other cultures and leverage them. Pokémon, which began as a card game, and Thomas and Friends toy trains, featuring Thomas the Tank Engine, are two such examples, and have helped to spin off a large number of successful books and digital products. Sanrio's Hello Kitty line of girls' accessories appears to spawn an endless number of books and interactive games. Michelin, for many years, has been another brand that has had great success with its publishing programs and remains as one of the standards in the travel book business, even though its core business is manufacturing tires.

The key to a real brand coup, of course, is to select a promising brand that has not yet become world-famous. If a publisher is lucky (or prophetic) enough to pick an emerging brand before it becomes well known, it might be able to take advantage of the brand's growing momentum in the marketplace before it becomes too expensive to leverage. If the brand has not yet reached its zenith, the cost of entry will be much lower. The goal is to spot the next SpongeBob SquarePants (a Nickelodeon property) before it becomes SpongeBob the brand or, at a minimum, before it becomes a high-priced premium brand.

Publishing's Branding Kings

Publishers can use their content to help companies outside of publishing promote their brand and also generate incremental revenue. DK has a separate division, custom publishing, devoted to helping companies align their brand with DK. In some cases, DK will remove or lower the visibility of its brand from the licensed product. A form of "white labeling," this can help a consumer product company associate its brand with quality content that consumers can use—such as recipes, automotive safety, or health information. DK has created customized products in a variety of print and digital formats with such diverse brands as Coca-Cola, Chevrolet, Pfizer, and Nestlé.

Arguably the branding king of publishing is a company that most people outside of publishing have not heard of, yet it dominates sales of books and interactive learning toys in big-box wholesalers like Costco and Sam's Club. Publications International (PIL), a Chicago-based company, has taken world-famous brands in the food and appliance sectors and created best-selling books, e-books, and apps. Using big brands like Campbell's, Hershey's, Crock-Pot, and KitchenAid, it produces illustrated books with recipes that utilize those brands' products. The marketing edge for PIL is based on the assumption that if people enjoy the soup, chocolate, and stews associated with these brands, they are likely to purchase the books that feature them. The consumer brands like these books for the opposite reason: if people buy the books, they are likely to buy the ingredients that are promoted in the recipes. For PIL, its own brand is not as important as the brand that helps sell the books. In many cases, the recipes themselves were already created for other books, but with some of the ingredients replaced with the sponsoring brand's products.

PIL has also licensed the Britannica name, logo, and content to create several best-selling products at the big-box retailers. PIL took existing Britannica content, repurposed it, and used it in interactive books that had specially coded paper and came with an audio device that, when placed on certain hot spots in the books, would play recorded text, so children could hear parts of the book read to them. Although PIL did all of the editorial work, manufactured the product, and brought it to market, the branding on the packaging would suggest that it was a Britannica production. Indeed, the content was Britannica's, but the vision for the product, the form that it was in, and the path to market belonged entirely to PIL.

This relationship between publishing and a brand, where content can be reused in different products, demonstrates how licensing can improve a publisher's ROI on its investment in content. Licensing the same content generates much better margins than the original publications, since the investment in content has been covered by previously published works. In the case of PIL, it had access to a certain market that Britannica did not sell in; but PIL needed the Britannica brand and content to create a successful marketing opportunity.

Brand Extension

Outside of the world-class brands that are established in a variety of consumer segments, niche-category brands offer real opportunities. Universities, for example, especially Harvard, Cambridge, Princeton, Wharton, the London School of Economics, and Oxford, have done an excellent job of extending their brands and making them relevant in non-academic areas by licensing their brands selectively for general business, language, and training books and manuals. Middlebury College, well known for its expertise in world language curriculum, has teamed up with K12 Inc., a digital publishing company, and created a joint venture called Middlebury Interactive Languages, which publishes online language courses for schools.

Associations and not-for-profits, such as the International Reading Association (IRA) and the American Medical Association (AMA), have been very effective in extending their brands based on their reputation among their members and the influence they have outside of their organizations. One of the best examples, both in the U.S. and the U.K., are their respective automotive associations, the AAA and the AA.

Corporations and celebrities have also been able to leverage the trust that their brands have built in the minds of consumers to generate easily recognized publications. Kraft Foods, General Mills through its Betty Crocker brand, Martha Stewart, Rachael Ray, Nigella Lawson, Gordon Ramsay, and Wolfgang Puck have generated numerous best-selling cookbooks, and Home Depot and Black & Decker have licensed their brands for popular home repair books. As an example of two publishers joining forces, where one is the more dominate brand, John Wiley & Sons has been the official worldwide publisher of the Microsoft Official Academic Course book series.

When corporate icons like Microsoft and Kraft partner with a publisher, two objectives are met: the corporations receive additional branding and marketing—in a sense, free advertising—in addition to royalty revenue generated from the publications; and the publisher leverages the brand with its content to help accelerate sales. Without a name-brand partner, the publisher's content (on software code or recipes) may not have the same use or reuse value. The corporate brands are not only well recognized and respected, but readers will be apt to have more confidence in the content if it is associated with a known brand. The branding identification helps to differentiate similar content from one publisher over another. A counterargument is sometimes made that some content can be diminished in value or viewed more like advertising than trusted editorial content if it is tied to a corporate brand. But if the alignment is a good one, like the examples above, linking a corporation to carefully selected content can be a benefit to the brand, the publisher, and the consumer.

Some alliances between a content provider and a brand could not be more natural. The *Official Scrabble Players Dictionary* (OSPD), published by Merriam-Webster, is an example of a perfect fit. In 1975, representatives of Scrabble Crossword Game Players Inc. wanted to provide Scrabble players with a specialized—or "official"—dictionary to adjudicate acceptable words. But as a game organization (even one with a best-selling product), they did not feel that they were in a position to publish a dictionary that Scrabble players would take seriously. So a Merriam-Webster product seemed like a good idea. The dictionary, which today displays both the Merriam-Webster and Scrabble brands (see next page), has been in continuous publication for 40 years.

Brand extension, like brand alignment, must be well managed and applied carefully so that it is not abused. Consumers must not only trust the brand, but they must be able to feel that they can trust the particular application or extension of the brand. The brand extension must be logical and well directed, and cannot be seen as a stretch, or it will fail as a marketing aid. As a hypothetical example, it probably would not be a good idea for McDonald's to put its name on a line of software products or for Lenovo, on the other hand, to help McDonald's sell burgers with a "McPC meal." While these examples might seem ludicrous, I can recall a popular cereal brand that failed when it tried to use its brand on educational workbooks and websites. Why did it fail? Cereal cannot logically bridge the divide between breakfast food and education, whereas LEGO—with its clear association with skill-building, architecture,

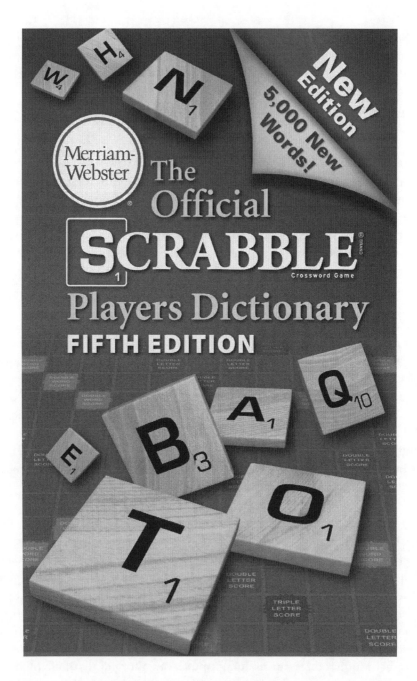

Figure 6.2   *Merriam-Webster's Scrabble Dictionary* **cover**[2]

---

2   Merriam-Webster®, and Circle with NW Monogram and Webster's, are trademarks of Merriam-Webster, Incorporated. All rights reserved. Used by permission. Scrabble® is registered trademark of Hasbro, Inc.

engineering, and design—can more easily be a partner to education. This is especially true with the growing popularity of STEM/STEAM (Science, Technology, Engineering/Art, and Math) courses.

A good example of brand extension, outside of the publishing field, comes from a colleague of mine in the licensing business. Andy Lieb, the founder of the JRL Group, represents Cobra Electronics, a market leader in automotive and outdoor lifestyle electronics. Cobra Electronics was seeking a co-branding partner for its CB radio line. JRL secured a licensing partnership with Harley-Davidson, a brand with significant equity that, given its customer base, would logically extend into CB radios. The parameters of the license included a specific distribution channel targeting professional truck drivers who have an affinity for lifestyle brands such as Harley-Davidson. Net result: a special limited edition Harley-Davidson/Cobra CB radio sold out and created pent-up demand in the market, thus achieving both goodwill and a successful product that generated good margins for Cobra and a royalty stream for Harley-Davidson.

Cobra's success with the Harley-Davidson tie-in with its CB radio caused it to think about a similar strategy for its two-way radio line, or walkie-talkies. For this product line, JRL evaluated numerous outdoor lifestyle brands and negotiated a licensing partnership with Realtree, an outdoor gear and lifestyle brand with an impeccable reputation for quality. In particular, Realtree is well known to the outdoor enthusiast for its unique outdoor artwork patterns. At the same time, even though the Realtree logo and artwork are enormously popular, with almost a cult following, having an electronic market leader like Cobra as the manufacturer of a branded product gave it instant credibility and recognition in a product category where Realtree had no presence. In this case, both companies brought their unique branding and market position to a new line of products. Realtree brought design, outdoor lifestyle appeal, and a strong following, while Cobra brought technology, innovation, and dependability. Net result: a full line of Cobra/Realtree two-way radios was successfully launched and continues to gain market share with outdoor enthusiasts.

Although brands can be significant assets in establishing immediate intimacy with consumers and for gaining market share, not all brands, even the most recognized ones, play equally well in all markets. For any market, a decision has to be made as to who has the best brand for selling the most products in that market. In the case of publishing in international markets, the local publisher is usually in the best position to make the right choice, especially since it is taking most of the risk.

The surest way to gain market share is by leading with the most recognized local brand and to keep egos out of the equation. If necessary, the power of a brand can be validated by using focus groups and surveys, especially for fine-tuning the demographic reach of certain brands. In general, assuming a reasonable amount of effort in time and resources, brand publishing can be a very effective tool for building awareness in any format—print, digital, or mixed media.

Chapter 7
The Virtue in a Virtual Town Hall

The public is the only critic whose judgment is worth anything at all.
Mark Twain, "A General Reply," The Galaxy

The primary business of international publishing is the buying and selling of content in one form or another. Beyond making their sales forecasts from their own markets, publishers who have developed a sizable list of publications should consider leveraging the investments that they have made by establishing a relationship with a company to license or distribute their content in another market. It is possible for a publisher in one market to partner with a publisher in another market that might actually be interested in licensing an entire backlist of titles as well as a forward publishing plan. At the same time, publishers can supplement their existing portfolio quickly (or even start a new product line) without heavily investing in developing new products from the ground up by licensing products from a publisher with complementary product lines.

Whether leveraging existing content or supplementing an existing line of books—whether buying or selling rights—knowing where and how to identify a suitable partner is the first step in making product licensing an integral part of a publisher's strategy. Literary agents specialize in matching a seller with the right buyer by learning where there may be compatibility and interest. And, as I will discuss later in this chapter, publishers might want to consider working with an agent in some foreign markets. But for the most part, the best place to find a licensing partner is by making personal contacts at one or more of the major international book fairs.

Throughout the year, publishers have the opportunity to attend any one of two dozen or more book fairs that take place in every region of the world (see Appendix A for a list of the biggest fairs). However, many people have observed that, over the years, general attendance at these events has been waning, which can be attributed to a number of causes: since much of the trade business has moved online, fewer distributors and retailers remain in the business; publishers have been cutting back on marketing expenses, and book fairs are an obvious target for reducing costs; and the publishing industry in general has experienced considerable consolidation and contraction over the years, resulting in fewer publishers overall. But another reason is our increasing dependence on instant communication, which we may (falsely) think has decreased the need for in-person meetings with potential partners.

We can easily fall into the trap of believing that virtual meetings provide an adequate alternative to physical ones, even though this might not always be the case. Today, not only can we easily contact almost anyone in the world with email or have face-to-face meetings using telecommunication technology such as Skype, but we also have available a variety of social media options, such as LinkedIn and Facebook, to search for and locate potential partners. We can make presentations to strangers across time zones with online webinars. Virtual trade shows, which provide interactive environments—fully loaded exhibit booths, including branding, demo stations, and avatars—and real-time data to keep track of "attendance," are gaining popularity and substituting for live events.

As the cost of getting to and exhibiting at book fairs has risen, publishers have become much more strategic about which fairs to attend and how many employees to send to them. Measuring leads and determining the benefits from a fair usually results in cutting down on future trade show attendance. Many of us feel that we can learn as much as we need to know about available products from corporate websites and that we can be introduced to key contacts through LinkedIn or email.

Still, publishing, just like any business, has much to gain by promoting physical encounters between potential partners. For those who still regularly attend book or technology shows, live events provide invaluable opportunities for buyers and sellers to have meaningful exchanges, to share the benefits of their respective publications, and to form relationships based on mutual interests. Accomplishing this in an exclusively online environment is difficult. The issue is not just an old-school-versus-new-school approach to communication, or a quaint sense of the importance of continuing a long-standing, annual tradition of meeting at a particular fair. Trade shows in any business still give us a unique opportunity to strengthen existing relationships, get a closer look at new products, and network in the company of colleagues who are engaged in the same activity and believe that there is value in sustaining a global, publishing community.

Developing long-term business relationships without attending book fairs or trade shows is possible. But these frenetic congresses of like-minded people provide a unique, stimulating atmosphere that allows us to measure our own ideas on a world stage, test our assumptions about what is marketable, and even get lucky by locating, serendipitously, just the right product or partner. Most people who frequently attend them agree that being at book fairs is still essential to establishing meaningful relationships and building a competitive publishing program.

To help stem the decline in attendance and to remain relevant in an increasingly digital world, book fair officials have been reinventing the purpose of the fairs and adjusting to changes in the market. More shows today feature digital solutions along with print, and promote a growing number of fair spin-offs that focus exclusively on technology in publishing and e-learning platforms.

When e-books and digital solutions first started to gain popularity, many of the book fairs had completely separate areas dedicated to digital exhibits, and in some cases publishers had to double their exposure by exhibiting at both the traditional print and digital stands. Now the tendency is simply to combine them in one exhibit and to acknowledge that publishing has a dual track with equal stakes in digital and physical solutions. By embracing the new norm—where digital outputs do not necessarily threaten physical ones—and letting the market decide what formats to choose, book fairs should remain relevant, even in a world in which broadband and wireless connectivity is taken for granted.

The virtue in a virtual town hall is in extending our ability to interact with one another—to increase the frequency with which we are able to communicate and to provide a vehicle for being in more places without going everywhere—not in replacing one-to-one contact.

International Town Halls

To promote the annual exchange of IP in all categories of publishing, four international book fairs have traditionally stood out among all of the others: the Frankfurt Book Fair, which takes place in October; the London Book Fair, which takes place in March; the Bologna Children's Book Fair, usually in late March or early April, after the London Book Fair; and Book Expo America (BEA, formerly the ABA, or American Bookseller's Association), which takes place in late May, and which used to rotate among New York, Chicago, L.A., and Washington, D.C., settled in New York for a while, and will move to Chicago in 2016 and other cities, including New York, thereafter. Other large book and rights fairs in locations such as Japan, Korea, Singapore, India, China, and recently the Middle East have attracted worldwide attention, but these tend to be more regional rather than major international events, even though they mount extensive PR campaigns to increase their international audience. Officials of some of these events have even been known to pay VIP publishers from the U.S. and the U.K. to attend. Certainly the Beijing International Book Fair (BIBF) is gaining in popularity as China becomes more of a global player and makes visible progress in its respect for, and protection of, international copyright laws. The BIBF is probably an essential destination for publishers that are serious about doing long-term business in China. But the big four—Frankfurt, London, Bologna, and BEA—are the events that most publishers, large and small, from all over the world still attend in substantial numbers.

With the growing worldwide importance of digital publishing, some technology fairs and conferences have gained popularity: BETT (more often written as "Bett"), the British Educational Training and Technology Show, which takes place in London in January; ISTE (International Society for Technology in Education), which is the American equivalent of Bett; and Digital Book World in New York.

The Frankfurt Book Fair (FBF), which has been held continuously at the Frankfurt exhibition complex (the *Messe*) since 1949, is the grand-daddy of the fairs. It is by far the biggest and the most talked about, and is the one fair that has maintained its industry prestige even as attendance has dropped slightly over the years. Because the fair attracts so many exhibitors from all over the world, very few other venues besides the Frankfurt *Messe* are large enough to play host to it. At one point talk circulated that the book fair might move to Munich, which also has a large exhibition hall. But the Frankfurt fair officials have been proactive in making improvements to keep the fair where it is, such as getting concessions from the hotels to stop inflating their rates during fair week and shortening the fair's duration from six days to five in order to keep exhibitor costs down. The shorter fair week also means that the fair's organizers accept the reality that six days is just not needed anymore, given how easy it is for people to plan for the fair in advance, communicate online, and follow up after the fair has ended. (In fact, since the last two days of the fair—which starts on Wednesday—coincide with the weekend, when the general public is allowed to attend, by Friday night most of the senior publishers' representatives return home.)

Given the tradition behind the fair, the mammoth undertaking in moving a fair of this size, and with the recent flexibility on the part of the fair's officials to make changes, this preeminent rights and book fair is likely to remain in Frankfurt for some time to come.

Approximately 7,000 exhibitors from more than 100 countries attend the FBF each year, in addition to hundreds of German publishers. Publishers are spread out among a complex of a dozen massive buildings or "Halls," which are accessible by minibus or a maze of moving sidewalks and escalators. To avoid the congestion and maddening confusion inside the Halls and the connecting corridors, many attendees take the minibuses when going from Hall to Hall. Although they can be crowded, the buses circle the fair continuously and frequently. The Halls are well marked on the exterior of the buildings, so the buses, which move freely from building to building, are the easiest way to get around the fair and locate exhibitors.

Because of its size, reputation, and longevity, the FBF is regarded by most publishers as the beginning of the annual book-fair cycle, even though it takes place in the fourth quarter of the calendar year. Big titles from best-selling authors like Brazilian novelist Paulo Coelho get their initial international exposure at Frankfurt, and many of the more substantial deals are sealed or announced at the fair. Some of these deals are highlighted in a daily newsletter that the fair distributes to all exhibitors. For all practical purposes, the new publishing year begins with this fair, and publishers finalize their spring lists at this time.

When digital solutions first arrived on the publishing scene, the FBF officials seemed uneasy about how to accommodate the new medium, as if the format would be temporary and hadn't yet earned its place at the table. So a separate floor in one building was devoted to digital publishing. Recently any reluctance to mainstream digital formats with print seems to have disappeared. Last year, the Director of the fair, Juergen Boos, boasted that the fair has turned the corner and has made changes to accommodate more digital publishing events around e-books, apps, and publishing platforms.

The FBF is something of a brand in the industry, so officials of other major events carefully observe how FBF leaders adjust to the changing landscape and follow their example. Three years ago, in a strategic move by the FBF officials to take their brand outside of Germany to get closer to trends in other markets and to better respond to local needs, they launched an annual event in São Paulo, Brazil, called "Contec Brazil," which focused on education, technology, and children's media. I spoke at this event last year and was impressed at how much innovation was taking place not only in Brazil, but in other countries in

Latin America as well, and how eager educators were to integrate technology into their schools and classrooms. As a response to the growing global need to understand how best to combine print and digital publishing solutions, a similar event is being planned for Colombia and other locations in the near future.

The London Book Fair (LBF), now in its 44th year, takes place in early spring and is a significant event for the European consumer book trade. It used to be held at the Earl's Court Exhibition Centre and has relocated to the newly refurbished Olympia, in West London. One year fair officials moved it to ExCel London in the Docklands area, a modern facility with quite a bit more space than the Exhibition Centre that also provided attendees with a far less crowded networking environment. That move failed to please fairgoers, however, who found the location inconvenient for going to the finest London hotels and restaurants. Olympia, where all former Earl's Court events have moved to, has the benefit of both plenty of space and a central location.

The LBF is quite a bit smaller than the FBF, with fewer than 1,000 exhibitors, but it's arguably the best place to discover and learn more about the most innovative book designers and publishers in the English language as well as the U.K. retail market. Workshops that are offered before and after the fair are also popular with publishers and other industry professionals who prefer networking in smaller, more targeted groups. These focused seminars provide insights into the latest innovations and trends that are likely to impact their business, and give attendees a chance to mingle with industry thought-leaders.

The Bologna Children's Book Fair is also worth attending for children's and educational products. This fair has always been a favorite among publishers who also enjoy the charming medieval architecture of the city, the superb Bolognese cuisine, and the relaxed pace of the fair, especially compared to the frenetic environments that characterize Frankfurt, and, to a somewhat lesser degree, London. The weather is normally better than it is in either Frankfurt or London. It gets roughly the same amount of attendance as the LBF in a more expansive space. With a focus on children's publications, it is inherently less daunting than the other fairs and allows publishers who specialize in children's publications—either trade or educational products—to find one another more easily.

BookExpo America (BEA) is primarily for North American booksellers, distributors, and retailers. Over the years, as the large chains have either ceased their bricks-and-mortar businesses and more of the retail business has moved online, particularly to Amazon, BEA officials have been expanding the fair's role and its relevancy by including more of the same types of activities that take place at Frankfurt and London. Increasingly it is an event for the exchange of literary rights, international promotions, big book deals, networking, and celebrity author signings. As the largest book publishing event in the U.S., it's an essential destination for trade publishers and distributors.

These fairs are all considered *international* book fairs because the major international publishers and packagers (people who make books for other publishers, but generally do not distribute under their own imprint) attend, and they attract publishers from around the world. For the most part, publishers will send their top executives, as well as their foreign rights managers, to these fairs. If a publisher, regardless of size, is looking for an international partner in any country, it is likely to find that partner at one of these events.

Over the years, Bett has become the most important international show for education technology (IT) products and services. Although the show goes beyond publishing with the inclusion of pure technology solutions, equipment, ergonomic furniture, and manipulatives, anyone who provides technology-driven content and publishing platforms needs to consider attending this event.

ISTE is roughly the American equivalent of Bett, and also attracts international attendees. Both Bett and ISTE combine presentations, seminars, and keynote speeches with vendor exhibits. Though Bett and ISTE are similar in many ways, from my experience, Bett, which is truly international in its representation, highlights its exhibitors more than ISTE does, while ISTE caters mostly to educators and focuses on knowledge transfer, school improvement discussions, professional development, and making connections. ISTE moves around to different U.S. cities (recent shows took place in San Diego, San Antonio, Atlanta, and Philadelphia), and almost all of the exhibitors are from North America. Neither Bett nor ISTE generates the business networking opportunities of any of the big-four book fairs, but they are both useful for understanding how various publishers and technology companies are meeting user needs and for following trends.

From its debut in 2008, Digital Book World (DBW) has become an important forum for consumer publishers, journalists, agents, and booksellers who want to keep up with digital innovation, learn how to manage a publishing business with a focus on digital content, and acquire and improve skills essential to creating and distributing digital content. It hosts an annual conference in New York and follows up with monthly webcasts and other publications. Mike Shatzkin, founder and CEO of the Idea Logical Company and one of the conference's organizers, publishes a regular blog, "The Shatzkin Files," in which he covers various issues affecting the global book publishing business, including topics that have been or will be addressed at a DBW conference.

Neal Goff, a publishing veteran and now President of Egremont Associates—a consulting firm that assists educational and children's publishing and technology firms with strategic, marketing, and product development issues, often helping them navigate the move from print to digital—attends the annual DBW conference regularly and finds that it has a unique role to play in digital publishing:

> Digital Book World is a great conference. As far as I know, it is the only conference solely devoted to e-books and their impact on the publishing industry as a whole. It's focused on the adult consumer book trade, but also touches on what's happening in children's publishing, K-12, and academic publishing.
>
> The presentations and panels are always interesting, and a lot of the top people in publishing attend, so it's often a good networking opportunity as well.

Regional Meeting Places

For publishers in a highly specialized market—or those looking for a specific type of book from a certain country or who believe that their publication is particularly suited to a specific foreign market—attending one of the top regional book fairs around the world might make sense. Local book fairs such as those in Paris, Tokyo, Guadalajara, Singapore, and Jerusalem may be worth attending if finding publishers from those regions is a priority. The Beijing Book Fair has been aggressively promoting itself as more than just a regional fair. And certainly, given the size and complexity of that market, it's bound to be an increasingly important event. In addition, the Chinese government's recent emphasis on children learning English is making that fair an important destination for British and American publishers that specialize in developing programs for English as a foreign language (EFL).

Publishers interested in interactive media, video, and digital content might consider attending MIPTV (Marché International des Programmes de Television), which takes place in Cannes, France. It used to be called MILIA—when multimedia first hit the publishing stage—and then morphed into an audiovisual marketplace when CD-ROMs and DVD-ROMs started to decline. Today it describe itself as "the world's most established TV and digital content market," focusing on deal-making, partnerships, networking, and distribution deals.

Preparing for a Fair

Although I have indicated the dates when these fairs take place in Appendix A, they do change from time to time. The FBF is an October tradition and is unlikely to make a major calendar move in the near future—though the fair officials ensure that the dates do not conflict with the Jewish high holidays. The exact dates when these fairs take place, along with a list of past attendees and their publishing focus can be found on the fairs' websites.

Most publishers invest in exhibiting at a fair so they can be easily located by their colleagues and have a permanent place to show their books or concepts to potential partners. But many first-timers or small publishers prefer not to rent exhibit space. Instead, they simply "walk the floors," visiting one stand after another, browsing the offerings, and hoping to meet a potential partner.

Exhibiting with a "collective," which provides a turnkey solution for exhibiting at a minimal cost, is a good alternative to either setting up a personal stand or wandering around, lugging book concepts, promotional materials, and "best-sellers" in a wheeled Samsonite. Collectives rent and manage a large block of stands and offer a menu of services including branding, marketing, a place to ship products, and a message service. Collectives are available at all of the major fairs, some of which are organized by countries and others by marketing groups or publishing associations. Information on these collectives can also be found at the book fairs' websites.

First-time fairgoers should not feel compelled to have a private, fixed presence at the fair. Plenty of people go without renting real estate, just to see how fairs are organized, get the lay of the land, and make initial contacts. However, only so much can be learned from websites or other people's experiences. So, once the right fair is identified, attending it without a fixed location is better than not attending at all.

A publisher's strategy for approaching an international book fair and what kind of expectations to have depends, to some degree, on whether they are buying or selling. More people attend a fair to sell than to buy.

Unlike other markets, where supply and demand tends to fluctuate, book fairs always provide a buyer's market. Publishers will find buying a product that fits in their line of publications easier than selling even their most successful publications.

Certain factors, however, will always favor the seller. For example, finding a publisher in a relatively small market like Belgium willing to acquire the translation rights to a best-seller from a major market such as the U.S. or the U.K. should not be difficult. Sought-after brands and trademarks, as well as new publications from well-known publishing houses, do better than those from lesser-known or untested sources. However, publishers of specialty products in a narrow market (e.g., music history) or a category experiencing a temporary downturn (e.g., Middle East travel) will have a harder time finding someone in a foreign market willing to take on the translation rights or even distribute the books in English.

When deciding to attend a book fair, planning ahead by making as many appointments as possible, and starting the process several months in advance of the fair, will make the event more valuable. By the first week of September, many people worth meeting at the FBF, for example, will have full schedules, so getting on their calendars as early as possible will make finding a buyer easier. Most people would advise anyone who is looking to sell products not to attend a fair cold or to expect to find a suitable buyer serendipitously.

A good source for tapping into a network of publishers, editors, and rights managers is the LMP (*Literary Marketplace*), online or in print. The print and electronic versions are available in domestic and international editions; the latter is called the *International Literary Marketplace* (ILMP). Most public libraries will have a hard copy, but the LMP website may be a better place to look since it's likely to have more up-to-date information. The ILMP is a good starting point for locating publishers in other countries and getting a sense of the kind of publishing they do.

The larger book fairs, such as Frankfurt and Bologna, offer (onsite and online) their own fair publications, digitally and in print, which include capsule descriptions of the publishers that attended in the past. In addition, the book fair websites, which are kept up to date, offer their catalogue databases free of charge. The FBF site, for example, has three catalogues online: the main Frankfurt Catalogue, which contains the approximately 7,000 companies that attend; the *Who's Who Catalogue*, which lists around 14,000 publishing and media professionals who attend the fair; and a *Rights Catalogue*, which is a directory of more than 19,000 titles available for subsidiary rights. The online directories make it easy to contact fair attendees to help make appointments.

Working with Agents

Although international book fairs can be invaluable for making the right connections, attending all of them would not be practical—or even desirable. For this reason, a good way to "keep things moving" in distant markets while staying home is to work with a locally based agent. Agents can be found at the "rights" sections of the major book fairs or at joint country exhibits (the "collectives" mentioned above), which tend to consist of a consortia of publishers, packagers, publishers representatives, and agents from one country or region. They are also listed in the same industry publications as publishers and editors. Agents usually have an in-depth knowledge of their market, can access an up-to-date network of publishers, and can efficiently match publishers and products. The downside of working with agents, however, is that they usually represent a virtual basketful of products from a variety of publishers and cannot always give a single publisher a satisfactory amount of attention; getting to the top of their priority list can be frustrating for all but the largest publishers or the most successful clients. Once agents do get a nibble, they have a tendency to oversell and overpromise, and they may be willing to accept less than ideal terms just to get a deal done. In many ways, they can be similar to real estate brokers and favor the quick over the ideal sale. Still, in many regions, agents can play a useful role in a publisher's overall licensing efforts—they just shouldn't be a company's primary or only representatives.

Agents should be paid only when they conclude a deal and funds have been transferred, not on the signing of a contract. The usual agent commission is in the range of 15–25% of net royalties, including any advances against future royalties. Commissions can be higher depending on how much travel and exhibiting the agent actually does in the course of arranging a partnership and in maintaining it once it has been solidified, including any due diligence required in managing the account. The agent normally makes the deal with the local publisher directly on the publisher's behalf. In this way, the transaction itself goes through the agent first—the local publisher pays the agent, then the agent takes his or her cut and passes the balance to the publisher. The agents I've done business with have all been honest and competent in handling these kinds of transactions. I avoid working with an agent on a retainer basis. More often than not, this is a formula for disaster. It generally breeds complacency, and only in rare cases will the content owner recover the investments in the agent's fees, travel costs, and other expenses from any deal that may arise. Paying only for results is the best structure, and the basis on which the most productive agents will expect to work.

Although an agent may play a substantial role during the negotiations—and sometimes as the project moves into the development or production phase—the publisher needs to establish a personal relationship with the partner and take over as early in the process as possible. The agent will not be as invested in the relationship as either of the partners will be. A long-term publisher–partner alliance will depend on a strong working relationship from the beginning, based on trust and common goals, not on the agent's enthusiasm to earn a commission. Even if, for expediency's sake, a project is initiated prior to a face-to-face meeting between the two parties, plans should be made to get together soon after the start of the project to clarify roles and responsibilities—and to ensure that the relationship has all of the ingredients to be a win-win.

Chapter 8
Luck is Not a Strategy

There are two times in a man's life when he should not speculate: when he can't afford it and when he can.

Mark Twain,
Following the Equator: Pudd'nhead Wilson's New Calendar

When publishers set out to create a product, they normally do the research necessary to determine in advance the size and receptivity of their primary market to the product and plan on selling it through their usual channels of distribution. They also determine the minimum investment they will need to return a profit in an acceptable period of time. But unless they have had some international experience or have company-owned operations overseas, they may not have built into their business model incremental revenue from licensing deals in foreign markets. This is especially true for publishers with large domestic markets, like North America, where additional revenue from other markets may not have a significant impact on a product's P&L, or at least not enough for the effort of creating a foreign-market version to appear on management's radar. I know several successful mid-size U.S.-based companies that do not give a second thought to international markets and have yet to attend the Frankfurt Book Fair. However, whatever their main market, publishers should not overlook the potential value of product licensing. Almost every product's earning potential should provide revenue from licensing, for no other reason than if the initial publishing plan falls short of forecast, licensing could end up filling the gap.

As I have been discussing, licensing, or the buying and selling of IP rights in the form of published products, is the foundation for co-publishing deals and partnerships. Why one product has more success in some markets than in others is a function of culture, trends, and sometimes the inexplicable. Publishers or content providers on the selling side look for compatible buyers who have the ability to maximize the potential of their products in a new market. A content provider can improve the odds of selling a product in other markets by identifying unmet market needs—and then aligning itself with a partner who is in the best position to address those needs with a local version of its product.

The nature of licensing assumes that the licensor and the licensee have mutually beneficial goals. The seller's, or licensor's, primary goal in licensing is to establish a presence in markets that it cannot easily reach through its normal distribution channels, and to generate revenue from a sunken investment in a product without incurring the additional sales and marketing costs in unfamiliar territories where it has neither the means nor the expertise to sell its product on its own. By licensing its product to a publisher in another market, it shifts the burden of adapting, translating (if necessary), producing, marketing, and selling to the licensee. If the right partner is identified, the licensor benefits from the local partner's understanding of, and ability to serve, its market. The revenue, in the form of royalties that the licensor receives from this relationship, goes right to the bottom line.

The licensee, on the other hand, is able to take advantage of the IP holder's "vision" in bringing the product to market in the first place and can benefit from the investments already made in conceiving, writing, and developing the product. At the same time, the licensor must rely on the licensee to make any incremental investment necessary to launch the product into its market successfully and, in so doing, to generate revenue from a market that was previously inaccessible to the licensor.

Sellers at trade shows who have a particularly desirable property that resonates in another market may attract the attention of more than one potential buyer and may be able to entertain several offers for their property. However, except for best-sellers or publications by well-known or celebrity authors, licensors normally should not expect to receive multiple interested buyers; attracting even one compatible co-publishing partner would be considered an accomplishment. Publishers often have to kiss a lot of frogs before they find a prince.

Publishers exhibit at trade fairs to promote and license their products, and to obtain commitments as quickly as possible. Because sellers outnumber buyers at these events, the latter are in great demand. Publishers who are looking to make an acquisition, either for pure distribution or for the purposes of translation or adaptation for their market, will be able to make appointments at a book fair easily. Unless a property has already established itself as a best-seller with unusual marketing potential, publishers won't hold off too long to gather and compare competitive bids. If two parties can generally agree on the terms of a deal, they will assume that they will proceed to the formal contract stage and will not anticipate that a better offer will preempt the negotiations.

Licensing is one way to acquire content, but "acquire" is somewhat of a misnomer. A licensee actually rents content for a certain period of time and under specific terms and conditions, which I will discuss in the next chapter. But content can also be bought and sold outright, either in the form of finished products or individual assets. And because so much content is now available in a digital format and can be showcased on publisher websites, it can be evaluated quickly, remotely, and collaboratively by any potential partners.

At any given time, a number of companies may be looking to divest themselves of assets that no longer fit into their strategic plan or corporate profile. These properties may be of high quality and still relevant, but for a variety of reasons—including exiting the business entirely—the company's management has decided to sell rather than maintain and market them, or even manage the in-house licensing process.

Many companies have been built on making serial acquisitions of this type, and some have been able to grow or to expand into new markets by acquiring a number of product lines. For publishers who are looking to grow quickly and have available capital—or if they are in a mature market segment and need to make a move into a higher growth sector—looking at potential acquisition targets may be a sensible strategy.

Book fairs, however, may not be the best place for making large acquisitions, since the focus at these events is on licensing individual properties rather than the divestment of entire publishing divisions or multiple product lines. A better approach for identifying substantial acquisition targets is networking with investment banks or private equity firms that specialize in brokering IP or that are purchasing media companies for their own portfolios. Other good contacts include various publishing associations, such as the Association of American Publishers (AAP), the U.K. Publishers Association (PA), or the Software & Information Industry Association (SIIA), which can help locate potential opportunities. Investment banks, private equity, or venture capital firms that specialize in the publishing and media sectors, such as Berkery, Noyes & Co., DeSilva + Phillips, the Carlyle Group, or Veronis Suhler Stevenson, are often affiliate members of these types of associations and sponsor networking events at their conferences, sometimes in conjunction with major book fairs. Industry publications, such as *Publisher's Weekly* or *The Book Standard*, follow acquisition trends and can be useful sources for learning about who is buying whom and what companies or product lines may be up for sale. But in order to get a jump on the process and to take advantage of opportunities at the earliest possible stages, most publishers try to find their way on to the brokers' A-lists to signal that they are in the market to make an acquisition.

First Steps Toward Partnering

In advance of shopping for products at book fairs, potential buyers should target publishers that are most likely to have the kind of product that they are looking for. Publishers and packagers can sell only what they have in their lists and they may not have exactly what the buyer or licensee needs. For a potential buyer to assume that a publisher or packager digging into its backlist will come up with a jewel among obsolete or irrelevant products is usually an overly optimistic strategy.

Some book packagers will be willing to customize an existing product or even build a new one according to the buyer's specifications. But this can be expensive and risky, and doesn't take advantage of an existing product's track record or the usual economies of co-publishing.

A buyer should be alert to opportunities to participate, along with other partners, in the publishing of a new product in the field of its specialization that has the potential to appeal to a variety of markets. In most cases, book packagers prefer to license the same product in as many languages and for as many markets as possible, and to control all aspects of the project, including the production of both print and e-book versions, if required. With multiple deals lined up, they can combine the various versions at production time to manufacture all of them at once—thereby increasing the number of units they can produce and, as a consequence, reducing costs and increasing their margins. The more versions that the packager can gang together, the greater the profit will be. The licensees also benefit from the cost savings due to the longer print-runs and the resulting lower unit costs. Similarly, accounting for as many language or market adaptations as possible from the beginning of the production process is a more cost-effective way of generating the same basic product in digital formats.

Local Market Expectations

Publishers should have realistic expectations when establishing the basis on which they are going to license their properties into foreign markets. They could very easily come to the wrong conclusion based on false assumptions about the size of an unfamiliar market or the kind of barriers that a distributor or publisher in that market may face. For example, since India has a population of 1.3 billion, a non-Indian publisher might assume that the market for its product in that country is four times what it is in North America. But since the earning power per capita in India is much lower than that of the U.S. and Canada, expectations should be managed down proportionately. Of course, price sensitivity exists in most countries, but to appreciate what that means in places like India or South America, pricing pressure has to be viewed from inside the market—not from a North American or European perspective.

Publishers may have to make unplanned adjustments in their expectations beyond pricing and methods of distribution. In some markets, such as China, Thailand, and India, the risk of piracy or the requirement to sample products well in advance of a selling cycle are still real factors and have a substantial impact on profit margins. An experienced local partner should alert the original publisher to any additional obstacles that aren't immediately apparent and propose possible solutions.

Even though China, Thailand, and India may require special consideration with greater inherent risks than many other markets, almost every market will have its own unique set of factors that will affect the potential success of a product; as such, the goal should be to establish a relationship with the best possible partner who can provide the most transparency about local considerations and knows how to plan accordingly. A well-connected partner should be able to navigate the vagaries of the local market and avoid pitfalls that may not be anticipated. In the end, a relationship that can eliminate or at least dramatically reduce the problems that are unique to a specific market is more important than the specific terms of any written agreement.

Preventing Buyer's Remorse

The process of formalizing a deal is fairly straightforward and should be applicable in any situation regardless of the publishing segment or target market. But the written contract itself will be of little value unless it reflects the desire of the parties to build a strong business relationship. With this in mind, both parties can achieve their goals: licensees can expand their list of publications economically, and licensors can generate incremental revenue by licensing their IP into other languages and markets. These mutual interests are the building blocks of successful co-publishing relationships.

Both parties should have equal confidence in their partner. If the relationship is new, they should talk to other publishers, vendors, and customers, if possible, and validate each other's credentials. The best bet may not always be with a large, well-known publisher with an excellent reputation. Depending on the product, the most appropriate publisher might be a smaller, more focused publisher that understands the particular market niche in which the product fits. It's worthwhile doing some research by checking out the best-selling products in the market and the most successful publishers to establish an unknown partner's credibility.

The licensor should be able to assume that the licensee will treat the property as if it owns it. The licensor should expect the partner to give the same kind of editorial and production effort, as well as marketing attention, to the licensed product as it would one of its own publications.

The licensee should make similar assumptions. If it doesn't have full confidence in the product and its potential, for whatever reason, it should walk away from the deal. It is better to turn down an opportunity than to make a regrettable decision that results in extending only a half-hearted effort into the success of the product.

For a licensee, even after it has conducted the requisite homework to determine that the product is worth having, a receptive corporate environment has to exist at its company in order to actually take all of the necessary steps to complete the deal and to proceed in a timely fashion. To be able to "green light" a licensed product, the company has to have the right skill sets and processes in place. Let's assume the following: the licensee understands the economics of publishing the product and its internal financial hurdles; it has clearly identified the licensed product's benefits and how it is distinguished from competitive products; and, finally, it is prepared to take some measured risks in bringing the product to market. Still, to take the process to the finish line, the licensee's company needs to be able to embrace an international co-publishing project. Many companies have a "not-invented-here" syndrome, which can undermine licensing activity very quickly.

In order to build momentum for co-publishing projects in any company, management needs to prioritize this activity and to install and lead the right individuals willing to work enthusiastically on projects that did not originate from internal development. In smaller publishing companies, the impetus comes from a strong founder or CEO who is personally committed to the licensing business. But with or without the top-down energy behind international projects, individuals have to be empowered to make decisions and, equally important, have the ability to get intercompany buy-in so that outside projects are received, developed, and marketed no differently from internally produced, proprietary products.

The following is a scenario that I've seen played out multiple times. This situation tends to occur more frequently in larger companies, where a single strong personality driving international projects isn't present and product decisions are made more by committee.

A Case in Point: Knowing When to Take the Plunge

An editor who is responsible, and accountable, for spearheading acquisitions and buying rights for her company goes to a book fair and discovers an Italian publication that she likes and that she believes will fit in perfectly with, and add value to, her company's current list of publications. After studying the product carefully, she determines that, other than needing to be translated into English, it will require only a modest amount of adaptation.

She begins to negotiate for the publishing rights, making sure that she covers all of the known bases: the publisher agrees to grant her worldwide English-language rights, and ensures her that all of the photo rights have been cleared and that there are no restrictions on the maps and other illustrations; the publisher agrees to a fair royalty rate with no minimum guarantees for the initial term of the agreement, which it defines as 18 months from the publication date of the English-language edition; and the publisher also accepts a very modest advance against royalties because of the high costs that the editor must incur for the translation.

To make the overall co-publishing deal even more attractive, the Italian publisher has an arrangement with a printer in China that can manufacture the books at an extremely favorable per-unit cost if the editor agrees to have her version printed at the same time as the French and German editions go to press. The editor agrees and, in theory, has a co-publishing arrangement that she believes will provide an excellent new publication with the potential of returning very good margins on her investment, with a reasonable capital expenditure in a short initial print-run.

The editor returns to her office, sends the Italian publisher a mutual non-disclosure agreement (NDA) to counter-sign, clarifies a few minor points with an exchange of emails, and, a short while later, she receives a term sheet from the publisher covering the deal points that they had discussed at the book fair. After it confirms that the term sheet is accurate, the publisher sends the editor a first draft of the contract to review. It appears to represent the agreement accurately. Everything seems to be in place to proceed to the next steps.

At the same time, the editor shares the product and term sheet with her colleagues, who do not respond enthusiastically. They don't like the idea of publishing a product that was not developed in-house. They feel that they cannot accurately evaluate it because it's in a foreign language. They don't reject the idea completely, but they don't embrace it either. They figure that if they ignore it, their colleague will drop it.

The editor doesn't know how to respond to her colleagues' indifference and lack of response to her requests to review the project so that she can proceed. Now she has her own doubts. She worries that she didn't make the right choice after all and that she was too hasty in focusing on the Italian publication. She wonders if there isn't something better available, on the same subject, from another publisher. She asks the publisher to give her more time to think it over. The momentum and enthusiasm for the project begins to wane. In the end, she didn't have to cancel the deal because the Italian publisher informed her that someone else was interested in worldwide English-language rights and was ready to move forward immediately. So much time had gone by that the decision was made for her.

To some degree, the scenario above is understandable. We often have doubts about making major buying decisions, whether it's a house, a car, or a license to publish a book. Some of us, who don't trust our gut (and don't have the right processes in place to confirm our instincts), have a harder time making decisions than others. Decision making is even harder when the results can affect an entire company. We don't want to make the wrong decision, so we make no decision at all.

Sometimes a rights manager will pay a non-refundable advance—a holding fee—just to review a product on an exclusive basis for a certain period of time and finally decide not to proceed. In some cases, especially if the product requires a substantial investment, paying a holding fee can be a good strategy;

it may be better to spend a little up-front to review a product carefully—to assess whether it's right for the market and to reconfirm the decision with additional research and data—than to later regret making a major commitment of time and resources.

However, publishing is more of an art than a science, and regardless of how much validation is done, one can seldom know for sure whether a product is going to be a success. There will always be some guesswork at play and some risk. Numerous publishers have turned down even some of the most popular recent best-sellers before someone took a chance on them. This was true for J.K. Rowling, who received many rejections before Bloomsbury took a risk on her now iconic series of books, and, more recently, for Hugh Howey, the author of *Wool*, who bypassed the mainstream publishers altogether and chose to self-publish what became a runaway best-seller on Amazon.

Publishing requires good instincts backed up by as much experience and data as possible. But if a publisher seeking to license a product doesn't feel that it has developed the instincts necessary to identify a good product when it sees it, it won't get much out of a book fair.

However, good instincts are not enough; even though educated intuition can be a valuable tool, there should be additional validation to support a decision to proceed with an acquisition. Checkpoints need to be in place within the company that can help validate whether the proposed licensed product has a good chance of succeeding. Malcolm Gladwell in his book *Blink* argues that there is more value in expert gut feeling than we might think. Following his theory, an experienced publisher's initial reaction to a product concept is often going to be the right one. But a publishing project is always a team effort and, when working within a corporate structure, other people need to get behind a project; it's a good insurance policy to get initial reactions verified. At the end of the day, good data should support, not contradict, an experienced publisher's gut feeling.

Rallying the Troops

The licensee must find a balance—good instincts vs. validation—and make sure that the processes are followed before finalizing a deal or requesting additional concessions from a future partner. Once a publisher has identified a product that it likes, it should get internal buy-in before beginning detailed negotiations. It should bring the product specifications and samples back to the office, and share them with the key decision makers and the people who will be doing the work, including the sales managers as well as the distributors. If necessary, the publisher might assemble focus groups that include potential buyers for the various markets that the product can address. The publisher should be able to articulate the features and benefits that will build enthusiasm for the product—and why it will be a good addition to the existing publishing list.

The editors and marketers need to believe that the adaptation of the product can be accomplished with minimal resources and effort, and that it has the potential to achieve positive results. Licensing should save time and money. But every project—whether licensed or built from the ground up—has opportunity costs; if a project requires too much work and too many resources, starting from scratch may be a better option. This is why the finance department needs to believe in the project as well. They will need to review the impact that the project will have on cash flow, margins, and profitability. Whatever resources are required, the project should have a minimal effect on other cash flow obligations, with the prospect of an above-average ROI with the lowest possible total capital investment. If these metrics are met, finance shouldn't hesitate to support the project.

A comprehensive marketing plan will ensure that marketing, sales, and promotions people are positioning the product to meet the needs of the market and can differentiate the product from the competition. The plan should include approximate marketing costs and pre-publication pricing and sampling, if necessary, as well as sales collateral and social media initiatives.

The licensee has to be sufficiently disciplined to go through the steps of the buy-in process and make sure that everyone involved takes their share of ownership in the project, which will greatly increase the chances that the licensed product will be successful.

Taking "Yes" for an Answer

The licensee's ability to master the process of buying rights to a particular product or IP is only half of the equation in bringing a co-publication to life; the other half is controlled by the licensor, which must decide to whom, and under what conditions, to sell the rights to its IP—or "baby"—either in part or whole.

When selling rights, the licensor has to learn how to let go of a proprietary asset and allow someone else to take control over its fate in another market.

A licensor will naturally regard the original product or database as a piece of the publisher's identity; it culminated from a measured risk and a serious investment of time, resources, and sweat equity. In addition, it represents the publisher's brand and reputation. Presumably, it is also bringing in revenues from its primary market. Even in the case of a limited license, in a clearly defined new territory, for a limited period of time, a leap of faith is required to say yes to a co-publishing partner and, by doing so, let someone else take over the responsibility for generating revenues and building the product's value.

Most products do not begin to take advantage of the huge global market that is available. Objections to extending a product's presence in a new market or channel by licensing the rights to a third party are usually not valid, or they can be easily countered in favor of the many benefits that licensing can produce.

The goal should be to reach as many markets as possible with the least amount of risk and the greatest ROI. The publisher should be able to maximize the market opportunities that it is capable of reaching on its own—with the best margins possible—but at the same time, it should identify those markets in which it will need to partner in order to exploit a product's full potential. By licensing a product to someone else, it may be decreasing its margin and giving up control, but it will presumably be penetrating markets that would be otherwise unattainable. In this case, margins are sacrificed for what is essentially found money.

Of course, partners should be selected very carefully. Their reputation and ability to penetrate a market or channel will need to be validated. Assuming that due diligence is built into the process, licensing should not only be a proactive part of business development, but should also be a strategic activity—a corporate priority with full upper-management support for building brand loyalty and adding new revenue streams.

If the company has not yet developed a culture dedicated to licensing, people at all levels of management may have questions and objections when licensing opportunities are presented that aren't aligned with existing corporate goals. Some may assume that by licensing the product, or a portion of the product, they might lose sales opportunities in their existing channels. They raise a variety of concerns that they believe might interfere with current marketing efforts, which causes unnecessary delays in making the deal and can ultimately lead to the deal's demise—and lost opportunities. This need not happen in any company, large or small. Licensing products has been a staple for many companies for decades. We are long past the proof-of-concept stage. And technology has only made the entire process more efficient and less risky. Still, the various objections or even perceived conflicts have to be taken seriously so that licensing can become a growth opportunity that is embraced by the entire management team.

Dealing with Real and Perceived Conflicts

Here are 10 common objections that often surface when a deal is up for review:

1.   The licensee does not have a large enough market share in its own markets.

2.   The deal might have a negative impact on our brand.

3.   The deal will confuse existing customers.

4.   The deal will cannibalize internal sales efforts and take commissions away from the sales teams.

5.   The licensee's pricing structure cannot be controlled and will lower the value of the product in existing markets.

6.   The territory the licensee wants is too broad and will inhibit other licensing deals.

7.   The royalty rate isn't high enough.

8.   The royalty advance isn't large enough to risk channel conflict.

9.   The minimum guarantees are not sufficient in demonstrating the licensee's confidence in the product.

10.   The term of the agreement is too long without an adequate upside.

These are all legitimate concerns and they need to be fully addressed and answered so that all licensing deals can proceed according to a strategic plan that will permit a publisher to take advantage of every possible opportunity to monetize existing products and generate incremental revenue. For these specific objections, and others that may arise, those tasked with selling rights need to be prepared to respond to them and justify the terms of all projects so that every final agreement is closely aligned with corporate goals.

This can be done by establishing parameters that allow the rights people enough flexibility to deal with a wide variety of situations, but are also specific enough to cover corporate requirements. These rules of engagement have to be made available and communicated so that everyone who needs to know is aware of them.

The following is an example of a 10-item checklist that can help the licensing team ensure that the product is a good candidate to license and the partner has the experience necessary to satisfy management's standards, with the caveat that the specific items in the list are meant to be a starting point and should be tailored to the company's individual requirements:

☐   All IP rights have been cleared for the target territory.

☐   There are no conflicting agreements in the target markets.

☐   Files are in a format that can be easily transferred.

☐   The amount of investment required for monitoring the licensee's progress and the quality of the output is acceptable.

☐   The licensee has a proven track record and is a market leader.

☐   The licensee is willing to commit adequate resources to complete the project at a high-quality standard.

☐   The licensee has a business plan that will meet corporate objectives.

☐   The royalty rate is within a pre-set range established by management.

☐   Advances and minimum guarantees will provide an ROI that is commensurate with the size of the market.

☐   The initial term limit does not exceed corporate mandates.

These guidelines, or something similar to them, should be adopted for licensing IP, and then represented in a "decision tree" designed to accept good deals, make essential adjustments so a deal can proceed, or reject inadequate ones in a timely manner. An effective decision tree will stop a deal before a potential partner has been unnecessarily encouraged or a deal is made in principle. It will also serve as an empirical aid to validate the publisher's judgment about the value of the licensing project and the role it may play in meeting corporate objectives.

The goal is to take advantage of as many opportunities as possible to monetize the initial investment in a product. Whatever guidelines are finally adopted for getting to yes, they should be as unequivocal as possible. Once the guidelines satisfy that goal, the rights people should be empowered with as much latitude as possible within that framework so that they can proceed with minimal interference and second-guessing.

As they are finalized, the details of licensing deals should be communicated immediately to the sales and marketing teams so that they are fully apprised of new markets that are being served and are not surprised if their existing customers become aware of them. The selling teams are naturally inclined to think only about product introductions that will affect them personally, but they also need to understand that the world is a very large market and that partners are imperative to penetrate the number and variety of global opportunities available. Most sales teams won't object to the reality that, whenever possible, various products will be licensed for translation or adaptation if they realize that the translated product won't conflict with their sales efforts. At the same time, they must also accept the fact that some products or portions of products, particularly from large databases, may also be licensed to third parties and niche channels within the publisher's own language and markets. These efforts may appear to have the potential to cut into the company's main sales channels. However, in a global marketplace with a vast array of needs to serve, licensing will not interfere with other sales and marketing efforts, and should have no impact on the in-house sales teams. Good communication and a strategic plan for making licensing deals that everyone understands and buys into will help to minimize objections and greatly reduce the perception of channel conflict, even among the most protectionist sales managers.

Avoiding the Blame Game

Before a licensor finalizes a new partnership arrangement, it should verify that the partner has four key attributes:

- financial stability;

- the ability to keep sensitive information, including the nature of the agreement, confidential;

- the technology necessary to keep IP secure; and

- excellent communication skills and processes.

All of these are critical qualities for mitigating risk and building the foundation for a strong relationship. Perhaps the most difficult of all of these to measure and to sustain over the course of a project is communication. Mostly it's impossible to over-communicate, even among co-workers—people who see, meet, and work together every day in the same office. Communicating with distant partners—mostly with emails or even frequent videoconferencing—is exponentially more difficult. Learning how to communicate takes effort, experience, skill, patience, and compromise. Its importance in a successful relationship, however, should not be underestimated and needs to be continually stressed with the in-house team as well. Otherwise a lot of time and money will be wasted, and the project and long-term relationship might be put at risk.

Therefore, as the relationship progresses from the contract to the development stage, the best communicators, regardless of which departments they come from, should be involved in the project. If necessary, the staff may have to be trained to build communication skills specifically for working with overseas projects and partners. These skills will help them avoid making assumptions and instead continually verify what they agreed to over the course of working together. Language and culture barriers need to be addressed openly so that they do not interfere with clear communication on the details of the project.

Effective communication also depends heavily on defining the partners' roles and responsibilities. To a large degree, this will be outlined in the contract, which specifies the transfer of the licensed IP and any additional material that is developed, and delineates mutual obligations to bring the product to market. But the contract cannot cover all of the processes and procedures that must be put into place for the relationship to be successful. Nor can it account for all contingencies or the various issues that may arise. The contract can specify intentions, the basic deliverables, and the costs or fees. However, it won't adequately cover *how* the project is going to get done and what the options are if things don't go exactly as planned.

After the contract has been executed by top management or the head of licensing, the individuals who are actually responsible for making the relationship successful, as well as implementing the tasks necessary to complete the project, rarely refer back to the contract itself. In fact, they may have had little or no input in writing or negotiating the terms and conditions of the contract in the first place, even though they may be responsible for the success of the project.

The relationship's ultimate success will be determined by the synergy between the parties—their enthusiasm for the project, shared expectations, a clear understanding of common goals, and frequent and open communication. This will require knowing each other's particular core competencies, agreeing on processes, and compromising when necessary. To keep this process healthy and transparent, the partners cannot lose sight of the initial vision that made the idea of exchanging IP a way to provide better products—and more customer value—together than they could separately.

Process Protocol

By clarifying who is responsible for what and, above all, who will pay for mistakes, corrections, or deliverables that may not have been anticipated in the contract, the partners take an important step in establishing a relationship that transcends the contract and allows both parties to resolve problems with as little friction as possible. In the course of completing any joint-effort project, issues will arise. The licensee may complain that files were not sent in the right format and that it has to convert them, which will result in extra costs, or that it had to hire additional writers to fill content holes that were not expected. To avoid bottlenecks or standoffs that may result from these kinds of complaints, it's incumbent on both parties to establish early in the process who will pay for what, including items that are identified in the deliverables list as well as changes or mistakes that are made along the way.

Defining an acceptable deliverable is at the heart of a smooth partnership and is key to avoiding the uncomfortable situation of blaming one another for something that went wrong and having to cover for the other side's unintentional missteps. People will make mistakes or change their minds—that's the nature of any project. Partners should expect this to happen, plan for it, and decide how they will handle "surprises," determine the areas of responsibilities as clearly and fairly as possible, and accept responsibility for the share of the project each has agreed to assume.

The partners should create a spreadsheet of responsibilities that will enable an effective and efficient process. The number of steps in the process and how detailed they need to be will depend on the type of product, the market, and the skills of the people implementing the project. Some basic protocols should be established that could serve as a roadmap for ensuring that milestones are met. Ideally, of course, it's best to prepare a roadmap of all known issues prior to finalizing a contract. Here is a list of items that should be included for a typical licensing project:

- Description of the licensed content, including text, images, and other media assets, e.g., the physical specifications—pages, number of assets, length of each asset, size in gigabytes, etc.

- Identification of the file formats of the licensed assets, a timetable for having them converted, and deadlines for delivering and receiving them.

- Samples of the original content, either in print or digital format, for every licensed asset.

- Listing of who needs to approve the deliverables and who determines whether a file or deliverable is not acceptable, and who is responsible for making any necessary corrections.

- Escalation tree of who should be contacted if there is a problem with a file, if something is missing or corrupted, or if something needs to be changed.

- Description of what needs to be adapted or translated.

- Identification of the skills and talents that will be necessary to carry out the adaptation.

- Appointment of the primary contact people and a definition of their main responsibilities.

- Identification of the primary stakeholders in the development process and their roles and responsibilities.

- Frequency of progress reviews and meetings—either in person or via phone or videophone (SightSpeed, Skype)—and people in charge of setting up the meetings and conference calls.

- Progress reports and how they will be made available, such as Web-based project management programs, spreadsheets, or other tools.

- Identification of any third parties involved.

- Identification of personnel responsible for applying for local copyrights and any other ownership issues.

- Posting of production and launch schedules.

The goal and measure of a successful relationship is delivering on the co-publishing plan. The sample listing above should be part of a mutually agreed-upon document that describes the various stages of the content exchange and development process, and who, on both sides, will be authorized to approve the various stages of the process. This document should identify specific benchmarks, checkpoints during the process, and a strict schedule for accomplishing the tasks—and agreement on exactly what has to be accomplished to determine that both parties have fulfilled their obligations to one another, like a "punch list" for completing a construction project. Of course, the contract will have some of this specified. But the list will grow as the project advances and changes shape, which means that the contract may not be able to account for everything. A good relationship will be able to accommodate issues that may not have been anticipated in the contract.

The following is a short narrative of what went wrong in the delivery of files to one of our licensees and how the problem was resolved. It arose from a misunderstanding of the kind of PDF that it required to create its finished product.

A Case in Point: Misunderstanding the Definition of "Layered"

We have a licensing arrangement with an app publisher that delivers e-books to consumers on a subscription basis. This is a market that we don't address directly, so we were happy to license it a number of our e-books of its choice. Since its product is aimed at very young learners who are first beginning to read, it selected 50 or so of our youngest, most highly illustrated books to convert to its platform. It wanted the files in layered PDFs because in its conversion process, it added a sound layer of a recorded voice reading the books. This was part of the value proposition of its offering—each book being read by an actor.

Somehow, we misunderstood its requirements and thought that it meant universal PDFs, which is a common file format that we use for our own platform and those of our other partners. All of our e-books are in both UPDF and EPUB formats. Unfortunately, the app publisher couldn't use our PDFs, but it could convert our files to layered PDFs if we would deliver the original application files, which we did have. (As you will recall from Chapter 4, the original digital files of a complete work should be stored in an asset management system for just such purposes.) But there was another problem. Although most of the application files were created in InDesign, which was just fine for the app publisher, some of the older books were in Quark, which it could not convert directly to layered PDFs. This was something that we had not anticipated. The app pulisher asked us to convert our Quark files into InDesign files so that it could then make the final conversion into layered PDFs. In theory, we could have done this, but at the time that it needed the files, our production team was fully engaged. The app publisher agreed to have a freelance designer make the conversions from the Quark files. It turned out that the costs to do this were very reasonable, and we agreed to have those costs taken out of our advances rather than to move our staff from other projects. The willingness and the ability of both parties to sort this out solved the problem with a reasonable impact on the project's schedule and budget.

Flexible, Not Open-Ended

For the content provider, one of the biggest considerations is how much freedom the partner will have in adapting the content. Some content providers have very strict rules for what can or cannot be changed, edited, or added. If these rules are too restrictive, the deal could collapse or they could prevent the partner from making the right editorial decisions to meet the needs of its market.

However, in a large organization, which may have several different business units responsible for licensing depending on the content type, subject, or market segment, certain restrictions, such as how the brand is used or how proprietary characters can be depicted, may be dictated as part of corporate guidelines and mandated by the legal department. If this is the case, the flexibility of what a licensing partner can do may be limited. In some cases, covenants surrounding the origination of the content may actually determine how much latitude can be permitted. For example, multiple authors or third parties may have a legacy stake in the product, in which case several approval stages may be required. Or specific cultural content that would not be appropriate for the licensee's market that the licensee might not be aware of might need to change—all of which should be made clear at the start of the project.

Naturally, a licensee will want maximum freedom and flexibility to make the changes and adaptations necessary so that the product can achieve its goals and be published without unnecessary delays. Whenever possible, and within clearly defined limits, the licensee should be able to exercise free will in adapting the product because its interests are completely aligned with those of the licensor.

Chapter 9
Making a Deal with Best Practices

The first thing we do, let's kill all the lawyers.[1]
William Shakespeare, Henry VI, *Part II, Act IV, Scene II*

The Elements of the Deal

I'm not aware of a universal blueprint to cover all possible types of licensing deals, but most publishers follow some standard parameters—which vary depending on which side the publisher is negotiating from. Just like the rug merchant who asks his son the sum of two plus two, and the son asks "Am I buying or selling?" the licensee's (buyer's) goal is to pay as little as possible and "even less" if it has to incur translating expenses, and for the licensor (seller), the goal is to make as much profit as possible. These are the starting positions from each perspective. But the objective for both sides in any negotiation should be to ensure that the economics work two ways. Each party needs to generate enough revenue to make the transaction worthwhile. The long-term goal is to establish a valuable relationship that creates a trustworthy basis for conducting many fruitful transactions.

Every deal should be market-driven. The licensor will want its potential partner to identify, quantitatively, the sales potential for the product in its market. From experience and knowledge of the territory, the licensee should be able to forecast how many units it can sell in a typical 12-month period and at a specific price point. An experienced partner should be fairly accurate in its estimates. Since the licensee is taking all of the risk, the licensor should accept the licensee's estimates, and give the licensee enough time in the contract to achieve its forecasted results. Of course, unknowns and a certain amount

---

1   Just so I don't get into trouble with all of my lawyer friends, I use this quote as a way of saying we all should find a specialist lawyer to make sure that we have a solid contract that covers our rights and is workable for all parties. My reading of this line from Shakespeare is consistent with the following interpretation by Debbie Vogel in the *New York Times*, June 17, 1990, which I paraphrase: "This quote was said by Dick the Butcher, who was a follower of the rebel Jack Cade, who thought that if he disturbed law and order, he could become king. Shakespeare meant it as a compliment to attorneys and judges who instil justice in society."

of guesswork in launching any new product are commonplace, but a local publisher will know how to minimize its risks.

Territory Considerations

By being immersed in a specific territory or region, a publishing partner represents a significant marketing expansion opportunity. Normally a territory is defined by language rather than geography. Publishers that license French-language rights, for example, might assume that Switzerland and Belgium were included in their territory, which should be defined precisely and take into consideration the partner's marketing capabilities. French-language rights could also include Quebec and far-flung French territories such as Mauritius and Madagascar. Identifying as many appropriate territories as possible from the beginning will benefit both sides.

Neither party should make assumptions about which territories are "automatically" implied. This should not be left open for debate and end up being in contention after the marketing and selling begins. Specific territory rights should be granted only if they are likely to be used. A publisher in France may expect to have distribution rights for the entire French-speaking world, but this would make sense only if it has the resources and distribution network to market in all of the regions that could be considered part of the territory. There are 33 French-speaking countries—not including the province of Quebec—which is second only to the 44 countries that comprise the English-speaking world. The question to consider is whether the France-based partner has the ability to reach all of these locations. If not, the agreement should specify in which markets distribution rights are granted, with any exclusions remaining with the licensor to handle on its own or to license to another partner.

American publishers normally define their territory as the U.S. and Canada, including unincorporated U.S.-owned territories, such as Puerto Rico and Guam. Frequently the Caribbean is also included, even though some Caribbean islands, like the Bahamas—only 60 miles (100 km) from the Florida coast—belong to the British Commonwealth of Nations. In any case, there should be a clear understanding at the beginning of any relationship where in the world licensing rights apply.

A good policy is not to seek or grant rights that are not going to be exploited. The goal is to sell as much finished goods or services as possible in as many markets as possible. The world is a big marketplace and very few products, as a matter of practice, get a wide enough circulation to worry too much about whose territory is whose, and in most cases, it's unlikely that channel conflict is more than a perceived issue. Still, giving away more territory than necessary can limit future opportunities.

Exclusivity vs. Non-exclusivity

With the aim of keeping as many options open as possible and of taking advantage of opportunities as they arise, exclusivity is an important consideration when granting licensing rights. Most licensees will ask for it even if it's not essential in achieving their goals. The theory is that with less competition, it will be easier to differentiate the product, control pricing and discounts, and take advantage of as many channel opportunities as possible. At the same time, licensees understand that exclusivity comes at a higher price. The buyer would have to be prepared to guarantee a certain amount of royalty revenue to the licensor to prevent other versions of the same product from entering the market.

If the licensor carefully defines languages and/or territories and it gets a large enough financial commitment, it may be willing to grant exclusivity. Instead of granting exclusivity broadly in an entire territory, a better idea may be to limit exclusivity to a specific format or technology (e-books *or* print, for example), or a clearly definable market, such as the school or library market. If the licensor grants the partner blanket exclusivity in a market and the partner is unable to take advantage of every channel and every format in the market, then the licensor has unnecessarily limited its ability to leverage its IP to its full potential. Non-exclusivity will result in smaller guarantees and minimums, but at least this leaves the licensor free to take advantage of other opportunities that the licensee couldn't handle anyway. The licensor should never give away more rights than necessary, and the licensee shouldn't ask for more rights than it can exploit with its own resources.

Although the conservative approach for the IP owner would be to make only non-exclusive deals, this may not always be the right strategy either. In some situations, the price of the freedom to license the property—or even a version of it—to someone else may be costlier than placing all chips on a single licensee. The most lucrative opportunity in some markets may be with a single, dominate player that requires an exclusive arrangement, which may be better in the long run than multiple non-exclusive deals. Because exclusivity comes with commitments and guarantees, the licensee who has an exclusive is highly motivated to succeed.

It boils down to understanding the market as well as possible and finding the right partner—maybe only one partner under an exclusive arrangement—or perhaps multiple partners, each with a clearly defined sales channel. Or maybe the right solution is to have an open market with everyone under the same non-exclusive arrangement. In any case, exclusivity should not be granted lightly and should be valued accordingly. It's another tool—perhaps the most important one—that the licensor has to help make the right deal for the best possible results.

Royalties and Essential Financial Commitments

In addition to territories and conditions for exclusivity, any deal should, at a minimum, address the following terms that have a direct impact on the financial success of the relationship: periodic royalties; advances against future royalties; and a defined term limit, as well as non-monetary commitments, such as deliverables and the roles and responsibilities of both parties.

Royalties can be at a fixed percentage, or they can increase, or even decrease, over time. Advances against future royalties can be paid up-front or periodically. For large projects that take place over a long period of time, advances may be paid upon reaching certain milestones: a percentage upon signing the contract; another portion at some stage during production; and a final payment due when the product goes to press. Minimum guarantees are not always a given. There may be reasons, which I will discuss later, to either insist on or forego them.

The deal should be structured so that the licensor receives a royalty stream based, in most cases, on the licensee's net receipts, which means the revenue that it keeps after deducting the cost of goods and any discounts, returns, and sales expenses. "Net receipts" should be explicitly defined so that there is no ambiguity as to what is or isn't deducted from gross revenue. Sometimes development costs or marketing expenses are deducted before calculating net receipts, which should be resolved during the negotiations. E-book revenue can be tricky since physical returns aren't a factor, but instead an order could be cancelled after royalty payments have been made and before any downloads were accomplished. So in the case of e-books, net receipts should account for any cancelled purchase orders or invoices.

Royalties are not always calculated on net receipts. Some publishers prefer to use the selling price of the book as the basis or, in some cases, a fixed amount regardless of the list price. Net receipts, when defined correctly, is usually the fairest standard for everyone, but most importantly it provides the licensee with the flexibility it needs to offer normal discounts or to make bulk deals without drastically reducing margins or possibly losing money on a sale because of fixed royalty commitments.

If a publisher doesn't have the flexibility to maximize all marketing opportunities, neither the publishing partner nor the licensor will benefit in the long run. The publisher may simply have to turn down business opportunities because royalty obligations make them financially unviable. This scenario can be avoided by defining net receipts in a way that allows the publisher the ability to take advantage of opportunities (perhaps in collaboration with the licensor) that may not be anticipated at the time that the agreement is made. In exchange for providing maximum flexibility to the licensee to respond to market conditions and sell products at varying margins, a minimum royalty can be established so that the licensed product isn't excessively discounted or used as a loss leader, or premium, to enhance the sales of other products.

Royalty rates can vary quite a bit, but the typical range is between 5% and 20%, depending on development costs and any ongoing third-party expenses that might provide additional financial burdens on the licensee. They can start at one rate and go up (or down) after hitting defined revenue milestones. For example, they may start at 10% for the first $100,000 of revenue and shift to another percentage after the next $100,000. If the licensee has invested a considerable amount of money at the start of a project, it may insist on a lower rate for the first year so as to recoup some of its investment, and agree to a higher rate once it has broken even.

Royalties are normally distributed either quarterly or semi-annually, and are usually paid, along with the submission of an accounting report, on defined dates. Once the royalty rate is established—as a fixed, escalating, or descending percentage—and the basis for the calculation determined (e.g., net receipts, list price), some consideration should be given to advances that will be applied against future royalties.

Advances can be useful in helping to determine the partner's seriousness and to motivate performance. The more that it is willing to invest up-front in the product, the more likely it is that it will bring the product to market quickly and finance a meaningful marketing campaign. However, any advances should not be too onerous and should take into consideration the investment that the partner has to make to accommodate its market's expectations, including the cost of translation, which can be substantial depending on the project. In the end, advances should be in line with anticipated earnings. If, for example, both parties agree to quarterly royalty payments, a typical royalty advance should be equal to the royalties expected from the first quarter's forecasted revenues. What should be avoided is a situation where the advances are so high that it takes the licensee an unreasonable amount of time before its earnings equal the paid-out advances.

Advances against future royalties aren't an absolute requirement in the agreement, nor is a fixed ratio against a sales forecast a standard. In cases where sales prospects are largely unknown and where the licensee has to make a substantial investment to bring the product to market, advances should probably be avoided. Usually an advance is a good-faith number and a token expression of commitment. Sometimes, especially in a competitive situation, an advance can well exceed any definition of "token" and can be a serious commitment that may be difficult to recover. In the long run, both parties should be more interested in the lifetime value of the product in the market, not in the size of a speculative advance.

Another way a licensee can be motivated to perform without creating the unnecessary burden of an advance is to specify a target date for publication and to make the first royalty payment due by a certain date after the signing the agreement. Either way, the objective is to confirm that the licensee really intends to publish the work and not just hold onto the rights to prevent someone else from publishing it in its market. This doesn't happen very often, but it can, depending on the market and the competitive environment. On the other hand, the licensee may have had all intentions of publishing the product, but simply ran out of funds or had a change in priorities. Regardless of the intentions or reasons for missing a publication date, the result is the same. The licensor cannot receive revenue if the licensee doesn't publish the product with a solid marketing plan in place. Commitments built into the contract with time requirements help to create some urgency for the licensee to publish by a specific date and not just let the license to publish languish.

The benchmarks for advances and royalty rates described above apply mainly to educational titles, general reference works, travel books, and most children's books. When it comes to blockbusters—fiction or nonfiction—celebrity books, or "star" titles with unusual marketing hype or potential, payment terms may be very different. Although the royalty rates may be similar, non-refundable advances can be very substantial and highly speculative. In these elite publishing categories, where there is often competitive bidding for the original publication as well as foreign-language (and even movie) rights, advances can reach six and even seven figures.

In some cases, these advances may not be recoverable over the life of the publication, and publishers can wind up incurring huge losses on the books when sales fail to meet the astronomical expectations driven by the advances. A good place to follow the trends in royalty advances with these types of books is in *Publishers Lunch,* a free online newsletter (with an optional premium upgrade), or *The Book Standard,* which is also available online.

In addition to royalties and advances against future royalties, two other essential economic factors in a deal include the term limit of the contract—the length of time the agreement remains active before it expires and action needs to be taken to allow it to continue—and minimum guarantees.

Three- or five-year limits are standard initial terms in most licensing agreements. After the initial term, contracts can automatically renew or expire unless renewed by mutual agreement. Minimum guarantees can be established during the initial term of the agreement as a way of setting revenue expectations. The length of time a publisher is willing to give up rights for a product in a market is sometimes determined by set minimum guarantees. In other words, the term limit could be automatically extended provided that defined revenue hurdles have been reached. In this way, the licensee can continue to publish a product that is finding success in its market without having to renegotiate the contract. There is no need to allow an agreement to terminate as long as both parties are benefiting from the arrangement.

By establishing term limits, the licensor puts the burden on the partner to maximize the value of the original product in its market. If both parties are satisfied with the financial performance of the product at the end of the term, the agreement should be renewed or extended for an additional length of time.

In a conservative deal where the licensee is held accountable for success, the term of the agreement will not renew automatically unless the specified minimum guarantees are achieved or a new term limit is substituted. In this case, the term of the agreement automatically expires, and the license does not renew unless the parties take definitive action to renew it. An expiration date gives both parties an opportunity to re-examine the relationship and quantify the viability of the product for both sides. In addition, it prevents the unhappy situation where the architects of the original deal may have since departed from the company and left others with an open-ended, perpetual agreement that they cannot undo. Since I have faced this situation myself, I make sure that I don't put others in this position. No one should be obligated to live with something that they inherited and that cannot be undone. There are usually ways to get out of a bad deal, but having a fixed expiration date provides some flexibility for everyone.

As in the case of advances, minimum guarantees must be realistic. But even if they are still not achieved during the initial term of the contract, both parties may decide to continue the relationship, either on an exclusive or non-exclusive basis. Unfortunately, just like in other consumer businesses, many unknowns exist in publishing, and how a specific market will actually respond to a new product, or how long it takes for the product to achieve critical mass, is not always predictable or may take longer than anticipated.

Determining minimum guarantees that are realistic is more of an art than a science. Both sides should avoid the outcome where minimum guarantees actually exceed the amount of the earned royalties. High minimum guarantees may sound desirable for the licensor, but in this scenario, the licensee will probably not be motivated to renew the agreement after the initial term, ending a revenue stream for the licensor and putting the licensor in the position of having to start all over with another partner. It is far more preferential to have earned royalties outpace the minimum guarantees, which means that the product is exceeding expectations. If this is the case, both parties will be eager to continue the relationship beyond the initial term.

The process of establishing minimums and reporting earned royalties assumes, of course, that the accounting is trustworthy. Some publishers will insist on having minimums if they feel that they cannot trust the licensee's royalty reports and therefore will use the minimums to be certain of the financial value of the relationship. They will set the minimums high enough so that they do not have to question the accuracy of the royalty reports. (It's natural to be skeptical of royalty reports that show earnings just short of the minimum guarantee.) Or, to be even more conservative, some publishers will even forego an upside altogether and will accept a fixed amount of revenue up-front in lieu of royalty income. This may be a lower-risk strategy, but it's not a good basis for building long-term relationships. A relationship that lacks trust in any part of the process—from the transfer of the IP to the disbursement of payments—is not worth having. Sooner or later it will fail. I have had several licensing deals where the earned royalties from a licensee never surpassed the minimum guarantees and had to decide whether to continue with the deal or not. As long as the minimums are paid, it usually makes sense to continue the partnership.

Minimum guarantees can be useful for motivating performance and to provide an incentive on the part of the licensee to exert best efforts. However, they put a lot of pressure on the licensee, and therefore reaching a mutually agreeable number may be difficult. But the subject should be raised as part of any good negotiation. Sometimes minimums start low and escalate over time as the licensee builds momentum in its market and recovers its initial investments in launching the product. Its ongoing product investments will naturally decrease over time, which will then allow for greater guarantees as the product matures and gains traction in the market. Since most products have a lifecycle, at some point sales will begin to decline, which should be reflected in the minimum guarantees.

With or without established minimums in a contract, both parties should always have expectations in mind that will trigger the renewal or termination of the agreement at the end of the established term limit. If minimum guarantees are built into the agreement, both parties will go through a learning curve to determine whether the minimums were appropriate or not, and sometimes failing to achieve these minimums may not be anyone's fault. Before the licensor pulls the plug on a partner for not meeting minimums, especially a partner that operates in good faith, it should make sure that it really understands the market, that it has evidence that the product is being undersold, and that it believes that the product is better off in someone else's hands. I wouldn't change partners without a good reason. It's much better to fix a product problem or a poor marketing plan than to develop a new mutually beneficial relationship.

The following "Case in Point" demonstrates how minimum guarantees allowed both parties to work through a problem in the marketing of a product that neither had anticipated.

A Case in Point: Shifting Market Requirements

Over the years we had developed a successful multilevel mathematics program that was one of only a few programs in the marketplace that taught math through real-life contexts. The program was the result of a unique collaboration between U.S. and Dutch mathematics scholars who had received a National Science Foundation grant to create a program that made the connection between mathematical concepts and everyday life. Because of its pedigree, the program received notoriety in the international mathematics community, which helped us in our licensing efforts. One of our first licensees was the top Korean mathematics publisher, which was quite a coup since Korea was already a global leader in teaching mathematics.

The publisher did an excellent job of translating and adapting the program so that it conformed to the way in which math is taught in Korea. The program was well received by its sales force, which forecasted ambitious sales numbers.

In Korea, before schools will decide on purchasing one program over another, they test the competitive products thoroughly in hundreds of classrooms—requiring publishers to provide a large quantity of samples free of charge. During the sampling process, an executive at our Korean publisher noticed that our licensing agreement had a free sampling cap of 10% of the print-run, which meant that it would have to pay royalties on any free products that it distributed in excess of 10% of the manufactured quantity. No one on either side had paid much attention to this restriction during the negotiation process. If the publisher were to be constrained in this way, however, it would feel compelled to limit its sampling initiative; it would be an onerous burden to pay royalties on free samples while bearing the costs of manufacturing, marketing, and distribution. Having to do so would put it at a disadvantage to a local competitor that was in a position to sample more liberally.

No one makes money by giving product away, so understanding why the 10% ceiling on sampling may have been in the contract in the first place was important. In theory, a sampling restriction would make sense in preventing someone from giving one product away in order to sell another one. A licensor doesn't want its product used as premium to sell another product if the only way it gets paid is by earned royalties from revenue. If the product is being heavily sampled, the licensor is at risk of not earning very much.

But in this case, we had a three-year agreement with a substantial minimum annual guarantee, regardless of the earned royalties. This meant that we had protection against abusive sampling. At the same time, with minimum revenue hurdles in place, the publisher had no incentive to give away more products than was absolutely necessary to gain market share.

Therefore, there was no reason to enforce a ceiling on sampling. We had mutual interests, and the only way that we could both win was to gain as much market share as possible. If the publisher felt that it needed to sample freely in order to maximize its future sales, it should have the flexibility to do so.

It was an easy decision to make an adjustment in the contract and give the publisher complete discretion with sampling without having to pay royalties so that it could compete in the market without a handicap. If we hadn't given it the freedom to do so, we would have put the long-term viability of the product at risk.

In the end, we told the publisher to treat the program as if it owned it and, as long as it met its minimum guarantees, to do what was necessary to meet the expectations of the market. This paid off. The program was so successful that our royalties exceeded the minimum guarantees and the program became the market leader within 18 months of launch. At the end of the initial term of the agreement, we entered into a long-term commitment with our Korean partner. The sampling program ended up being a small investment in developing a valuable equity for both of us.

Royalty-Inclusive Deals

One way to license a product without the burden of calculating royalties or establishing minimum guarantees is to buy finished goods on a royalty-inclusive basis. In this way, the publisher is actually purchasing a finished product (paying for manufactured goods), but with the same rights that would be granted from a straight licensing deal. In other words, payment for the license includes both the IP rights and the physical product itself. This is a basic turnkey deal. The originating publisher or packager constructs a deal for a specified number of finished books for a set unit fee—and also takes a margin on the manufacturing. The fee in this case is "fully loaded," meaning that the royalty is already built into the cost of goods.

This is a very simple way for everyone to calculate their risks and to keep the post-publication accounting issues to a minimum. It also simplifies the entire process for the licensee, since it doesn't have to do any development work. It's also a common way for a developer to work with multiple licensing deals at the same time; it can print several language versions at once to take advantage of printing economies.

But there are downsides to this type of deal. The amount of adaptation that the licensee can make is limited since the structure or layout and design of the content is predetermined and is used by more than one licensee. In addition, the buyer will have to commit to a substantial print-run up-front in order to secure a favorable unit price point. Usually these print-runs are higher than the publisher would normally contract for if it controlled the production and manufacturing itself.

The Licensor Holds All the Cards

Terms for buying and selling rights are grounded in the basic economies of general publishing and take into consideration what both sides are able to bring to the table. As the originator of a product, the licensor has not only taken on the initial risks of the project, but has invested time and resources that the licensee does not have to invest. Even if the licensee now has to translate and perhaps even reconfigure the product, the original IP holder has provided a fully developed concept and decreased the licensee's time to market.

My view is that as the originator of the product, the licensor is entitled to own any derivatives of the product, including translations and additional content regardless of the format. Any work that the licensee does to meet its market requirements is still based on the licensor's original work and is "fruit of the same tree." The licensee can have the rights to the translation as long as the contract is active, but once the contract has terminated, all rights, including the translated materials, should revert to the licensor.

If the licensor feels that there is value in the licensee's adaptations in its own market, the agreement made between the two parties should allow the licensor to use any or all of the licensee's derivative work in exchange for royalties back to the licensee or for a share of the revenue.

From a seller's point of view, licensing products into a new territory extends the earning power of a product in which it has already made a substantial investment. Publishing has a high fixed but relatively low variable cost, and licensing is the optimal "variable," because the revenue it generates is purely incremental. From a buyer's point of view, licensing a product is an excellent way to take advantage of someone else's capital risk in development. When compared to the publisher's original investment in research, development, and production, the licensee's additional costs to make the product appropriate for its market are minimal. Since royalties are paid only after working off initial advances and after actual sales are made, royalty expenses do not negatively impact cash flow.

With highly successful products, licensees may get to the point where they cringe at making high royalty payments, but they have to keep in mind the much smaller risk they took in the first place. And sending large royalty checks means that the bet on the original property is paying off. So, in reality, the higher the royalty checks, the happier both sides should be.

Sealing the Deal

The process for formalizing a workable licensing or co-publishing partnership consists of having three documents in place:

- A mutual non-disclosure (NDA) agreement.

- A term sheet.

- A binding agreement or contract.

MUTUAL NON-DISCLOSURE

Regardless of the nature of the deal and how eager both parties are to conclude the negotiations, it's always prudent to sign a mutual non-disclosure (NDA) or confidentiality agreement. An NDA is meant to be a preliminary document that can serve as the first step in executing a term sheet and ultimately a final, binding agreement. An NDA will permit potential partners to exchange information freely, including any data or documents that might be considered to be proprietary or confidential. Although an NDA is more common, and essential, in software licensing, where exchanging code can present real business risks to the developer if the code were to be made public, it's a good idea to have a written document for the exchange of IP that lists any proprietary issues and specific content or creative output that are tied to the publisher's brand, patents, trademarks, or copyrights.

The NDA must be mutual, meaning that both parties are equally responsible for maintaining the confidentiality of the discussions until a contract is signed, and for securing all documents and correspondence that are exchanged during the negotiations. The NDA should require both parties to destroy any documentation related to the other party's IP or the nature of the relationship in the event that they could not come to an agreement. An NDA should have a term limit of between two and five years regardless of whether the deal goes forward or falls apart for any reason, including simple apathy.

THE TERM SHEET

Assuming that both parties have determined that they are going to proceed with a formal contract, they should exchange a concise list of terms and conditions, or a term sheet, that describes the basic elements of the deal, what the mutual obligations are, and expectations of a successful outcome for both parties. This can be as simple as a bulleted list or outline of intentions, roles, and responsibilities, the resources that will be employed, and the anticipated financial commitments. The primary purpose of the term sheet is to expose any issues or areas of disagreement that need to be resolved prior to formalizing an agreement and to get a sound, mutual understanding in place before the partnership is official. Often it's easier to "see" the structure of a relationship in a term sheet prior to setting in stone the formal language in a legal document. The term sheet should be a simple listing or outline, a basic description, in plain language, of commitments that each party is willing to make. I would not begin to generate a formal document until the term sheet is agreed upon by both parties.

Using the mutually agreed-upon term sheet, both parties can proceed to formalize the relationship and make it legal by recording the terms and conditions in a binding licensing agreement or contract. Small publishers that do not have a legal department or even a standard licensing agreement on hand do not have to rush out immediately and hire an attorney to have one produced. Chances are the partner will have one that will be perfectly acceptable. However, before anyone signs anything, especially someone else's standard form, both parties should have an IP attorney on each side ensure that the document accurately represents the agreed-upon business goals and the spirit of the term sheet, and protects joint corporate interests.

A STANDARD AGREEMENT

Most international publishers that license their content or products out to other publishers as a regular part of their business activity have a standard agreement—in English—that should serve both parties' purposes well. The same will be true of publishers that are accustomed to licensing content *from* other publishers. Whatever the starting point, after the terms and conditions are agreed upon and incorporated into a formal document, it needs to be reviewed and approved by an attorney who specializes in IP, particularly if the agreement came from a basic boilerplate template that is used for multiple types of partnerships or vendors.

In the course of doing several agreements, publishers new to licensing are eventually able to piece together an agreement that satisfies most of their licensing purposes. Over time, it will likely need to be refined and revised as they gain more experience or as new situations demand. But I don't know of any publisher who is particularly possessive about the agreement itself or rigid about the specific language of the agreement. If it seems to meet the needs of both parties and covers the general business goals, it should be able to serve most licensing situations. These kinds of documents are not highly regulated, so the particular language used in them will vary from publisher to publisher.

Licensing agreements normally consist of five sections:

- *definitions* of terminology and other legal covenants that are described in the agreement;

- the *terms and conditions* of the business transaction itself, or what the partners are agreeing to buy or sell from each other;

- the *specifications* of the IP that is being licensed as well as the format in which the content will be transferred;

- the *roles and responsibilities* of both parties; and

- the *termination triggers*, which attempt to address what happens if and when things go wrong—or causes the relationship to end—to avoid any unnecessary legal intervention at the end of a relationship.

Although the business terms of the agreement are not subject to any prescribed legal standards, an attorney should make sure that the relationship does not put the company at risk and that the commitments being made are enforceable. Attorneys can clarify legal terminology or warranties and incorporate standard terms and conditions that may be required by the firm.

If the licensing agreement also allows for the transfer of code, or if it includes ongoing software or Web services, someone from the IT staff should review the agreement as well.

Assuming that the legal parameters of an agreement are covered, the business manager, not an attorney, should assume responsibility for justifying and explaining the basis of the transaction to upper management and the execution team. Articulating the terms and conditions of any agreement should be a business function, not a legal one. An attorney can help structure the language so that it reflects the business manager's intentions and goals, protects the IP, and ensures that the deal is consistent with any other legal commitments that others in the company may have made. But the final acceptance and sign-off should be made by the business manager.

I've included a sample licensing agreement in Appendix C, at the back of this book, which is a standard form that I have used in several situations. Below is a brief summary of the main points and standard terms and conditions that need to be included in any agreement, and which are more fully rendered in the sample form:

- Identification and place of business of the parties entering into the agreement, as well as where the parties are incorporated if different from the place of business.

- A clear description of the IP.

- The grant of rights, or what the owner of the IP is interested in providing to the licensee. (This may require detailed elaboration in an appendix to the licensing agreement.)

- Specific rights that are excluded.

- The territory or places where the licensed property can be sold and any re-licensing rights.

- Warranties indicating that the licensor owns the property in question and has the right to enter into a licensing agreement, as well as any restrictions or encumbrances that may apply.

- The term of the agreement—how long the licensee will have rights in its territory—and what performance hurdles will be required in order to extend those rights.

- The quantity and price agreed to if the licensee is buying finished goods.

- Deliverables required, such as electronic files, transcripts, or original art, if the licensee is handling production and manufacturing.

- Terms of payment, specifying royalty rates and any advance against those royalties as well as minimum guarantees.

- Copyright and trademark notices, including specific language that both parties require.

- A final publication date.

- Notice of the reversion of rights, back to the licensor, when the term of the agreement expires or if the publication date isn't met.

- The state's/province's or country's laws that govern the agreement and where any arbitration will take place in the event of a dispute.

- Actions, or negligence, that constitute a breach of the agreement, and the remedies—and required timeframe for making the remedies—in the event of a breach.

In addition to the above, the contract must allow for worst-case scenarios—for example, in the case of copyright or trademark infringements, bankruptcies, acts of war and God, and other dire events. These rarely come up in licensing deals, but they must be considered: companies can go bankrupt; they can be bought and sold soon after a deal is signed; and books and other physical materials can sometimes be lost at sea, literally. Most boilerplate agreements will have these clauses spelled out; an attorney should make sure that they are either slanted in the client's favor or, at the very least, apply equally and fairly to both parties. At the end of the day, the best agreement is one that enables both parties to achieve their goals, sets the stage for additional deals, and provides the basis of a trusting relationship and not just a one-time transaction.

Since licensing agreements are often between companies that operate in different countries, three common issues may need to be negotiated:

- which country's laws govern the agreement;

- where legal disputes are to be resolved;

- the currency that payments will be made in.

Usually whoever is marketing the licensed property will expect the agreement to be governed by the laws in their country and to have any legal disputes settled there as well. In addition, the licensee, in this case, will probably prefer to make payments in its local currency to avoid taking any risks with exchange-rate fluctuations.

One way to resolve the venue problem, and how to determine whose laws to adopt, is to apply the laws of a neutral country, such as Switzerland, and to choose a location that is equally difficult to get to by both parties. This avoids favoring one side over the other and helps to keep the resolution of problems where they belong—out of the courts and between the business groups of the two parties.

Regarding the currency used in making payments, most people will agree to convert to U.S. dollars or British pounds if they can be shielded from an unfavorable foreign-exchange rate. Naturally, international publishers will calculate their royalty obligations in their local currency and then convert the amounts owed prior to making payments. Often the conversion rate is written into the agreement. If it is, it shouldn't be fixed for the entire term. The contract should allow for the conversion rate to be reviewed quarterly or prior to the due date, and adjusted, if necessary, against the current prevailing rate. The parties may have to agree on a fluctuation range that will be mutually acceptable.

The following is an example of how we addressed the volatility of the U.S. dollar against the Canadian dollar in one of our licensing deals.

A Case in Point: FX Rates

I once ran into an issue regarding the currency to use with a Canadian publisher from which we licensed a series of interactive learning materials. The publisher's concern was legitimate because of the fluctuations in the value of the Canadian dollar against the U.S. dollar. The publisher was a small company and it couldn't afford to lose critical margins because of an unfavorably trending exchange rate.

Here's how we resolved the problem. Instead of assigning a royalty rate against our total revenue from sales of the deliverables, we established a fixed payment for units sold in Canadian dollars regardless of the exchange rate at any given time. We dealt with the exchange rate issue on our side and paid in U.S. dollars, but the unit value in Canadian dollars was always the same. In this way, our partner could determine exactly what it was earning, in its currency, based on the number of units sold.

In short, the same flexibility that is built into the development and production process must also be applied once the product is rolled out for sale. Here too, regardless of what is explicitly stated in the agreement, unexpected issues will arise and both parties may need to make adjustments to save the relationship and the viability of the product. At all times, common sense should prevail, and every participant in the relationship should assume that both sides are operating in good faith, and work towards an amicable resolution to unanticipated challenges from market conditions, competitive products, and any outside event.

Chapter 10
Consumption Models

There is only one boss. The customer. And he can fire everybody in the company from the chairman on down, simply by spending his money somewhere else.

Sam Walton

When negotiating rights to a product or to individual assets, the best starting position is to include every conceivable format—print and electronic, known and unknown. If a publisher is absolutely certain that it is interested in one format only and cannot anticipate publishing in any additional formats, it might be satisfied with having limited rights. This strategy assumes that it will save money by acquiring rights for a narrowly defined market or specific format. But if the publisher plans on making the product available in more than one format or language sometime in the future, then the objective should be to obtain broad rights to cover as many use cases as possible.

Similarly, any third-party assets added to any publisher-owned products should be acquired under terms that provide the publisher with as much flexibility as possible. In particular, these assets should not create unnecessary restrictions or limit the publisher from taking advantage of any marketing or licensing opportunities that may arise. A definition of the rights being acquired in an agreement should take into account all existing formats as well as formats that may not exist at the time the licensing deal is negotiated. When combining proprietary and third-party content, publishers should ensure that no asset unit in the database will prevent them from marketing, licensing, or sub-licensing the product in any territory or in any format.

In the sample contract included in Appendix C, Clause 3 describes the rights that are being granted. In this hypothetical example, the licensee is purchasing 5,000 copies of the product and acquiring worldwide print, e-book, and all electronic rights in English: "The Licensee shall publish, sell, and sublicense third parties to sell the said Work as defined in Appendix A in the above-mentioned language throughout the world in print or electronic form through all channels. Electronic form includes all known and unknown digital formats, including CD-ROM, DVD-ROM, flash or thumb drive, e-books, databases, and electronic storage devices."

Electronic rights can be described variously and will evolve as the technology advances, but being platform agnostic should be the goal, and the contract needs to indicate that so that the publisher does not have to refer back to the contract each time a new distribution channel opens up for a format that had not been anticipated. The reason for capturing as many formats as possible is simple: publishers should be prepared to monetize their products in any format that consumers prefer and, as we have seen, preferences can change over time.

For decades, the revenue models for publishers were relatively straightforward, even if they were not very efficient. Published products, whether they were books, magazines, or newspapers, were printed and sent to homes or retail outlets where they were purchased, returned, or sometimes destroyed and recycled. Once the same or similar content went digital (and included various media elements), distribution and purchasing options changed dramatically, and publishers were forced to reinvent how they reached customers and who they charged for their products. The buyer might not always be the end user; advertising pays for some products and, in the case of educational institutions, libraries or schools purchase products for use by teachers and students.

A variety of models have emerged, including downloading to own or to rent (as we have discussed with e-books), free access on the Internet (via websites or apps), and various subscription models. For many consumer websites, the most popular model is free with advertising, not unlike a television or radio broadcast. "Freemium" is another model, where a publisher offers some content for free, but charges for premium content or additional functionality or benefits, such as storage space. Access to premium content, without advertising (as offered on cable or satellite TV), is usually a timed subscription, either monthly or annually. Through annual subscriptions, newspapers and magazines are able to charge for access while still embedding advertising, which is a carryover from their print models. With magazines, however, the subscriber owns all of the past editions that are purchased as part of the subscription.

Publishers also have to account for the fact that consumers are using a variety of devices to access digital content, with the trend increasingly toward mobile devices, essentially handheld computers with phone and texting capability. This means that the content that publishers generate must be optimized for a variety of screen sizes in order to be readable on any device.

Customizing content on devices with different screen specifications is purely a technical issue, with several options possible, including responsive design, where the pages fit perfectly on the screen regardless of its dimensions. The publishers' true dilemma is finding the right digital models to adopt and the best way to reach customers—wherever they are and on whatever devices they are using—to create customer loyalty and generate ongoing revenue.

Let's take a familiar example. It's probably safe to say that every one of us has used and owned a dictionary at some point, and until technology made it possible to have other formats available, the dictionary we typically referenced was a thick, printed volume or two that we kept close at hand on a desk or shelf where we worked or studied. Today, we are more likely to use the Internet—from a computer or mobile device—if we want to look up a definition. Using a search engine, we can get the definition directly (sometimes from an unknown source), or go to our favorite, trusted source, like the Merriam-Webster or the Oxford English Dictionary (OED) website. If we are using a tablet or smartphone, we might have a dictionary app; or if we are reading an e-book on a Kindle, iPad, or other electronic reader, the device's platform is likely to have a built-in dictionary.

For more than 150 years, as a print product, Merriam-Webster's *Collegiate Dictionary* and *Collegiate Thesaurus* has been the most popular dictionary with consumers and students in North America. For most of its history, the brand enjoyed the majority of the market share in the reference section of every bookstore and was the dictionary of choice for students and professional knowledge workers. By the mid-1990s, the company was also offering a CD-ROM product, often bundled with the print version. By the end of the decade, with the growth of the Internet, Merriam-Webster's management had the challenge of maintaining the popularity of the brand in light of the proliferation of other dictionaries on the Web, most of which were free. Even if Merriam-Webster's was a preferred brand, it was too easy for Internet users to look no further than the first definition that popped up when they entered a word in a search engine rather than take an additional step to enter a URL for a specific dictionary site. For the brand to continue to resonate with the user, management understood that Merriam-Webster had to be as popular on the Internet as it was in print.

John Morse, the President of Merriam-Webster, faced this challenge head-on. He was determined to find a model that would attract and satisfy consumers, and would also make sound business sense. He started out with the assumption that, given an even playing field, people would choose Merriam-Webster. Now, what was the best way to level the playing field and still provide adequate revenue for the company to continue to invest in research and talent?

As early as the mid-1990s, even though Merriam-Webster had the best-selling dictionaries in the North American market, sales of its print products were declining. John felt that the company had to have a strong digital strategy, as it was seeing the same trends with its print sales as Britannica did (described in Chapter 2), and it knew that the downward slope of the curve would continue as the public increased its use of e-book readers and depended more on the Internet for information, including dictionary definitions. Like Britannica's management, those at Merriam-Webster too were convinced that the CD-ROM was only an interim technology. In reviewing his reports on product strategy from that period, when the company was in the middle of creating an HTML version of the CD-ROM product, John found the following memorandum: "Have begun examining options for establishing a Merriam-Webster World Wide Web server and service … Initial plans are being made to offer a limited version free on the Internet and develop a service around a full-featured version."

While John and the Merriam-Webster team were debating whether to offer free online access to the full text of the *Collegiate Dictionary* and the *Collegiate Thesaurus* or to make it a subscription service, other non-branded dictionary databases as well as the search engines themselves were occupying the word definition space on the Internet. Offering Merriam-Webster's family jewels for free would be gambling that the traffic on a Merriam-Webster website would be sufficient to generate enough revenue from advertising to make up for the fall in print revenue without accelerating the decline even further. But it was a gamble that John felt had to be made.

The Merriam-Webster free website was launched in February 1997. Looking back at the site's debut, John had these thoughts: "It was done as a result of technology; couldn't have been done without technology; changed or adjusted our business strategy; had a very positive effect." As a way of examining the value proposition of different revenue models for digital products, and how the models have evolved over the last decade or so, it's worth recounting what John and his team grappled with in those early days as they were making the transition from print and CD-ROM to online delivery.

According to John: "Reading between the lines of the reports [at the time], it's easy to detect the tensions, frustrations, and fraying tempers amongst various people and departments" —and for good reasons, which we will look at shortly. However, they didn't seem worried about the impact of the website on print sales, partly because, as John remembers it:

> *The Web business was still small at that point. The number of people using websites had just recently risen above 10 million, so from that point of view the threat to print was small. But I also think that we looked upon the Web a little like we looked at Microsoft Bookshelf¹ (which we were not part of), which is that the availability of the dictionary in digital form was in effect an endorsement of its quality, and hence actually supportive of print. In other words, if you like us on the Web, you'll be more inclined to buy us in print. The phrase "Age of Also" hadn't been coined yet, but I think we were guided by that concept nonetheless.²*

John was also aware that although the move to the Web may not have been disruptive to the short- or even medium-term revenue projections, it was "profoundly disruptive to the new skills that we were going to have to acquire, which is where the Sturm und Drang of the period comes from." The move to the Web was going to require changes in three aspects of the business: a new *revenue* model; a new *distribution* model; and new business *partners*.

Once they set the wheels in motion to produce a Web service, several revenue models were discussed. Selling advertising on a free site was a leading candidate, but others were considered and contested within the company: a subscription service; micropayments (a charge for individual downloads or look-ups or time-based fees); site licenses for institutions—revenue models that are currently in use by many website publishers—all had their champions. Since this was the mid-1990s, emphasis was placed on a relationship with AOL, which dominated access to the Web via a dial-up ramp. Even though the debate continued for months, the loudest voices were in favor of an advertising-supported model, which, in spite of the increasing competitiveness on the Web, was buttressed by very optimistic growth projections.

---

1   Microsoft Bookshelf was Microsoft's first CD-ROM title, and comprised a series of licensed titles: a dictionary, thesaurus, style book, quotation book, and almanac. The product was originally developed by Cytation, a San Francisco-based company, which Microsoft purchased.
2   "Age of Also" is a term coined by Richard Saul Wurman, the founder of the TED conference on technology, entertainment, and design, and refers to the availability of several formats at the same time: books, magazines, TV, CDs, DVDs, etc.

The challenge to find the right distribution model may have been even more difficult because, although the company knew a lot about technology and depended on it for running every part of the business, with a website as the primary means of generating revenue, it would actually have to *become* a technology company. If the company's future was going to rely on the functionality and appeal of its Web service, it would have to take control of its online fate regardless of the revenue models it settled on. It could no longer outsource the Web design and implementation work, and it would have to build up its own internal staff and take responsibility for the user experience and a robust serving capacity that would of necessity be running 24 hours a day, 365 days a year. This was not going to happen overnight. Going online raised the stakes for all kinds of development issues, which was the root cause of many of the tensions that arose during that period. But it would soon become the company's top priority.

Finding new business partners was probably the easiest change to make, but it required the company to have relationships with people it had never dealt with before, including technology partners for hosting services, advertising sales executives, and search engine optimization (SEO) consultants. This was the pre-Google era, before advertising links were as automated as they are now. Still, websites like Merriam-Webster's needed to have links from the search sites of that time to reach a critical mass of traffic to attract advertisers and increase advertising rates.

Today, Merriam-Webster is primarily a Web-service company, with strong advertising revenue from its free offerings and a steady revenue stream from subscribers who prefer an advertising-free site with the full suite of premium dictionary products. And it still has a robust print business, with most of those sales coming from online retailers and direct from institutions.

John believes that the print and various online revenue models can co-exist for three reasons: need, use, and value. He described it to me this way:

> There was a particular gamble here, and it involved believing in the value of what we do ... We gambled that people actually use their dictionaries, that they don't just take them home and leave them on the shelf; because if people didn't use their dictionaries a lot ... then we were in trouble. Sooner or later they would tell themselves that they didn't need to buy the dictionary, because it was available on the Web, but they wouldn't come to the website because they really didn't need to use the dictionary. However, we bet that people did use their dictionaries, and

that even if, in time, they came to buy fewer [print] dictionaries because the dictionary was available online, that was OK. As long as they were coming to our site, we would still be getting the eyeballs, and the only challenge then would be to figure out how to monetize the traffic. That turned out to take longer than anticipated ... but we figured an answer would emerge, and it did.

What John means by "an answer" was more advertising revenue as an increasing number of people used the site because of its rising ranking position on a search engine results page (SERP), and they stayed longer after having gotten the definition or spelling that they looked up because the site was compelling, or "sticky," with vocabulary quizzes, videos of editors discussing word usage, and debates about controversial new words entering the lexicon and popularized on social media.

To serve a variety of consumer preferences, Merriam-Webster currently has several online products: a free mobile app with advertising; a subscription app without advertising; a free website with advertising; and a subscription website without advertising that also contains a complete line of Merriam-Webster dictionaries, including the highly lauded *Unabridged International Dictionary*.

Merriam-Webster had to make the shift from print to the Web at a time when revenue models for digital products were largely untested. But what about companies whose products started life in a digital form (without a print legacy) very early on in the evolution of digital technology? How would a company with that profile be able to adjust to various revenue models, and would its path to the Web prove to be more or less difficult than it was for publishers that started with a strong print base?

Marlowe Teig, formerly Managing Director of the investment bank Berkery, Noyes & Co., worked with just such a company in the 1980s, which produced a computer-based language arts program to teach reading skills in the classroom. The program that the company sold to schools was delivered on floppy disks originally, but as the complexity of the program increased and as the technology evolved, it was converted and delivered on CDs and hard drives for installation on the schools' file servers.

Although the product was digital in nature, a physical component was still being delivered—software in the form of either CD-ROMs or hard drives. The company asked customers to pay a one-time fee for a perpetual license to the IP on the delivered software and a time-limited fee for maintenance and upgrades of the software.

As technology evolved in the first decade of the 21st century, the company could distribute the product over the Internet as an online, browser-based instructional program, providing a better experience and eliminating the physical deliverables. On the advice of its auditors, the company tried to maintain and separate the perpetual license from the software piece, but this no longer made sense in an online world, where the program did not operate in the same way on the customer's own computer system. It was no longer a downloaded static program living on the schools' networks, but a streaming, continuously updated subscription service. As a result, the company had to change the way it recognized revenue and what the customer was actually paying for. The subscription service provided the customer with access to the program 24/7, but only during the time that the designated subscription period was in force, with no actual ownership of, or perpetual license for, the product. Because of this, when the customer paid for the subscription, the publisher was obligated to provide the service for the life of the subscription period and therefore had to amortize revenue over the length of the subscription.

At this time, the broad acceptance of subscription sites was not necessarily a given, particularly with schools and libraries, which were accustomed to purchasing products, not renting them or paying for timed access. In the case of libraries, online subscriptions were a big leap because their acquisition budgets were based on purchasing single titles, multivolume sets, and content collections. Further, one of their value propositions is being a repository; libraries pride themselves in maintaining comprehensive archives of their acquisitions. A patron would expect to be able to research documents, manuscripts, books, newspapers, magazines, and audio and video content at the library. Many of us can recall the days when we researched news items and past editions of journals and magazines using microfiche, for example. Today, the newspaper publishers themselves maintain their archives on their own servers and provide subscribers with access to them, and if libraries want to archive their online magazine or journal subscriptions under this model, they have to have their own on-site servers.

Nevertheless, the market has made the transition to accepting and trusting subscription services, particularly as a way of accessing premium content and archival material. Judging by the number of online services that academic and public libraries subscribe to today, it's clear that they believe that they can be true to their mission as a central repository and research hub, even though much of the research material resides on off-site servers. And consumers have become comfortable with a model where they relinquish the ownership of content in exchange for continuous updates and software improvements. Digital magazine subscriptions, however, follow the identical model as print; you can always access any magazine edition that you download as long as you have enough digital storage space, either on your own devices or in the "cloud" from a third-party provider like Amazon, Google, or Apple.

At our house, we subscribe to newspapers only online, having stopped delivery of the print versions. We also subscribe to a variety of magazines online, but in these cases the print versions are included in the subscription price. If, in the future, these magazine publishers charge separately for the two formats, we will probably opt in favor of the online version. (We also subscribe to other online services when we are about to make a large consumer product purchase or need access to a network of vetted service providers for a major home repair.)

Educational institutions have embraced subscription models, especially for their large database products, and have dropped many types of print alternatives. Even as public, academic, and school libraries continue to build their e-book collections, with single-, multiple-, or unlimited-use licenses, schools are opting for e-book subscriptions, where new e-books are added, updated, or exchanged over the life of the subscription. The platforms on which these e-books are accessed provide additional functionality, including highlighting, bookmarking, and note taking, as well as assessment engines. In response to market demand, educational publishers are offering some of their e-book collections only as subscriptions.

Many classroom teachers have become strong advocates of both e-books and online subscriptions because of the advantages they both have over textbooks. In a recent newspaper article about the growing adoption of e-books, a teacher in the school district where we live put it this way: "The cost savings are huge … and students don't have to lug around many books. As long as they have Internet access, they can access their text and account from any location. This solves the problem of students forgetting their texts at school or at home."

LightSail, an e-reading literacy platform, conducted a survey in December 2014 on the state of the e-book market.[3] Based on the responses from over 400 educators, it concluded that the e-book market was "surging." A total of 52%

3   See: www.lightsail.com. September 20, 2015.

of the respondents expected that within two years, e-books would account for more than 40% of books read in the schools. They anticipated three types of buying models: the library model, where the texts were owned by the school or library and checked-out by the students; a subscription model, perhaps a monthly fee per student, with broad access to a comprehensive library, like Netflix; and rental, with a single, time-limited checkout period, e.g., one book for one student for 30 days.

E-book retailers are also experimenting with subscription models. Amazon has added a subscription service through its Kindle device, which allows unlimited access to approximately 700,000 e-books for $10 a month. Oyster, which began as an all-you-can-read subscription service, has started to sell e-books that are not available on its subscription services, which is a reflection of the current reality of the market. Not all authors or publishers are willing yet to have their books made available on a subscription service where payments are derived from a share (based on usage) of a royalty pool; instead, they prefer to have their revenue calculated on individual sales, just like they do with their print products. In the case of Oyster, up until this point, it has been able to strike deals for its subscription service with three of the "Big Five" trade publishers – HarperCollins, Simon & Schuster, and Macmillan – but not Penguin Random House or Hachette, whereas it is selling e-books published by all of them.

These publisher–distributor arrangements are still changing, however, and whatever they are today, they are likely to be different tomorrow. To find the most productive ways for working together and reaching the maximum number of consumers while protecting their margins, publishers and distributors are still experimenting with revenue models. Digital publishing may not be in its infancy, but that isn't preventing some participants from acting like it is.

Subscription services are gaining ground, even though the pricing models are still fluid. We see pricing models vary as the market tries to understand the value proposition of digital products—streaming content that is "borrowed" versus purchased content that sits on shelves or servers. The many advantages of online products, including continual updates, additional functionality, and access from any device, to name but a few, are still hard for consumers to value relative to products in print or e-books, which makes pricing a challenge for publishers.

Some print or e-books in specialty subjects such as law and medicine, or academic and pedagogical titles, can be priced at a premium based somewhat on the nature of the content. Most fiction and general nonfiction books, children through adult, are priced in a range relative to other books in the category and to some degree on page count and other specifications, such as the number of illustrations or physical characteristics—hardcover titles are priced at a premium over softcover, for example. However, it's difficult to establish pricing equivalency between online and offline products because their value propositions and user experiences are so different. It's equally hard to compare any two online products by conventional standards or to measure the content of a product that is constantly changing and growing.

When publishers add or revise articles, media, etc., in their online services, they can rarely charge more. By constantly updating their products, they are counting on customer loyalty and retention. When investing in new technology and more content, publishers are looking to the lifetime value of their loyal customers, which means ensuring that customers see continual improvement in their subscription sites so that they stick with them year after year. The thinking is that customers will experience and appreciate the value and will be willing not only to renew their subscription but also to pay more for it over time.

One common educational pricing model is a site license, where the publisher charges a flat fee per building. The cost per building could be based on the total number of students and teachers. Some publishers charge based on full-time equivalents (FTEs), where the price the school pays is determined by the actual number of full-time students in attendance at the beginning of the school year. For example, for a fee of $3 per student per year, everyone attending the school would have access to the product regardless of how many students or teachers actually use the site, how many computers or terminals there are, or whether the population in the school changes over the course of the school year. Some products are used only in certain subjects and certain grades, which would require classroom rather than building pricing.

Site licenses and FTE pricing vary wildly across the globe, depending on a variety of variables, including the price sensitivity of the market—prices are higher in the Middle East, for example, than they are in South America—and how much additional service is provided along with the product. For example, students and teachers who use educational products online often benefit from professional development, including online visits, and webinars that are provided by the publisher free of charge with the subscription. Sometimes a publisher, after having gone through an accreditation process, is able to provide continuing education (CE) credit to teachers who attend professional development sessions. Online services often require on-site consultations from sales representatives. These types of extra services are built into the FTE or site license fee and often take into consideration bandwidth costs for delivering the service as well as travel and expenses related to in-service calls by consultants.

Usage of online products has become an increasingly important factor in determining pricing. Because of the nature of online products and the back-end technology built into them, publishers can track the amount of time users spend on their sites and can collect data on user behavior, e.g., the number of sessions, queries, page views, and document downloads. If an online product gets little or no usage, then it is at risk of being canceled. For example, if a school with 1,000 students paid $1,000 for a school-wide building license to an online product, it paid the equivalent of $1/student, which may sound like a good deal—especially if it is accustomed to paying about $75 for a typical textbook. (Even if the textbook is used for five years, that's $15/year/student, or 15 times the cost of the online service.) However, if usage showed that after a full school year, a total of only 100 documents were viewed, then the school paid $10/per document. That would not constitute sufficient usage or good value for the school. Armed with this data, the school would very likely cancel its subscription.

The rule of thumb is that the average cost to a school should be less than $0.10 per document. This metric would mean that the product is being used often and is worth having. To demonstrate value, publishers need to make their products as compelling as possible and easy to use, and to provide ample training and support to increase usage.

Other factors besides usage can determine online subscription purchases in academic settings. Sometimes obscure or specialized online products (just like the long-tail print titles I discussed in Chapter 1) required as part of a curriculum are purchased even though they are not widely used. If a college is offering a course on Hungarian poets, for example, and only one known online source is available, that product may be given priority over something else that is more widely used and even less expensive. In this case, assuming that the interest in Hungarian poetry is limited, a product used by just a few people will be absorbing budget dollars that could be used for products that could be used by a larger audience. Online products, just like any other purchase, will run into budget barriers or competing priorities, which is why free online services (non-profits, government-supported sites, etc.) are not only widely used but also sometimes recommended.

However, generally speaking, the value of online products, whether they are free or subscription sites, is increasingly being determined by use. Whatever models arise as subscription websites and e-books gain in popularity, usage will continue to become an important metric for determining value.

Usage, and the ability to track usage, is a tool born of the digital age and it allows buyers to make objective decisions about product value, or at least the value to them. What may not be as easily measured is quality or reliability, and sometimes the relationship between popularity—measured by usage—and quality is not entirely clear. Reliability and quality are not attributes that can be determined by technology, which is why it's useful to understand who is creating products, how they are created, and the processes in place that made them available. If we are aware of the origins of the products that we consume, then we should be able to choose what we read and where we can spend our time more wisely—and have a better sense of what we can trust.

Chapter 11

The Lion and the Mouse:
The Professional vs. the Amateur

If you think it's expensive to hire a professional to do the job, wait until you hire an amateur.

Red Adair, international oil well firefighter

With the dramatic increase in the number of websites, including those that are advertising-supported, subscription-based (amateur and professional), or free from well-respected organizations—government and non-profits—as well as those with commercial or political agendas, it is challenging to identify unbiased, reliable sites just by randomly searching the Web. Search engines make the process of differentiation difficult in several ways. First, they are what they are called – *search* engines, not *find* engines – enabling us to conduct a search, but not necessarily research. Also, they favor websites that pay for higher placements on search results pages by purchasing text and graphical advertising—search-engine marketing (SEM), including paid listings and keywords, with the most popular keywords going to the highest bidders. And because of the way search-engine algorithms are designed, the more links a site gets from other sites (in-bound links), the higher the site will rank on the SERP. Free and open sites with a sizable amount of content will accumulate the greatest number of links and high SERP rank; therefore, the very best content, or the content most relevant to what users are looking for, may not always be at the top of the SERP. As a result, website producers are forced to compete on the Web by constructing their sites and writing text copy using keywords and phrases—search-engine optimization (SEO)—in a way that helps them improve their site's SERP position.

In order to be successful, website strategy has to follow search engine methodology. For the most part, websites that master SEO strategies will get more traffic than other sites with similar content, which may have little to do with how relevant the content is to the user. This is unlikely to change in the near future, so until search tools are better able to respond to users' personal needs or interests—and quickly locate the websites that correspond with those interests—amateurs and professionals must adapt to the way search engines prioritize content to maximize their opportunities on the Web.

Publishing's Relationship with User-Generated Content

In this environment, the challenge for publishers is to convince consumers to seek out their sites either from positive experiences with the publisher's offline products and services or from their most current offerings online. In theory, frequent online users will turn to the brands and products that they can immediately associate with reliability and accuracy, especially if the products were proven trustworthy prior to having a Web presence.

But pre-Web trust and popularity may not necessarily transfer to the Web. Indeed, many Web startups eclipse brands online that had strong brand value offline by being better at search engine strategies, social media, and multi-device marketing. For example, according to EbizMBA, the top three news sites based on unique monthly visitors are Yahoo!News, Google News, and the Huffington Post, which were all born on the Web and are more heavily visited than such well-established news sources as the *New York Times* (#5), *The Guardian* (#10) or BBC News (#13). Similarly, the top three most popular political news sites (the Huffington Post, the Blaze, and the Drudge Report) also had no offline presence or mind share. However, popularity is not the same as accuracy or credibility, and the jury is still out on whether the most popular sites are also the most trustworthy.

In a poll of almost 2,000 British adults conducted by the research group YouGov in August 2013, Wikipedia contributors rated slightly higher than traditional journalists. A total of 64% of respondents said they trusted Wikipedia to be truthful "a great deal" or "a fair amount" of the time, compared to 61% for BBC news journalists, 55% for ITV news journalists, and 45% for "upmarket" newspapers like *The Guardian*, *The Times*, and *The Telegraph*. This bias toward Wikipedia—ranging from slight to significant—could be the result of how the public perceives information on the Web in general, or it could be due to the nature of news itself, which, regardless of the source, is not always completely accurate the first time it is reported, and certainly not as evergreen as material published after a reasonable amount of time has passed and additional facts have emerged.

In the same poll, however, Wikipedia did not stack up as well against *Encyclopaedia Britannica*. When asked how much they trust the information on Wikipedia or *Britannica* to be accurate, 87% said they trusted Britannica "a great deal" or "a fair amount," versus 67% for Wikipedia.[1]

In spite of the popularity of some user-generated content (UGC), including Wikipedia, some research suggests that UGC is not perceived to be as credible as professionally produced content. Andrew Flanagin and Miriam Metzger at the University of California in Santa Barbara conducted a study that examined the perceived credibility of Wikipedia versus more expertly provided online encyclopedic information from Citizendium and *Britannica* across generations of users. They concluded that "although the use of Wikipedia is common, many people (particularly adults) do not truly comprehend how Wikipedia operates in terms of information provision, and that while people trust Wikipedia as an information source, they express doubt about the appropriateness of doing so."

The study indicated that children too rated information from Wikipedia to be "less believable" when they viewed it on Wikipedia's site than when that same information appeared on either Citizendium's or Britannica's site. The authors conclude that "despite the promise of social media in general and Wikipedia, in particular, to harness the 'wisdom of the crowd,' ... users are not ready to fully relinquish traditional models of information provision. Results [of the study] indicate that adults' perceptions of credibility are strongly anchored in the idea of expert-generated (or vetted) content, as shown by their apparent singular focus on the method of information provision."[2]

This study suggests that for a site to be credible, the content needs to be the result of a process or method dedicated to accuracy and objectivity. This is good news for both the amateur and the professional. Content should be able to earn trust over time if it is produced from a process that builds in checks and balances, and reduces the risk of introducing bias, which is certainly the role of the professional, but is not out of the reach of the amateur. Creating trustworthy content is not a question of authority per se, but rather the rigor of a standards-based process that can consistently generate reliable content that will inspire users' confidence and ultimately earn their trust.

---

1   Taken from *The Telegraph*, August 12, 2014. © 2013 YouGov plc. All rights reserved.
2   Andrew J. Flanagin and Miriam J. Metzger. From "Encyclpaedia Britannica to Wikipedia." *Information, Communication & Society*, 14(3), April 2011. © Taylor & Francis.

As an example, Britannica has adopted a process that starts with its expert contributors and involves various editors, information architects, fact-checkers, designers, artists, cartographers, and, finally, the users themselves. The process relies heavily on user feedback, and the input from readers is the final test of the integrity, usability, and readability of the content. Below are two infographics of the end-to-end process.

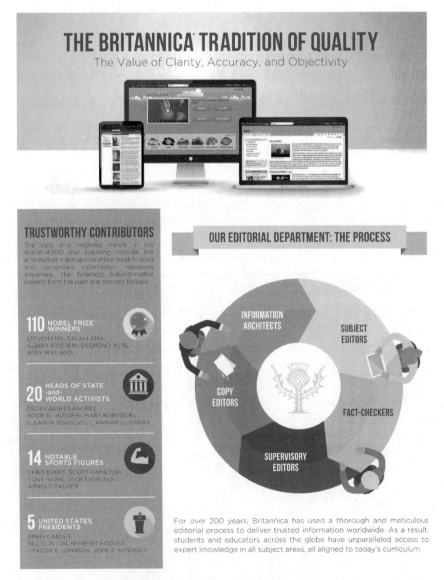

Figure 11.1   Infographic 1: Britannica's editorial process

Figure 11.2   Infographic 2: Britannica's editorial team

I offer this as an example of a rigorous editorial process only because it's the one with which I am most familiar, and I can verify that it produces the intended results—not perfect results, but consistently high-quality results with minimal bias. This process is not set in stone, but it is likely to be similar to the processes employed at other publishing houses. Of course, the details in getting to a final product are not spelled out, but the overall method corroborates what Flanagin and Metzger identify as the main elements of credibility—"trustworthiness and expertise"—which they say are "difficult to assess in the Wikipedia environment."

What follows is an example of how this process worked when it was tested in a real-life encounter with a user.

One of our editors received an email from a subscriber who was teaching students how to evaluate Internet sources. She was unhappy because she thought she found a feature in the Britannica website that caused her to doubt the product's quality and credibility. Here's what she wrote:

> I warn [my students] about sites like Wikipedia in which users can change entries. I was very disappointed to discover that the Encyclopaedia Britannica also has an "edit" option. Your print publication has the best reputation, so this option you are allowing is shocking to me as an educator. The Internet has enough bad information on it. We need sites students can trust. What are your criteria for edits? Who reviews them?

The teacher did not understand the purpose of the "edit button" on Britannica's website. It was designed to allow the user to submit comments or queries, similar to a "letter to the editor" feature in a newspaper—not make changes. Here is the basis of the response that our editor provided (which I have changed slightly for concision):

> Thank you for contacting Encyclopaedia Britannica.
>
> The Edit link [on the Britannica website] allows readers to submit their own suggested revisions of Britannica articles. Unlike edits made to Wikipedia, however, these changes are not published to the site automatically. Instead, they are channeled through an online system that allows them to be reviewed by Britannica's editorial staff.
>
> It is my personal responsibility to review submissions as they come in. Submissions that are obviously inappropriate (spam, vandalism, etc.)

are immediately rejected. Submissions made with what appears to be a legitimate intent to improve the article are typically referred to editors with expertise in the article's subject area. The editors review and fact-check the submission; and if an editor determines that a submission has some value, he or she will revise the article accordingly. Sometimes, a reader's submitted text is fully integrated into the article. In most cases, however, the editor decides to include only part of the submission and/or rewrites the text to conform to Britannica's rigorous standards for style, tone, accuracy, etc.

We welcome submissions from readers for the simple reason that many of our articles have been demonstrably improved because of them. We are especially thankful to readers who edit articles to correct errors or to provide us with updated information. Maintaining a database of some 150,000 articles is no small task, and input from the outside world can be of great help.

I hope I've addressed your concerns. If you have any other questions, please do let me know.

Best,

Readers' Editor, Encyclopaedia Britannica.

The teacher was delighted with our editor's response and replied accordingly:

Thank you very much for your timely response and for the detailed information you provided about your review process. I now feel very comfortable allowing students to use your site. I will also share this information with my colleagues. Thank you.

This email exchange illustrates how accountability makes a difference to users, and what distinguishes a credible site or publication from one of dubious quality.

The New Breed of Publishing Entrepreneurs

For publishers to have popular websites, they have to attract expert authors and contributors, use the Internet to exploit their business models, and build a reputation for responsible and engaging publishing. Publishers need to increase their awareness and be visible on the Web, whether their primary outputs are Web content, print products, e-books, or a combination of several formats.

But doing all of these tasks well will not guarantee that their products will be used. Consumers of offline and online products ultimately will decide what they can trust or not and what their favorite sites and products will be. Publishers were once in control of the information faucet. Now, with technology and the Internet, the faucet is always on, and information is coming from amateurs, self-publishers, and professionals.

Technology and the Internet have enabled publishers to perform at a high level, but the power has shifted to consumers, who have thousands of choices for the information and content they want, and they can experiment with little or no commitment. In addition, publishers cannot always take advantage of every publishing opportunity, nor do they always understand what will make a publication or product offering successful.

Technology has opened up a gap between professional publishers and demand—which is increasingly being filled by publishing entrepreneurs and self-publishers. Nature abhors a vacuum, and the void that needs to be filled was created from the publishing industry's limited capacity to produce enough products to meet demand. In fact, in publishing, demand itself is an illusion. If an excellent product arrives on the market, it can create demand, and demand can be almost limitless. Regardless of how many resources a publishing company has, it will always have a limited capacity; it will not be able to publish everything it wants to publish, and, for subjective reasons, may not want to publish every manuscript or product that comes its way. Or, because those working in publishing companies are human, they will simply miss opportunities or make the wrong choice.

Because the technology is available to anyone willing to use it, self-publishing has grown tremendously over the years. Even if they have a publisher willing to take on their project, some authors prefer to self-publish anyway to maintain control of the process from end to end and, if the project is successful, retain all of the profits rather than share them with a publisher.

Authors have the choice to do everything on their own or to hire a company to perform the various publishing services for a fee. Such companies offer a variety of services, from manuscript development to printing and e-book conversion. They allow authors to keep all of their rights and royalties, and to have unlimited access to wholesale and retail outlets. In addition, authors can purchase a variety of services, a la carte: press releases; publishing imprint and personal ISBNs; book design; print-run flexibility—from POD to traditional runs.

Here is how one author embraced disruptive technology and came out ahead. Jennie Walters wrote a trilogy of "Upstairs/Downstairs"-type novels, under the series title "Swallowcliffe Hall," aimed at the tween/young adult (YA) market. The books were published originally by one of the Big Five trade publishers. Hers was a case study of what can go wrong in the publishing experience and how it can be made right.

Jennie is an experienced children's editor herself, but that alone didn't help with the publisher. Her commissioning editor went on maternity leave, the covers were dreadful, and there wasn't much of a proactive marketing effort, so sales were horrible.

In 2011, five years after publication, sales had been so low that Jennie was able to request that the rights be reverted back to her. She still believed in the potential of the novels and one year later decided to self-publish the books only on Kindle. Even though she was a publishing professional, she was not particularly tech-savvy, so it took her a week to format the books (which she says she can now do in a day). She also took new cover photographs and commissioned much more attractive cover artwork. She used the bit of light meta-tagging allowed on the Kindle format to make the obvious connection between her books and the then smash TV hit *Downton Abbey*, which was a logical marketing gambit that the original publisher did not take up, thinking the TV series would not be of interest to children.

Optimistically, she thought that she might sell a few hundred downloads—at most, maybe, a thousand or two. However, during the last three years, she has sold 40,000 e-books, and has written and published a fourth title in the series aimed specifically at adults, which has also been successful. Of course, we hear about E.L. James and Amanda Hocking selling millions of units, but Jennie represents a mid-list author who was able to break through the noise in the market and find a niche for her work after the original publisher gave up. And of the 40,000 units she sold, Jennie, as a self-publisher, retained all of the profits instead of earning a 15–20% royalty rate from a publisher.

To understand her sales history in context, even at those modest sales levels, she is still in the top 1% of self-published authors on Kindle, and for her, this achievement has been transformational. Not only has it been a confidence builder, but she has been able to identify her true market. Yes, the YA readers constitute a portion of it, but mainly it is women of a certain age—three Americans to every one Brit—who want to curl up in front of the fire with a slice of British tradition.

Authors are very often the forgotten part of the disruption story, partly because content appears to grow on endlessly available trees as far as many of the disruptors are concerned. Yet, some authors have actually been able to turn the disruption into a distinct advantage.

An unintended consequence of Amazon's disruption in the marketplace was providing a solution for a problem it didn't set out to fix. The second life of Jennie's series was enabled by a distribution option that did not exist in the pre-digital era. After being disappointed by the traditional publishing system, she used technology to become a self-publisher and the Internet to provide distribution. Because of these new publishing "tools," she didn't need anyone's permission, nor was there an outside publisher or distributor to reject her.

While Amazon's main value propositions were fixing a problem in the supply chain and offering outstanding customer service, it also provided a means for willing authors to serve as their own publishers and distributors, and to take control of their publications' destiny.

Amazon's disruption created a new opportunity for people like Jennie. But Amazon's rapidly attained hegemony of the market also had negative consequences for some small and mid-size independent publishers and forced them to alter their marketing strategies.

Bill Evans, President and founder of Evan-Moor Publishers in Monterey, California, describes how Amazon's business practices caused his company to make a dramatic change in how they priced their educational products.

Thirty-five years ago, when Evan-Moor was founded, most supplemental educational materials were sold through 10 large regional catalogs. In the late 1980s, an explosion of small educational retailers, generally referred to as teacher stores, burst onto the market. The industry went from being dominated by 10 large customers to a dispersed network of over 1,250 small businesses. This created great stability for publishers because no one customer had 10% of the market. Up until about 10 years ago, Evan-Moor received 78% of its revenue through the educational retailers, 20% through direct response (teachers and schools), and about 2% in special sales, like book clubs.

About five years ago, the channels of distribution began to change again. With the emergence of Amazon into book distribution, more and more of Evan-Moor's business went through this single retailer. It also saw the pool of smaller educational retailers shrink. This same phenomenon occurred with the general bookstore in trade publishing, with fewer and fewer independent bookstores surviving. Today there are only about 350 viable educational retailers left.

The problem with this shift is in how Amazon takes sales from the smaller distributors. Amazon demands high discounts from publishers (eroding profitability), deeply discounts the products, and offers free shipping. Evan-Moor's customers peruse its catalog and browse at their local educational retailer, but they buy from Amazon. Some 95% of Amazon's customers arrive on its website already knowing what they are going to order. Basically Amazon takes orders that other channels have generated. If Evan-Moor allowed this to continue, it would see the people and organization that actually marketed its products go out of business. It needed to reward the person who generated the sale, not the entity that simply took the order.

Evan-Moor took the bold step to cease selling directly to Amazon as well as to Ingram and Baker & Taylor (two wholesale distributors that supply Amazon). These three accounts represented around $1.2 million in revenue. Once the company took this action, it took a while for the existing stock to be depleted. However, it has seen traffic to its website double compared to the same period in the previous year and actually grew direct sales by 4% over budget. Bill has talked to other publishers that have taken this action. Similar to Evan-Moor's experience, theirs has been a dip in revenue in the short term, but greater growth three to six months later.

Whenever disruption occurs to bring about a positive change, some people and businesses will be able to take advantage of the change directly, and some indirectly. In the case of Jennie, the independent author, and Bill, the independent publisher, disruption forced them to reinvent how they went to market, but in the end, the changes they had to make were for the better.

Epilogue

Things do good and bad, but I really love the fact that somebody invented the hammer. I think the invention of the hammer was terrific because the hammer and the chisel allowed Michelangelo to create beautiful things. Of course the hammer and chisel can also kill somebody, so I can't just say I love technology. What I can say is that I love the fact that technology can have very positive implications and implementations. Technology itself is nothing; it's a word. Words in themselves are nothing.

Richard Saul Wurman, founder of the
TED conferences on technology, entertainment, and design

The digital age and disruptive technology has either created or accelerated several trends that have had a dramatic effect on publishing. These trends have all created opportunities for businesses to grow and for consumers to benefit from more diverse and engaging content.

Outsourcing

Over the last 15 years, we have seen the emergence of companies, particularly in India, but also in Eastern Europe and the Philippines, that can provide high-quality services—at lower costs—with little startup time and in response to almost any need. These services, sometimes referred to as business practice outsourcing (BPO), often began as call centers, and mostly provided customer service and support. Today, BPOs that cater to the publishing industry provide comprehensive and highly scalable publishing services from keyboarding, scanning, and file conversion to illustration and page layout, to copyediting, proofreading, and indexing, and to Web development and software engineering, and the best of them are able to extend a company's resources on an entirely variable basis.

The growth of BPOs seems almost limitless, but they are only one of a cadre of outsource services, including CPOs for content development, PPOs for pre-press and printing services, and KPOs (knowledge process outsourcing), which offer legal or accounting resources.

Publishers now have a choice. They can build their own systems and invest in services that they will use only for themselves and thus end up with cost centers and fixed costs, which can erode their bottom line. Or they can take advantage of the infrastructures and best practices that outsourcing companies have built from working with many publishers—on a wide variety of content sources—and use these services only when they need them. In this way, publishers don't have to staff up or down as projects come and go; they can use outsourcing companies that can scale according to clients' needs and move resources from job to job. For publishers, having certain in-house proprietary services is becoming less economical and less productive when, in many cases, more efficient services are available elsewhere at a fraction of the cost.

The flexibility provided by outsourcing groups allows publishers to invest in the higher end of the value chain, such as innovation and superior content, core competencies that are differentiators in the marketplace.

Seeking less expensive ways to manufacture books, publishers have been printing off-shore for decades, first in Hong Kong, then in Singapore and China, and, increasingly, in South America and Eastern Europe. Although this is not new, the amount and variety of printing that is moving off-shore continues to increase. Printers in various countries have invested heavily in pre-press and printing to handle any kind of printing requirement. Consequently, printing and manufacturing off-shore is a sure way for publishers to save money and increase their margins—while maintaining quality and, in most cases, improving the level of service they receive.

Printing is an obvious commodity to outsource because, for most printing tasks, consistently high-quality output is available from many different suppliers. As long as printers remain under pressure to keep their physical assets in constant use and compete aggressively for every job available, publishers can take advantage of the excess supply of printing options. Because this competitive environment is likely to continue, especially as certain kinds of printed products are dropped in favor of electronic publications, opportunities to lower printing costs on any given job—from off-shore suppliers—will abound. To stay competitive and retain high-volume printing costs, many of the largest global printers based in North America have purchased printers in South America, Eastern Europe, and Asia, and can now move jobs to these plants.

Consolidation

Over the last decade and a half, we have seen a proliferation of small, boutique, and independent publishers that are nimble and, without legacy issues, can take advantage of the opportunities that have emerged from digital growth in the market. Traditional publishers could not develop all of the skills or products necessary to address the market as it evolved. As a result, the industry has contracted as some of the largest publishers have merged and consolidated to compete.

In particular, large- and mid-size publishers are buying smaller or lesser-known publishers that have competence in digital content development and distribution, and expertise in migrating new and existing content to the Internet. In this way, traditional publishers gain the following:

- Content that is either on the Web or is Web-ready.

- Technology and core competencies that they don't currently possess.

- Presence in an existing market that is already subscribing to or buying digital content.

- A fast track to new markets.

They also eliminate potential competition.

Often, by acquiring niche publishers, major publishers leave a vacuum in the market. If they have acquired too many companies too fast, they sometimes have difficulty optimizing all of their activities and neglect the new markets that they were trying to target. As a result, smaller, boutique publishers jump in to fill the gap. By focusing on this small niche market, they end up doing a better job of serving the market than the larger publisher could. However, large publishing houses can usually absorb minor missteps, so the appetite for acquisitions in new markets that build additional competencies continues to grow.

Adapting to Information Overload

The easy accessibility of digital content is due to the Internet. The Internet has not only changed the actual speed with which we exchange information and content, it has also altered our expectations of how fast information can be created and shared, as well as how much information we have access to. It has also changed how we regard static versus renewable content and the value we place on information.

If publishers are going to be successful in the digital age, they must learn to adapt to an environment where the amount of information is doubling almost daily; where updates are nearly instantaneous; where we are approaching universal access to almost any kind of information; and where business models are in a constant state of flux. Thus, publishers have to remain keenly focused on how they can add value, which may be different from how they accomplished that in the past. They not only need to know how to create and distribute quality content worldwide, but they may also have to leverage key relationships in order to acquire and aggregate relevant third-party content and attract and involve an international community. In short, publishers will have to be skillful at organizing, synthesizing, and connecting diverse forms of content that, at its most engaging, evolves from an intimate knowledge of the end user.

But beyond developments in technology that have changed the tools of publishing, digital content has enabled a cultural shift that has transformed what we publish and has redefined who and what a publisher is. For average consumers who use or create content, digital content and the Internet have brought about two significant events: the convergence of interactive media and the empowerment of the individual to act like a professional publisher. These are far-reaching phenomena that will continue to influence the way we consume information and are bound to have an impact on what we will experience in the future—even if we don't know exactly what form the products or devices will take.

The Convergence of Media

It is no longer the case that publishers can work in only one medium and expect to reach all of their markets effectively. We consume information in diverse ways—depending on where we are, the time of day, the kind of technology available, and our preferences. Still, depending on the information or its intended audience, sometimes one medium is more appropriate than another.

We should not force the simultaneous use of more than one media when it will not improve the communication or enhance the user experience.

However, for an increasing amount of information that we consume, it is common to have several media available to us at once. For a typical news item on a website, for example, we might read a few columns of text, view photographs with captions, watch a narrated video, listen to a podcast, click on an interactive graphic, respond to a real-time poll, follow a link to another website with related content, explore a map, and perhaps send an instant message to the editor or author of the item. For common sources of information on the Internet, on our mobile device, or via cable or satellite TV, media have converged to provide experiences that we take for granted today.

Individual Empowerment

Enabled by a variety of digital media, easy-to-use software, and the Internet, individuals can appear indistinguishable from publishers. Custom publishing programs combined with custom printing—POD—allow individuals to create, print, market, and distribute content and even books with very little development cost and no investment in inventory. Through custom publishing, along with websites and online fulfillment houses as a distribution vehicle, individuals are able to do everything that major publishers can do. Many individuals—independently filling gaps in the market not being addressed by larger publishers and accessible through the Web—can have a visible impact on buying behavior and the economics of publishing.

While individuals armed with the right software can behave like publishers, publishers, on the other hand, are beginning to follow suit and are behaving more like individuals. The result is that many titles that publishers could not afford to publish because of their narrow appeal or low demand can now be developed. If major publishers do not have to make an up-front investment in a minimum print-run in order to publish economically, they can address niche markets in the same way that boutique publishers do; they can create and publish more books, and serve a broader market. In this model, publishers do not have to be entirely focused on producing best-sellers. If they can increase the number of titles that they offer by taking advantage of custom publishing and POD technology, and thereby serve a wider market, they can afford to sell fewer units of more titles. They can also continue to keep published books with a low demand available if they don't have to maintain a large stock of each title or manage inventory levels. "Out of print" can be a thing of the past.

Fifteen years ago in an interview with Ubiquity, an online IT magazine, Richard Saul Wurman discussed a book about the U.S. that he had self-published long before it was fashionable to do so. His comments on his path in creating that book are prophetic:

> *Well, this book could only be done because of information technology. I have to laugh at the many people who think printing and publishing are not high-tech. In fact, a book is a very high-tech product, and only by using a lot of technology was I able to do this book with the lavish kind of color and the collaboration of people all over the United States, and do it in just three months' time. Five years ago, the book couldn't have been done. So technology plays a large part in what people are able to do, what I'm able to do. And I try to work at the edge of what I'm able to do. This is a book of understanding and explanation.*

Then he makes a prediction about the future:

> *The next 10 to 15 years will be the age of "also." I mean, we're going to have print; we're going to have books. We're going to have better magazines and more magazines; better newspapers and different newspapers. We're going to have TV and we're going to have satellite. We're going to have computers. We are going to have computers that are TV. We're going to have DVD. We're going to have lots of things. Will there be some falling outs? You bet. We don't have eight-track sound anymore, and in the future tapes will eventually die out because everybody will have CDs, and then CDs will die out because there'll just be one thing, which will be DVD for both images and sound. But for the next 10 to 15 years we'll also have a bunch of things going on, all at the same time. And that's fine. There isn't a best answer for things anymore. There's not a best way to have transportation. There's not a best way of communicating. There's not a best way for anything. There are just good ways.*

In the end, technology is only a tool, and it would be of no value if we didn't want to build something with it. I think that what's behind it all—the flow of information, the development of a talented, worldwide workforce, the acquisitions, the sharing of content in all media—is the desire to build a more transparent international community, one without cultural barriers, without censorship, and without traditional boundaries.

Appendix A:
International Book Fairs

Book Fairs by World Region

(Dates sometimes change from year to year)

AFRICA

Nigeria International Book Fair	May
Zimbabwe International Book Fair	July/August
South African Book Fair (SABF)	July/August

ASIA PACIFIC

New Delhi World Book Fair	February
Bangkok International Book Fair	March/April
Asia International Book Fair	April
Tokyo International Book Fair	July
Seoul International Book Fair	June
Shanghai International Children's Book Exhibition	November
Beijing International Book Fair	August/September

EUROPE

Salon du Livre: Paris Book Fair	March

Bologna Children's Book Fair	March/April
MIPTV (Marché International des Programmes de Television)	April
Bookworld Prague	May
Budapest International Book Festival	May
Warsaw International Book Fair	May
Göteborg International Book Fair	September
Frankfurt Book Fair	October
Moscow International Book Fair	November
Pisa Book Festival	November
Istanbul International Book Fair	November

CENTRAL/SOUTH AMERICA

Bienal do Livro de São Paulo	August
Feria Internacional del Libro de Guadalajara	November /December

MIDDLE EAST

Cairo International Book Fair	January/February
Tehran International Book Fair	May
Jerusalem International Book Fair	February
Dubai International Book Fair	May

NORTH AMERICA

BookExpo America	May

BookExpo Canada   June

Digital Book World   March

ISTE   June/July

UNITED KINGDOM

London Book Fair   April

Bett   January

Appendix B:
A URL A–Z for Information on Publishing and Licensing

The websites listed below are either mentioned in this book or relate to the chapter topics. All of these sites have useful information on educational and international publishing, licensing, digital publishing, or the Internet. The brief descriptions provided summarize their primary activity and in most cases have been taken or adapted from the websites themselves.

123RF www.123rf.com

123RF is a royalty-free digital media library that offers a wide variety of budget-friendly commercial and editorial images, video footage, audio clips, logo designs, and illustrations. Founded in 2005, it is a leading global provider of images.

The International Association for the Protection of Intellectual Property (AIPPI) www.aippi.org

The AIPPI (Association Internationale pour la Protection de la Propriété Intellectuelle) is a Swiss-based, worldwide, non-governmental organization for the research and advancement of intellectual property whose members are developers, academics, and owners of intellectual property.

The Association of American Publishers www.publishers.org

The AAP is the largest organization of American publishers and deals with matters of general interest to its members. It also acts as an advocate for the publishing industry. Its main concerns include intellectual property rights, emerging technology, censorship, international publishing rights, funding for education and libraries, as well as other issues of interest to the publishing community.

The Association of Educational Publishers www.edpress.org

AEP, formerly Edpress and now part of the AAP (AAP K-12 Learning Group), provides information on hundreds of educational publishers, especially those that specialize in supplemental educational resources, regardless of the medium. The association actively lobbies on behalf of its members. The AAP K-12 Learning Group hosts a variety of conferences during the year. Its product awards ceremony at its annual meeting in the summer has been referred to as the Academy Awards of educational publishing.

Berkery, Noyes & Co. www.berkerynoyes.com

Berkery, Noyes & Co. is an investment firm that specializes in the publishing sector and has strong relationships in the intellectual property community. It has brokered many mergers and acquisitions between large and small publishing companies.

Bett www.bettshow.com

Ranked as the leading learning technology event, with a worldwide audience of educators and publishers, Bett highlights the best in educational technology on a global scale every spring in London.

The Bologna Children's Book Fair www.bookfair.bolognafiere.it

This is the world's leading children's publishing and multimedia products event. Each spring, publishers, authors and illustrators, literary agents, packagers, distributors, printers, booksellers and librarians come to Bologna to buy and sell intellectual property, establish new contacts, strengthen professional relationships, discover new business opportunities, and get a closer look at the latest trends in children's books and new media products.

The Bookseller www.thebookseller.com

Very much like *Publishers Weekly*, this is a primary source of reliable news events in the book and publishing industry in the U.K.

Bowker www.bowker.com

The world's leading source for book, serial, and publishing data. The Bowker website contains comprehensive databases, including booksinprint.com, ulrichsweb.com, and globalbooksinprint.com. Bowker has more than 150 resources in all media and provides invaluable information for bookstores, libraries, wholesalers, distributors, and publishers. It also provides publishers with International Standard Book Numbers (ISBNs).

Digital Book World http://digitalbookworldconference.com/

Held in New York in the spring, DBW is the preeminent conference on digital publishing and is attended by the media, publishing, and technology professionals.

Digital Content Next http://digitalcontentnext.org

Digital Content Next is a weekly email that provides insights into the business of digital content and selected news and research on the digital media industry.

The Frankfurt Book Fair www.frankfurt-book-fair.com

Held every October at the sprawling Frankfurt *Messe*, the Frankfurt Book Fair is the largest and most important publishing event of the year. As the world's largest marketplace for trading in publishing rights and licenses, it is the one annual event that every decision maker in the publishing business must attend. Attendees include authors, publishers, booksellers, librarians, art dealers, illustrators, agents, journalists, information brokers, and the general public.

The Idea Logical Company www.idealog.com

Mike Shatzkin is the founder and CEO of the Idea Logical Company and is a widely acknowledged thought leader about digital change in the book publishing industry. He publishes the Shatzkin File, which is a digital publishing newsletter. He is also one of the organizers of Digital Book World.

The International Digital Publishing Forum www.idpf.org

This is the international trade and standards organization for the digital publishing industry. Its members consist of academic, trade, and professional publishers, hardware and software companies, digital content retailers, libraries, and educational institutions. Its primary goals are to build and maintain industry standards and to provide members with up-to-date information on digital publishing.

ISTE www.iste.org

The International Society of Technology and Learning (ISTE) is a not-for-profit organization dedicated to supporting the use of information technology to aid in learning.

The Licensing Executives' Society www.lesi.org

The Licensing Executives' Society (LES or LESI) is an international organization of dozens of national and regional organizations whose goals are to learn about and promote the licensing, managing, and marketing of intellectual properties rights and technology transfer.

The Library of Congress www.loc.gov

The Library of Congress (LOC) is a rich source of archival information, including documents, photos, videos, and speeches. It also provides a variety of services to publishers, including International Standard Serial Numbers (ISSNs), Cataloging in Publication (CIP) data, and copyright registration.

Literary Market Place www.literarymarketplace.com

Literary Market Place (LMP) is the most comprehensive directory of American and Canadian book publishing. It is a reliable and mostly up-to-date resource of industry data for publishing professionals, authors, agents, industry watchers, or those seeking to gain entry into the world of publishing. The International Literary Market Place (ILMP) provides similar publishing data for more than 180 countries around the world.

The London Book Fair www.londonbookfair.co.uk

This site provides information about the events surrounding the London Book Fair, which is the premier spring international book fair. It's a popular destination for publishers, distributors, packagers, librarians, and booksellers from all over the world. It's a compact three-day event that is always well attended.

National Aeronautics and Space Administration www.nasa.gov

The NASA website is a unique resource for images related to space and space exploration. Its images generally can be used free of charge. The website indicates that NASA imagery, video, and audio material can be used for educational or informational purposes, including photo collections, textbooks, public exhibits, and Internet webpages.

The Online Dictionary for Library and Information Science http://abc-clio.com/ODLIS

The Online Dictionary for Library and Information Science (ODLIS) is an A–Z dictionary of approximately 4,200 digital publishing terms. It provides useful, simple definitions to basic terminology used in the publishing industry and on the Internet. The entries define terms adequately, but sometimes contain dubious references. For this reason, it should be used with caution and entries should be double-checked against other sources.

The Podcast Directory www.podcast.com

More than just a directory, this is actually a database of playable podcasts. You can search by topic and keyword or browse the site alphabetically. You can upload podcasts, which then become part of the database.

The Publishers Association www.publishers.org.uk

The Publishers Association is the leading trade organization serving book, journal, and electronic publishers in the U.K. Like the AAP in the U.S., it brings publishers together to discuss the main issues facing the industry and to define policies that will advance the industry.

Publishers Lunch www.publisherslunch.com

Publishers Lunch is a free daily newsletter, available on the Web, that is now shared with more than 30,000 publishing professionals. Each report contains stories from the Web and print press of interest to the professional trade book community, along with original reporting and editorials. It is a reliable source for the latest information on publishing deals and royalties. It also offers a paid publication and service, called *Publishers Marketplace*, which provides expanded coverage on the same general topics that are sent out daily.

Publishers Marketplace www.publishersmarketplace.com

This newsletter is reputed to be the biggest marketplace for publishing professionals to find information and unique databases for conducting business electronically. It is a service of *Publishers Lunch*.

Publishers Weekly http://publishersweekly.reviewsnews.com

Available in print and online, *Publishers Weekly* (PW) is a good source of news on international book publishing and book-selling. It is part of the Reed Elsevier Group.

Reed Exhibitions www.reedexpo.com

Also part of the Reed Elsevier Group, Reed Exhibitions claims to be the world's leading organizer of trade and consumer events. It is the organizers of BookExpo America and the London Book Fair, among other publishing exhibitions.

SME Insider www.smeinsider.com

This is the premier news and analysis portal focusing on all the things that U.K. small business owners and managers should know in order to run their businesses.

The Software & Information Industry Association www.siia.net

The Software & Information Industry Association (SIIA) is the principal trade association for the software and digital content industry. It provides global services in government relations, business development, corporate education, and intellectual property protection to the leading companies in the digital age. It hosts a variety of technology events throughout the year, including an annual meeting and awards ceremony.

The Smithsonian www.si.edu

If you go to the "Archive" section of the Smithsonian site under the "Research Smithsonian" heading, you will find a rich source of content, some of which is in the public domain. The site claims that its archives hold an estimated 50,000 cubic feet of paper documents, seven million still photographs, and thousands of films and audio recordings.

The United Nations Cartographic Section www.un.org

Although this is a poorly organized and incomplete site, with dated material, it can be useful for identifying regions of the world that might have issues surrounding their official names and contested territories. It has links to other sites that have more detailed information.

Veronis Suhler Stevenson www.veronissuhler.com

Veronis Suhler Stevenson (VSS) is a private equity and mezzanine capital investment firm serving the media, communications, and information industries in North America and Europe. It also provides in-depth studies on industry trends.

Webopedia www.webopedia.com

This is an online dictionary of Internet technology and digital publishing terminology. It provides clear and concise definitions, a pronunciation guide, and a reference section of computer facts.

Wonder Book www.wonderbk.com

A bookseller since 1980, online since 1997, it sells used books, overstocks, and collectibles. No e-books. It claims to have more than four million books in its "Internet" warehouse and was featured in the press as "a model for the changing book industry."

The World Intellectual Property Organization www.wipo.org

The World Intellectual Property Organization (WIPO) is a global organization whose mission is the advancement and protection of intellectual property rights, trademarks, inventions, and copyrights.

Appendix C:
Sample Licensing Agreement

LICENSING AND PURCHASE AGREEMENT

Made this ___ day of _____, 20__

BETWEEN   _____

         For themselves, their assigns and successors-in-business

         (Hereinafter called "the Licensor") of the one part

AND   _____

For themselves, their assigns and successors-in-business (hereinafter called "the Licensee") of the other part regarding the illustrated Work at present entitled:

         "_____"

         (Hereinafter called "the Work")

WHEREBY the Licensor is the exclusive owner of all right, title and interest in and to the Work, and all prior editions and copyrights thereof;

WHEREBY the Licensor, plans to print a revision of the Work in accordance with the Revision Plan and to produce an e-book version of the Work in the PDF format;

WHEREBY the Licensee desires to acquire from the Licensor the right to publish and distribute the Work under the terms and conditions set forth in this Agreement and the attached appendices, which are incorporated by reference herein.

1) LICENSE. The Licensor, who guarantees to have full power and authority to make this Agreement, grants to the Licensee the exclusive LICENSE to publish, sell and sublicense third-party distributors, who must be approved in advance by the Licensor, the Work **in the English language throughout the world in all formats.**

2) **WARRANTY.** The Licensor warrants that the Work is an original work, that it contains nothing obscene or libellous and is in no way an infringement of existing copyright and that, upon revision, will comply in all material respects with the Revision Plan; that it has full power to make this Agreement and grant the Licensee the rights set forth herein and, in accordance with Clause 23 below, will indemnify the Licensee against any loss, injury or damage occasioned to the Licensee in consequence of any breach of these warranties.

3) **GRANT OF RIGHTS.** The Licensee shall publish, sell and sublicense third parties to sell the said Work as defined in Appendix A in the above-mentioned language throughout the world in print or electronic form through all channels. Electronic form includes all known and unknown digital formats, including CD-ROM, DVD-ROM, flash or thumb drive, e-books, databases, and electronic storage devices.

4) **ASSIGNMENT. SUBLICENSE.** This Agreement and the LICENSE granted hereunder may not be assigned or, except as set forth herein, sublicensed by either party without the prior written consent of the other party, such consent not to be unreasonably withheld. The Licensor hereby approves the sublicense by Licensee to _____ ("_____") of all rights to distribute the Work granted the Licensee hereunder.

5) **LICENSE TERM.** All rights granted under the terms of this Agreement shall automatically revert to the Licensor **5 (five) years from the signature of this Agreement,** without any further notice and without prejudice to any monies already paid or then due.

In addition, the rights granted the Licensee in this Agreement are subject to the proviso that if the Licensee places a reprint order of at least 3000 copies, the LICENSE period shall be extended by an additional three years from the date of the order, and by a further year for each additional 1000 copies up to a maximum of 5 additional years.

The LICENSE period shall automatically be extended by further periods of one year at a time, if the Licensee keeps the Work in print, unless terminated by either of the parties by written notice at least 3 (three) months before the date of termination.

The electronic rights granted in this Agreement shall remain in force as long as the print rights are retained as described herein.

6) **QUANTITY, PRICE & DELIVERY.** The Licensor shall produce and sell to the Licensee and the Licensee shall buy from the Licensor **5,000 (five thousand) complete copies** of the Work, _____, complete copies of which Publisher immediately will distribute to its sublicensee, _____, as indicated in Clause 4 above, at a price of **$00.00 (____ U.S. dollars) inclusive of royalty, CIF East Coast port** or such other place as the Licensee and Sublicensee shall designate in writing at any time and from time to time.

The copies of the Work shall be delivered **on or before** ___ ____, **20**__ to the East Coast port.

The copies shall be delivered on or before such date provided that the payments due under **Clause 7 below** have been made by the Licensee and that the material listed in Clause 12 below is received by _____ from the Licensee complete and in good condition by the date stipulated in Clause 12 below, as well as from all other parties participating in the same printing.

The Licensor shall make every effort to deliver the number of copies specified above, but delivery of up to **5% (five percent) over or under** the quantity specified shall constitute full delivery. The Licensee shall pay for the quantity of copies actually received. If the Licensor fails to deliver bound books in good condition **on or before** __ ____ **20**__, the final payment due **60 (sixty) days** after the delivery of full consignment shall not be made until **60 (sixty) days** after the actual delivery date; provided, however, the Licensor shall use best efforts to notify the Licensee of any changes to the final delivery date.

The Licensee and all approved sublicensees must complete the attached delivery information as requested in Appendix B.

For all sales of the e-book, or electronic version of the Work, the Licensee will pay the Licensor 30% of net receipts, which are defined as net revenue less cancellations or refunds.

7) **TERMS OF PAYMENT**.

The Licensee shall pay the Licensor the following guaranteed non-refundable sum for the quantity of sets specified in **Clause 6 above: $000,000 (_____ dollars), payable as follows:**

   $00,000 (____ dollars), payable within three (3) working days of signature of this agreement by both parties;

   $00,000 (_____ dollars), payable on completion of all editorial work and revisions (the "Editorial Changes") and approval by the Licensee of the Editorial Changes within the timeframe set forth in Clause 13 below;

   $00,000 (____dollars), payable on receipt of Printer Proofs (as defined below), including covers, by the Licensee and approval by the Licensee of the Printer Proofs within the timeframe set forth in Clause 13 below;

   $00,000 (____dollars), payable upon receipt of notice by the Licensee of the start of printing;

   $000,000 (_____ dollars), payable on delivery of finished sets to U.S. East Coast port or such other place as the Licensee and Licensor shall designate in writing at any time and from time to time or on __ ____ 20__, whichever is the sooner.

   The balance, taking into account any adjustment for the actual number of sets delivered, payable 60 days after delivery of finished sets to U.S. East Coast port.

8) **PRICE GUARANTEE.CONDITIONS.** The price for each copy specified in **Clause 6 above** is calculated using prices quoted to the Licensor by the suppliers on the basis of the following time limits:

Materials costs guaranteed until ___ ____20__

Labour and machining costs guaranteed until ___ ____20__ .

The final purchase price shall only be increased from the price specified in **Clause 6 above** if Licensor's suppliers have increased their prices by at least 5% (five percent) from __ _____ 20__.

9) **PAYMENTS**. All payments due under the terms of this Agreement shall be made by check in U.S. dollars to the Licensor's bank account as specified below or as subsequently notified in writing, without provision for returns and without any deduction in respect of taxation, exchange, commissions or otherwise, with the sole exception of tax withheld under bilateral fiscal agreements between the Licensor's and the Licensee's governments.

Bank:

Account number:

Sort Code:

10) **FULL TITLE**. The Licensor shall reserve full title in all volumes and materials supplied to the Licensee under the terms of this Agreement until all monies due from the Licensee for such volumes have been received. All materials supplied by the Licensor are solely for the production of the Work for Licensee; they cannot be used by sublicensees or others without the prior written consent of the Licensor, which shall not unreasonably be withheld.

11) **RIGHTS RESERVED**. The copyright in the Work shall remain vested in the Licensor throughout the term of this Agreement and all rights other than those specifically granted herein are retained and reserved by the Licensor.

12) **COPYRIGHT NOTICES**. The Work shall include on the verso of the title page the following copyright notice:

> ©20___, _____

> Devised and produced by _____

Together with the Licensee's or an approved sublicensee's own copyright notice and other relevant acknowledgments.

Due prominence shall be given on the cover and jacket and in the preliminary pages of the Work to the name of the editor(s).

13) DEVELOPMENT OF THE WORK; LICENSEE STANDARDS.

(a) **REPORTING AND APPROVAL PROCEDURES**. Periodically, as requested by Licensee, the Licensor shall submit to the Licensee a written report providing details of the Licensor's progress respecting the revision of the Work in accordance with the Revision Plan. Periodically, unless otherwise agreed in writing, the Licensor shall send to the Licensee printouts or electronic files of the text changes for approval. In the event that the Licensee rejects any Editorial Changes submitted to it by the Licensor, the Licensor shall modify such changes to the extent necessary to obtain the Licensee's approval. The Licensee recognizes that prompt approval of the Editorial Changes is critical to an efficient editorial process and agrees that its goal will be to respond within five (5) days after confirmed receipt. If the Licensee does not respond within seven (7) days after confirmed receipt, the Licensor may assume Licensee's approval of the Editorial Changes in question. Any revision required of the Licensor by the Licensee shall be completed by _____at its own expense. The Licensor agrees that no new or additional material shall be included in the Work without the prior written consent of the Licensee, which consent shall be provided or withheld at the Licensee's sole discretion. As soon as possible, the Licensor shall provide the Licensee with final color proofs of those parts of the Work that require new color images (the "**Printer Proofs**"). The Licensee shall have five (5) days after confirmed receipt to approve the Printer Proofs. If the Licensee does not respond within seven (7) days after confirmed receipt, the Licensor may assume the Licensee's approval of the Printer Proofs. In the event that the final Work differs materially from the Revision Plan, Editorial Changes or Printer Proofs provided by the Licensor to the Licensee and approved, either proactively or due to lapse of time, by the Licensee hereunder, the Licensee, in its sole discretion, can demand that the Licensor, at its own expense, modify the Work to the extent necessary to conform from the Revision Plan, Editorial Changes or Printer Proofs, as the case may be.

(b) **LICENSEE STANDARDS**.

(i) The Licensor recognizes that Licensee's reputation as an international publisher is based on the maintenance of high standards in editorial work, manufacturing and in the promotion, distribution and sale of its products (the "**Licensee Standards**"). The Licensor agrees that similar standards must be maintained in respect to its own production and publication of the Work.

(ii) The parties agree that the Licensee Standards for editorial material require that the Work be accurate in content, fair and unbiased, up to date and written consistent with the editorial quality of the Licensee's publications. Whether or not the edited material submitted by the Licensor to the Licensee meets the Licensee Standards shall be a matter for the Licensee to determine. The Licensor agrees, at its own expense, to revise any material so as to bring it up to Licensee Standards. The Licensee agrees that the prior publication of the Work meets the Licensee Standards.

(iii) The parties agree that Licensee Standards for manufacturing require that the Work be manufactured, printed and bound with good quality, sturdy materials comparable to premium materials currently published in the Territory. The Licensee acknowledges that the Licensor is well regarded as a quality developer and manufacturer of products similar to those contemplated hereby and agrees that the manufacturing standards generally used by the Licensor as of the date of this Agreement satisfy the Licensee Standards for manufacturing.

14) **DELIVERY BY LICENSEE**

(a) **IMPRINT, LOGO, BARCODE, and ISBN**. The Licensee shall supply the Licensor with a CD of its or its approved sublicensees' imprint details, barcode, ISBN and logo by ____ _____ 20__. Such material shall be for printing in black, to fit the Licensor's layout.

(b) **COVER.** The Licensor shall pass to the Licensee sample dummies for preparation of covers. The Licensee shall supply the Licensor with electronic files plus Printer Proofs of its cover design, or the cover design of any approved sublicensees, by ____ __ 20__.

It is the responsibility of the Licensee to ensure that said electronic files are full and complete and can be passed directly to the Licensor's printer.

15) **ADVANCE COPIES**. The Licensor shall supply the Licensee with **5 (five)** advance copies of the Licensee's and each approved sublicensee's editions of the Work prior to the date of delivery of the full consignment of books, two copies from each edition shall be free of charge and inclusive of freight.

Any additional advance copies and their delivery shall be paid for by the Licensee.

16) **COMPLIMENTARY COPIES**. The Licensor shall retain from the quantity to be delivered **10 (ten)** sets of the Work, these copies shall be paid for by the Licensee. The Licensor shall be permitted to purchase further copies of the Work from the Licensee at manufacturing cost plus cost of delivery.

17) **PUBLICATION**. The Licensee shall publish the Work **within 3 (three) months of delivery**. If the Licensee fails to do so, all rights herein granted shall automatically and without further notice revert to the Licensor and the advance payments provided for in **Clause 6 above** shall be forfeited without prejudice to any claim which the Licensor may have for damages, compensation or otherwise.

The Licensee shall give notice to the Licensor of the dates of first publication, the standard retail prices and all alterations to those published prices within two weeks of their happening.

18) **REPRINTS AND REVISIONS**. The Licensee shall notify the Licensor in good time when reprints are required, and subject to the terms of this contract the Licensee shall have the right to reprint the Work. The parties shall negotiate in good faith the terms including the price for such reprints subject to reasonable minimum quantities being mutually agreed.

19) **REMAINDERS**. The Licensee may not remainder the Work within two years of publication without the written consent of the Licensor. Before remaindering, all copies shall first be offered to the Licensor at the Licensee's manufacturing cost. The Licensor shall have 10 (ten) working days from receipt of the Licensee's notification of intent to remainder, in which to confirm that the Licensor shall purchase part or all of the remaining stock of the Work.

On remaindering the Work, all rights granted under the terms of this Agreement shall automatically revert to the Licensor without prejudice to any monies due to the Licensor from the Licensee.

For the purposes of this Agreement the term "Remainder" shall mean the reduction of 75% (seventy-five percent) or more of the price at which the Licensee's edition was first offered for sale.

If the Licensee wishes to remainder only a portion of its stock, he shall obtain the Licensor's prior written permission, which shall not be unreasonably withheld. Rights shall then automatically revert when the balance of the stock not remaindered is sold.

20) **REVERSION OF RIGHTS.** If the Licensee does not keep an edition of the Work in print and allows it to remain out of print for more than **6 (six)** months without coming to an agreement with the Licensor regarding a reprint, all rights in the Work herein granted shall immediately revert to the Licensor without any further notice and without prejudice to any monies already paid or then due.

For the purposes of this Agreement, out of print is defined as having less than 100 (one hundred) saleable sets in stock of the Licensee's editions of the Work.

The Licensee shall use its best efforts to inform _____in writing as soon as the Work goes out of stock, unless it has already placed an order for the immediate reprint of the Work.

21) **ILLUSTRATION RIGHTS.** The Licensor hereby notifies the Licensee that permission has been granted by the copyright holders to reproduce all illustrations included in the Work (including photographs, artwork, drawings, diagrams and maps) for publication in the above-mentioned territories, in print and in e-book format, but *only* in the form of the complete page layout supplied to the Licensee on _____. This includes permission to reproduce single or double page layouts from the Work for use in catalogues, promotional brochures, as part of a review in a trade or specialist magazine, or as part of a press campaign.

Permission has *not* been granted for the use of illustrations other than in the form of the complete single or double page layout. On request from the Licensee regarding specific illustrations, the Licensor shall, where possible, supply the name of the rights holder(s).

Where rights are controlled by the Licensor, specific illustrations may be reproduced by the Licensee for jacket, publicity or other purposes *only* after having obtained the prior written consent of the Licensor, and on terms to be mutually agreed in writing. Reproduction of artwork shall, when possible, be permitted by the Licensor free of charge.

For illustration rights that are *not* controlled by the Licensor, permission and payment for the use of such specific illustrations shall be negotiated directly between the Licensee and the rights holder(s).

In the event of unauthorized use of illustrations of any kind by the Licensee, the Licensor shall not be liable for any action by the rights holder of such illustrations arising from any such unauthorized use.

"Unauthorized use" means use of illustrations of any kind on promotional literature, advertising or on jackets except in the form of the complete page layout supplied by the Licensor without the written consent of the rights holder and payment of any fees due. "Action by the rights holder" means legal action, increased fees or any other kind of punitive action arising from use of illustrations without the prior written consent of the rights holder and payment of any fees due.

22) **RIGHT OF FIRST REFUSAL.** The Licensor hereby grants Licensee a right of first refusal to the exclusive license to publish, distribute and sell any single-volume work in print or e-book form that is comprised of the entire first set of the Work. The licensor agrees to give Licensee written notice of the terms upon which it is prepared to license such rights to a third party, and Licensee shall have forty-five (45) days to deliver its notice of acceptance of such terms. If Licensee fails to accept the offered terms within such forty-five (45) days, the Licensor shall be free to enter into an agreement with a third party for the license of such rights, provided that the terms granted such third party shall be no more favorable than those offered to Licensee.

23) **MUTUAL INDEMNIFICATION.** Each party (the "**Indemnifying Party**") will defend, indemnify, and hold harmless the other party, and its officers, directors, agents, affiliates, and employees, and each of them (the "**Indemnified Party**"), from and against any and all losses injuries, claims, demands, liabilities, costs or expenses, including reasonable attorneys' fees and disbursements ("**Claims**") to the extent arising out of: (1) the dishonest, fraudulent, negligent, willful or criminal acts of the Indemnifying Party or the Indemnifying Party's employees, agents or representatives acting alone or in collusion with others; and (2) any breach by the Indemnifying Party of any of its representations, warranties, covenants or other obligations under this Agreement. In addition, the Licensor hereby agrees to indemnify Licensee from and against any and all Claims to the extent arising out of any allegation that the Work infringes the intellectual property rights of any third party. The Indemnified Party agrees that it will (i) provide prompt written notice to the Indemnifying Party of any Claim with respect to which it seeks indemnification and (ii) permit the Indemnifying Party to assume the defense of such Claim with counsel reasonably acceptable to the Indemnified party. If such defense is assumed, the Indemnifying Party will not be subject

to any liability for settlement made by the Indemnified Party without the Indemnifying Party's consent (but such consent will not be unreasonably withheld). If the Indemnifying Party elects not to assume the defense of a Claim, the Indemnifying Party will nonetheless be obligated to pay the fees and expenses of the Indemnified Party's counsel. The Indemnified Party reserves the right, at its own expense, to assume the exclusive defense and control of any matter otherwise subject to indemnification by the Indemnifying Party hereunder, and in such event, the Indemnifying Party shall have no further obligation to provide indemnification for such matter hereunder.

24) **CONFIDENTIALITY**. The parties acknowledge that during the term of this Agreement, either of them may receive from the other "Confidential Information" of the other. As used herein "Confidential Information" means information and know-how related directly or indirectly to the disclosing party, its business, or its products that is conspicuously marked "CONFIDENTIAL," "PROPRIETARY," or with other words of similar import, or that the receiving party knows or reasonably should know is not publicly available. The receiving party shall not use or disclose Confidential Information except in connection with, and as contemplated by, this Agreement. The receiving party shall use at least the same degree of care to avoid disclosure or unauthorized use of Confidential Information as it employs with respect to its own most confidential and proprietary information, but at all times shall use at least reasonable care. The receiving party shall not have any obligation of confidentiality with respect to any information that (a) is already known to the receiving party at the time the information is received from the disclosing party, as proven by prior documents or records of the receiving party; (b) is or becomes publicly known through no wrongful act of the receiving party; or (c) is rightfully received by the receiving party from a third party without restriction. Notwithstanding the foregoing, each party is hereby authorized to deliver a copy of any such information (a) to any person pursuant to a subpoena issued by any court or administrative agency, (b) to its accountants, attorneys or other agents on a confidential basis and (c) otherwise as required by applicable law, rule, regulation or legal process including, without limitation, the U.S. Securities Act of 1933, as amended, and the rules and regulations promulgated thereunder, and the U.S. Securities Exchange Act of 1934, as amended, and the rules and regulations promulgated thereunder. The parties shall not make public the terms of this Agreement except by mutual consent.

25) **FORCE MAJEURE**. Anything herein contained to the contrary notwithstanding, neither party shall be liable or deemed to be in breach to the other by reason of any act, delay or omission, caused by epidemic, fire, action of

the elements, strikes, lockouts, labor disputes, governmental law, regulations, ordinances or order of a court of competent jurisdiction or executive decree or order, act of God, or of a public enemy, war, riot, civil commotion, earthquake, flood, accident, explosion, casualty, embargo delay of a common carrier, inability to obtain labor, material, facilities, transportation, power or any other cause beyond the reasonable control of either party hereto, or for any act, delay or omission not due to the negligence or default of either party hereto; provided, however, that if any such cause precludes performance, in whole or in part, by either party for a period of ninety (90) consecutive days, the other party shall have the right to terminate this Agreement by providing written notice to the other party.

26) **FAILURE TO COMPLY.** Should the Licensee at any time himself, or anyone acting on its behalf, fail to submit or comply with the terms of this Agreement in any substantial way, or if the Licensee shall go into liquidation (other than voluntary liquidation for the purpose of reconstruction only) then this Agreement shall thereupon automatically terminate and all rights herein granted shall immediately revert to the Licensor without prejudice to any claims the Licensor may have for damages or otherwise.

27) **LATE PAYMENTS.** The Licensor shall notify the Licensee in writing of any overdue payments. The Licensor reserves the right to charge 1% (one percent) interest for each month or any part thereof on any overdue payments, without prejudice to any other measures the Licensor may employ to recover any and all monies due.

28) **INFRINGEMENT.** Subject to Clause 23, if at any time during the term of this Agreement any infringement or threatened infringement of copyright affecting the Work shall come to the notice of either party, thereupon such party shall promptly give notice in writing thereof to the other and the parties shall thereupon consult as to the course of action to be followed and each shall render reasonable assistance to the other.

Should notice be served by either party on the other for infringement of any Clause in this Agreement, such notice shall be sent both by fax and by express registered post to the address shown above or subsequently notified and shall be deemed to have been received within five working days from posting.

29) **LIQUIDATION.** Should the Licensor go into liquidation other than voluntary liquidation for the purposes of amalgamation only, then the Licensee shall have a continuing right to sell the Work for the duration of the Term granted

herein. If the Work shall not already have been completed and delivered to the Licensee by the date of any such involuntary liquidation, and if there is no prospect that the Work can subsequently be completed and delivered, then the Licensee shall have the right to offset against sums otherwise payable by it to the Licensor an amount equal to but not greater than the value of any advances paid by the Licensee to the Licensor as a contribution to the development cost of the Work.

30) **GOVERNING LAW**. This Agreement shall be deemed to have been made in _____ and any controversy which shall arise out of or relating to the interpretation or execution of this Agreement shall be settled according to the statutes of _____.

Any difference or dispute which may arise between the parties hereto as to the construction, meaning, operation or effect of this Agreement or any Clause or provision thereof or as to the rights, duties or liabilities of the parties hereunder or otherwise in connection with this Agreement shall be referred to a single arbitrator to be agreed between the parties hereto, or, failing agreement, to be appointed by the _____ and in accordance with and subject to the Arbitration Act, 1950 or any statutory modification or re-enactment for the time being in force. The Arbitration shall be held in _____.

31) **HEADINGS**. The Clause headings in this Agreement are solely for ease of reference and shall not affect the interpretation of this Agreement.

32) **VALIDITY**. This Agreement shall be rendered invalid and the Licensor shall be at liberty to license the rights herein granted to a third party if countersigned copies of this Agreement are not received by the Licensor within one month of the date of this Agreement.

For and on behalf of   For and on behalf of

Licensor: **Licensee**:

_____   _____

Bibliography

These are books that I have found useful in helping me understand the important milestones in digital publishing, Web development, Web marketing, and adapting to change in the business environment.

Choate, Pat. *Hot Property: The Stealing of Ideas in an Age of Globalization*. New York: Alfred A. Knopf, 2005.

Christensen, Clayton M., Michael B. Horn, and Curtis W. Johnson. *Disrupting Class: How Disruptive Innovation Will Change the Way the World Learns*. New York: McGraw-Hill, 2008.

Davis, Stan and Christopher Meyer. *Blur: The Speed of Change in the Connected Economy*. New York: Warner Books, 1998.

Goldratt, Eliyahu M. *It's Not Luck*. Great Barrington, MA: The North River Press, 1994.

Hagel, John III. *Out of the Box: Strategies for Achieving Profits Today and Growth Tomorrow through Web Services*. Boston: Harvard Business School Press, 2002.

Hagel, John III, and Arthur G Armstrong. *Net Gain: Expanding Markets through Virtual Communities*. Boston: Harvard Business School Press, 1997.

Hammond, Ray. *Digital Business: Surviving and Thriving in an On-Line World*. London: Hodder & Stoughton, 1996.

Hyman, Sidney. *The Lives of William Benton*. Chicago: University of Chicago Press, 1969.

McQuivey, James. *Digital Disruption: Unleashing the Next Wave of Innovation*. Seattle: Amazon Publishing, 2013.

Modahl, Mary. *Now or Never: How Companies Must Change Today to Win the Battle for Internet Consumers*. New York: HarperCollins, 2000.

Moore, Geoffrey A. *Dealing with Darwin: How Great Companies Innovate at Every Phase of their Evolution*. New York: Portfolio, 2005.

Shapiro, Carl, and Hal R. Varian. *Information Rules: A Strategic Guide to the Network Economy*. Boston: Harvard Business School Press, 1999.

Shepard, Stephen. *Deadlines and Disruption: My Turbulent Path from Print to Digital*. New York: McGraw-Hill, 2012.

Shirky, Clay. *Cognitive Surplus: Creativity and Generosity in a Connected Age*. New York: Penguin, 2010.

Stross, Randall E. *The Microsoft Way: The Real Story of How the Company Outsmarts its Competition*. Boston: Addison-Wesley, 1996.

Thompson, John B. *Books in the Digital Age: The Transformation of Academic and Higher Education Publishing in Britain and the United States*. London: Polity, 2005.

Thompson, John B. *Merchants of Culture: The Publishing Business in the Twenty-First Century*. New York: Plume, 2012.

Index

Note: Italicized page numbers indicate a figure on the corresponding page.

AbeBooks 15–16
Abreu, Julio 39–40
adaptation of existing product 63
Adobe InDesign 77
Advanced Book Exchange 15
advances against royalties 132–4, 136
agents *see* literary agents
Alibaba 16
Amazon 11–15, 15–16, 158, 173
A+ Media 39–40, 50–1
American Medical Association (AMA) 92
Anderson, Chris 13
animals in photos/illustrations 69–70
Apple Computer (Apple) 10–11, 17, 86
asset base and licensing content 83–4
asset management system 49–50
Association of American Publishers (AAP) 111

backlist titles 11, 12
Barnes & Noble 11, 14–15, 17, 18
BBC News 164
Beijing International Book Fair (BIBF) 100
Berkery, Noyes & Co. 111, 155
"bias-free" map content 71
black-plate changes 73

Blackwell Reference Online 44
Bologna Children's Book Fair 99, 102
Book Expo America (BEA) 99, 102–3
book fairs 98–104, 111
Books-a-Million 15
The Book Standard 111, 135
Boos, Juergen 101
brands and reputations: brand alignment 89–90; branding kings 91–2; consumer perception of 85–6; extension of 92–6, *94*; licensing conflicts 120; overview 85–9, *87*, *88*
bricks-and-mortar bookstores 11–13
Britain on View website 55
Britannica Digital Learning (BDL) 85, 86, *88*
Britannica Multimedia Encyclopedia 29–30
Britannica Online 27
Britannica School website 79
Britannica Student Encyclopedia (BSE) 79
British Educational Training and Technology Show (BETT) 100
browser-based instructional programs 156
business plans 7, 54, 73, 121
business practice outsourcing (BPO) 175–6
buyer's remorse 113–15

cannibalization concerns 25, 80, 120
car advertisements 68
Carter, Jimmy 65
CD-ROM technology: decline of 105,
    155; *Encyclopaedia Britannica*
    24–30; global partnerships
    79–80; Merriam-Webster 152;
    for school networks 35
censorship 4, 180, 185
clear image rights 75–7
cloud-based services 77
Cobra Electronics 95
Cobra/Realtree two-way radios 95
code development 36
Coelho, Paulo 101
collective entities 64, 105
communication concerns 123
compression technology 27
Compton's database 25
Compton's Multimedia Encyclopedia 25–8
Computing Tabulating Recording
    Corp 86
consolidation in publishing 177
consumer behavior 1, 46
content development 78–81, 175, 177
content flexibility 72–5
continuing education (CE) credits 159
Curriculum Associates 57
customizing content 151
custom publishing goals 57–8

database publishing 36
deal-making: case study 137–9, 146–7;
    elements of 129–30; exclusivity
    vs. non-exclusivity 131–2;
    licensing terms 140–1; mutual
    non-disclosure agreement
    141–2; royalties and financial
    commitments 132–7; royalty-
    inclusive deals 139–40; sealing
    the deal 141–6; standard

agreement 142–6; term sheet
    142; territory considerations
    130–1
Digital Book World (DBW) 100, 103–4
digital content devices 150–1
digital natives 45
digital publishing (digitization):
    introduction 1; marketing
    models 45; music industry
    9–11; online book sellers 11;
    overview 9; year-on-year
    growth in 38
digital tools of change: advantages
    with 51–2; custom publishing
    goals 57–8; DRM (Digital
    Rights Management)
    technology 53–4; *Encyclopaedia
    Britannica* 54–6, *55*; foreign
    language translations 58;
    organizing digital content
    78–81; overview 49–50; in
    photography 52–3; quality and
    scope of the content 50–1
Disney brand 88–90
distribution channels in publishing:
    bricks-and-mortar 45;
    electronic rights 150;
    introduction 3, 7, 9–10, 12–13;
    licensing and 95, 110; limits to
    26; online 47; product changes
    and 30
door-to-door sales channel 23–4
Dorling Kindersley (DK) publishing
    73–4, 89
DRM (Digital Rights Management)
    technology 53–4

earning power of a product 140
EbizMBA 164
e-books: customer expectations
    36–7; market creation 16–19;

net receipts 132; rising sales of 37–8, 157–8; subscription models 158

educational publishers 35

Education Market Research (EMR) 38

Egremont Associates 104

electronic rights 150

Encarta encyclopedia 28–30

Encyclopaedia Britannica: CD-ROM technology 24–30; collection of historical/contemporary images 54–6, *55*; competition 28–30; door-to-door sales channel 23–4, 26; edit button on website 168–9; ending print-run 32–3, 47; *ImageQuest* database 61–2, 72; licensing content 80–4; overview 21–3; publishing partnerships 60–2; quality of 165–8, *166*, *167*; Wikipedia 164–5

Encyclopaedia Britannica brand 86–7, *87*

Encyclopaedia Britannica/Logos Edition 56

English as a foreign language (EFL) 104

equity of access 52

Evan-Moor 172–3

Evans, Bill 172

excess inventory concerns 41

exclusivity in deal-making 131–2

Facebook 98

Faithlife Corporation 56

file-sharing of digital music 10

foreign-exchange rates 146

foreign-language rights 103, 134

foreign-language translations 58

Frankfurt Book Fair (FBF) 14, 100–2, 105–6, 109

Frankfurt Catalogue 106

Freemium model 150

free online access model 150–5

FTE pricing 159–60

FTP (File Transfer Protocol) 77

geo-publishing 70–2

global market partnerships: animals in photos/illustrations 69–70; car advertisements 68; clear image rights 75–7; content development 78–81; content flexibility 72–5; development of 60–3; domestic market and 64–5; examples 65–7, *66*; geo-publishing 70–2; illustrated product development 67; intellectual property 64; large markets 63–4; licensing content 80–4; metric *vs.* imperial measurements 67–8; overview 6, 59–60; people in photos/illustrations 68–9; small markets 63; standardizing formats 77–8

Goff, Neal 104

Google translation 62

granting of rights clause 144

Great Big Canvas (GBC) website 55

The Grove Dictionary of Art 44

The Guardian 164

Gutmann, Peter 14

Harley-Davidson brand 95

Hello Kitty brand 90

Hocking, Amanda 171

Houston Independent School District 57

Howey, Hugh 117

HTML (Hypertext Markup Language) 53

Idea Logical Company 103
ImageQuest database 61–2, 72
incremental revenue 63
individual empowerment 179–80
information overload 178
information technology (IT)
    department 78
Ingram, John 19, 43
Ingram Content Group 19
intellectual property (IP): annual
    exchange of 99; attorney for
    142; benefits of exchange 64;
    buying and selling of 109–13,
    118; context in use of 78;
    format of 83–4; leverage of
    131; payment for rights 139;
    perpetual license fee 155;
    specifications for 143–4; target
    territory 121–2, 140; transfer of
    rights 123–4, 136, 141
intellectual property units (IPUs) 52,
    53
international book fairs 99–104
International Business Machines
    (IBM) 86
International Literary Marketplace
    (ILMP) 106
International Reading Association
    (IRA) 92
International Society for Technology
    in Education (ISTE) 103
iOS files 53
iPad 17, 151
ISBNs (International Standard Book
    Numbers) 36, 171
iTunes 10–11

James, E. L. 171
Japanese music market 10
John Wiley & Sons 92
JRL Group 95

Kindle 16–17
KPOs (knowledge process
    outsourcing) 175

learning management system (LMS)
    provider 60, 62
legal disputes 145
LEGO brand 89, 93
LexisNexis subscribers 22
Library of Congress 77
licensing strategies: buyer's remorse,
    prevention 113–15; case study
    115–16, 126–7; conflicts with
    120–2; content 80–4, 97; in deal-
    making 140–1; finding balance
    in 117–18; flexibility in 127–8;
    local market expectations
    112–13; minimum guarantees
    with royalties 132, 136–7;
    overview 109–12; partnering
    112, 119; process protocol 124–6;
    publisher identity and 118–20;
    risk mitigation 122–4; target
    dates for publication 134; term
    limits 135; typical project list
    125–6; *see also* deal-making
Lieb, Andy 95
Lightning Source 43
LightSail 157–8
LinkedIn 98
literary agents 97, 107–8
LMP *(Literary Marketplace)* 106
local market expectations 112–13
Logos Bible Software 56–7
London Book Fair (LBF) 99, 102
Long-tail titles 13–14
Lovell Johns 71
Lucas Films brand 88
Lucky Chemical Industrial
    Corp (Lucky Goldstar)
    (LG) 86

McCartney, Paul 66
McDonald's 93
make-ready costs 40–1
market changes 2
market-driven deals 129–30
marketing in publishing 7, 35, 45
market share 96, 120
mark-up language 7
media convergence 178–9
Merriam-Webster 12, 93, 150–5
Merriam-Webster's *Collegiate Dictionary* 151
Merriam-Webster's *Collegiate Thesaurus* 151
Merriam-Webster's Unabridged Dictionary 44
metric *vs.* imperial measurements 67–8
Michelin brand 90
Microsoft CD-ROM technology 28
Microsoft Official Academic Course book series 92
Middlebury Interactive Languages 92
minimum guarantees with royalties 132, 136–7
Ministry of Education of Brazil 60–1
MIPTV (Marché International des Programmes de Television) 104
Moore, Dan 7
Morse, John 12, 152–5
MPEG (Motion Picture Expert Group) 53
MP3 players 10
music industry 9–11
mutual non-disclosure agreement (NDA) 141–2

Napster 10
National Geographic website 55
national science writing competition 50–1

net receipts 132–3, 195
Newscom 53
New Standard Encyclopedia 28
New York Times 164
niche publishing markets 44, 90, 177
Nintendo Playing Card Company (Nintendo) 86
non-exclusivity in deal-making 131–2
non-refundable advance 116
"not-invented-here" syndrome 114

OED (*Oxford English Dictionary*) 44
Official Scrabble Players Dictionary (OSPD) 93, *94*
online encyclopedias 30–1; *see also* specific encyclopedias
online information services 36
open-source software 78
Options Publishing 57
organizing digital content 78–81
out-of-print 51, 179
outsourcing 175–6
Oxford English Dictionary (OED) website 151
Oyster 158

PDF (Portable Document Format) files 53, 127
Pearson Publishing 85
Penguin Random House 73
people in photos/illustrations 68–9
physical book as paradigm 39
platform support 36
Pokémon brand 90
print-on-demand (POD) technology 42–3, 50, 179
print-to-digital continuum: benefits of 46–7; challenges with 36–8; consumer options 44–5; digital marketing models 45; factors affecting trends

39–40; overview 35–6; POD
technology 42–3; print-runs
40–2; profit margin concerns
40–1; web-offset printing 41
process protocol 124–6
Publications International (PIL) 91–2
Publishers Lunch 135
Publisher's Weekly 111
publishing entrepreneurs 169–73

quality and scope of the content 50–1
Quark 77

regional meeting places 104–5
return on investment (ROI) 37, 92,
119
revenue models: free online access
model 150–5; overview
149–50; site licenses 159–60;
subscription models 76–7,
156–9; tracking usage with 161
reversion of rights clause 145
Rights Catalogue 106–7
robust software platform 56
Rosen, Roger 51–2
Rosen Publishing 85
Rowling, J. K. 117
royalties and financial commitments
132–7
royalty-inclusive deals 139–40
royalty rates 120
Russell, Barbara 57

Say It in English project 74
Scrabble Crossword Game Players
Inc. 93
search-engine marketing (SEM) 163
search engine results page (SERP) 155
self-publishing 3–4, 171–2
Sesame Street brand 88
Shatzkin, Mike 103–4

site licenses 159–60
Skype 98
Smokey Bear character 66, *66*
Software & Information Industry
Association (SIIA) 111
Southwestern Advantage 7
SpongeBob brand 90
standard agreement 142–6
STEM/STEAM (Science, Technology,
Engineering/Art, and Math)
courses 94
stock photo agencies 75
strategies in publishing 7
subscription models 76–7, 156–9
supply-chain efficiencies 3, 13, 46

target dates for publication 134
target-language spelling 73
technical production in publishing 7
technology and publishing:
compression technology
27; DRM technology 53–4;
introduction 2–3; POD
technology 42–3, 50, 179;
wireless technology 80–1; *see
also* CD-ROM technology
Teig, Marlowe 155
term limits 76, 135
term sheet 116, 141, 142
territory considerations 130–1
third-party considerations 133, 178
Thomas and Friends brand 90
total cost of ownership (TCO) 42
trade publishers: book fairs and 103;
marketing decisions 35–6, 84;
self-publishing *vs.* 171, 173;
subscription services 158
traditional publishing: consolidation
in 177; non-traditional
publishers *vs.* 80; online
publishing impact 11, 29, 58;

physical book as paradigm 39;
self-publishing *vs.* 172
translation software 5

Ubiquity 180
U.K. Publishers Association (PA) 111
United Nations Group Experts
on Geographical Names
(UNGEGN) 71
Universal Images Group 53
UNIX files 53
used-bookbusiness 15–16
user-generated content (UGC) 164–9,
166, 167

virtual town halls: international book
fairs 99–104; literary agents
and 107–8; overview 97–9;
preparation for fair 105–7;
regional meeting places 104–5

Walters, Jennie 171–2
Warner Bros. brand 88, 90

warranties clause 144
Waterstones 15, 17
Web application maintenance 36
web-offset printing 41
website strategy: overview 163;
publishing entrepreneurs
169–73; search engine
methodology 163–4; user-
generated content 164–9,
166, 167
Westlaw/WestlawNext 44
Who's Who Catalogue 106
Wikipedia 4, 164–5
Windows operating system
28, 53
Wired Magazine 13
wireless technology 80–1
Wurman, Richard Saul 180

XML (Extensible Markup Language)
coding 53

YouGov 164